DIRECTED SELF-PLACEMENT
PRINCIPLES AND PRACTICES

RESEARCH AND TEACHING IN RHETORIC AND COMPOSITION
Michael M. Williamson and David L. Jolliffe, series editors

Basic Writing as a Political Act: Public Conversations About Writing and Literacies
Linda Adler-Kassner and Susanmarie Harrington

New Worlds, New Words: Exploring Pathways for Writing About and In Electronic Environments
John F. Barber and Dene Grigar (eds.)

The Rhetoric and Ideology of Genre: Strategies for Stability and Change
Richard Coe, Lorelei Lingard, and Tatiana Teslenko (eds.)

Identities Across Text
George H. Jensen

Against the Grain: Essays in Honor of Maxine Hairston
David Jolliffe, Michael Keene, Mary Trachel, and Ralph Voss (eds.)

Directed Self-Placement: Principles and Practices
Dan Royer and Roger Gilles (eds.)

forthcoming

Black Letters: An Ethnography of a Beginning Legal Writing Course
Randolph Cauthen

Marbles, Cotton Balls, and Quantum Wells:
Style as Invention in the Pursuit of Knowledge
Heather Graves

Multiple Literacies for the 21st Century
Brian Huot, Beth Stroble, and Charles Bazerman (eds.)

Classroom Spaces and Writing Instruction
Ed Nagelhout and Carol Rutz

Remapping Narrative: Techonology's Impact on the Way We Write
Gian S. Pagnucci and Nick Mauriello (eds.)

Tech Culture: Internet Constructions of Literacy and Identity
Gian S. Pagnucci and Nick Mauriello (eds.)

Unexpected Voices
John Rouse and Ed Katz

Who Can Afford Critical Consciousness
David Seitz

Principles and Practices: New Discourses for Advanced Writers
Margaret M. Strain and James M. Boehnlein (eds.)

DIRECTED SELF-PLACEMENT
PRINCIPLES AND PRACTICES

edited by

Daniel Royer
Roger Gilles
Grand Valley State University

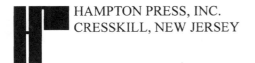

HAMPTON PRESS, INC.
CRESSKILL, NEW JERSEY

Copyright © 2003 by Hampton Press, Inc.

All rights reserved. No part of this publication may be reproduced, stored in a retrieval system, or transmitted in any form or by any means, electronic, mechanical, photocopying, microfilming, recording, or otherwise, without permission of the publisher.

Printed in the United States of America

Library of Congress Cataloging-in-Publication Data

Directed self-placement : principles and practices / edited by Daniel Royer, Roger Gilles.
    p. cm. -- (Research and teaching in rhetoric and composition)
Includes bibliographical references and index.
  ISBN 1-57273-532-5 (cloth) -- ISBN 1-57273-533-3 (pbk.)
 1.   English language--Rhetoric--Study and teaching. 2.   English language--Rhetoric--Study and teaching--United States--Case studies. 3. Report writing--Study and teaching (Higher) 4. Advanced placement programs (Education) 5. Basic writing (Remedial education) 6. Educational evaluation. 7.   Self-evaluation.   I. Royer, Daniel. II. Gilles, Roger. III. Series.
  PE1404.D57 2003
  808'.042'071173--dc21

                                                      2003044961

Hampton Press, Inc.
23 Broadway
Cresskill, NJ 07626

CONTENTS

Foreword *Edward M. White*	vii
Introduction: FAQ *Daniel J. Royer and Roger Gilles*	1
Part I: Principles	**13**
1. Directed Self-Placement in Relation to Assessment: Shifting the Crunch From Entrance to Exit *Peter Elbow*	15
2. Directed Self-Placement in the University *David Blakesley*	31
3. The Pragmatist Foundations of Directed Self-Placement *Daniel J. Royer and Roger Gilles*	49
4. The Role of Self-Efficacy in Writing and Directed Self-Placement *Erica J. Reynolds*	73
Part II: Practices	**105**
5. Directed Self-Placement at Belmont University: Sharing Power, Forming Relationships, Fostering Reflection *Robbie Pinter and Ellen Sims*	107
6. Introducing Directed Self-Placement to Kutztown University *Janice Chernekoff*	127
7. The Case of a Small Liberal Arts University: Directed Self-Placement at DePauw *Cynthia E. Cornell and Robert D. Newton*	149

8. Directed Self-Placement at a Large Research University: A Writing Center Perspective — 179
    Phyllis Frus

9. Directed Self-Placement in a Community College Context — 193
    Patrick Tompkins

10. Southern Illinois University Carbondale as an Institutional Model: The English 100/101 Stretch and Directed Self-Placement Program — 207
    David Blakesley, Erin J. Harvey, and Erica J. Reynolds

11. Responding to Directed Self-Placement — 243
    Michael Neal and Brian Huot

Author Index — 257
Subject Index — 261

FOREWORD

Edward M. White
University of Arizona

The testing of entering college and university students in order to place them in an appropriate college, or precollege, writing course has, for more than 100 years, seemed reasonable, responsible, and a nice compromise between high standards for the first-year course and social awareness of the needs of those with weak preparation for study. However, in recent years, a series of questions have been raised about this process, emerging from both the academic left (objecting to invalid testing, institutional tracking, negative labeling, and retrograde employment practices) and the popular right (objecting to the use of university resources for those defined as not ready for university work). As we attempt to think systematically about placement into the first-year writing course, we encounter a tangle of academic, professional, political, and social issues that makes it difficult to decide on an appropriate course of action in general or at our own institutions.

Part of the attractiveness of directed self-placement (DSP) is that it proposes a way through this tangle, one that might keep the advantages of placement yet avoid its disadvantages. The idea is deceptively simple. In place of testing students, the institution puts its efforts into informing students about the demands and expectations of the composition courses available to them and how they can meet the writing requirement. Then students make informed choices, and take full responsibility for their choices, instead of more or less grudgingly accepting test results and institutional placement. DSP assumes that students will be mature enough to choose the course that is right for them, if they have enough information and pressure to choose wisely. DSP also assumes that there may be many reasons besides test performance for students to choose more or less demanding writing courses in their first year of college. And—perhaps the most perilous assumption of all—DSP depends on the institution clearly defining the requirements and proposed outcomes of its different writing courses, maintaining consistency in those definitions, and then communicating them to entering students. For

DSP to be effective, the institution must develop some means of making that information meaningful to young students, generally bemused by the mass of lectures, warnings, greetings, and exhortations offered in the weeks before the opening of classes.

Thus, DSP is no panacea, although its promise is encouraging. Like many other solutions to educational problems, it offers new problems in place of old. Yet the new problems are those that postsecondary education should be meeting anyway: helping students take responsibility for their own learning, replacing reductive placement testing with sound counseling, developing clear curricular guidelines and outcomes, and becoming less paternal and more, shall we say, avuncular. At heart, DSP is a conservative proposal, one that maintains the first-year writing requirement as an essential introduction to college-level writing, thinking, and problem solving; DSP is an answer to those unwisely calling for an end to the requirement as unnecessary in modern times of technological and vocational revolution. At the same time, DSP proposes a radical solution to the persistent problems of overtesting, negative labeling, and student alienation from required coursework.

Will it work? At this point nobody really knows. Maybe entering college students are not really able to make wise course decisions; perhaps communicating with entering students about their choices is too difficult; maybe the curriculum is in too much disarray to become transparent. Many institutions will need to revamp their counseling procedures for new students to make DSP possible and such change is exceedingly difficult. All kinds of unforeseen problems lurk behind the implementation of DSP, perhaps most pointedly a shift in perception of who should be responsible for academic decisions. The concept is promising enough for widespread trials and we need to gather information about what happens as concept becomes procedure at real institutions.

Into this breach step Dan Royer and Roger Gilles, with the first book to seek to pose, and perhaps answer, many of these questions. Appropriately, the book seeks to document the experience of institutions, rather than force agreement about the answers, or even the questions. They, and many—but not all—of the contributors to this book are clearly in favor of DSP and seek to promote its use. I have no doubt that this book will be the first of many on the topic because DSP is bound to take widely different forms on different campuses. Certainly, DSP is the most creative and exciting development in placement since teachers began trying to replace the dreary multiple-choice usage tests with student writing, first with impromptu essays and then with portfolios. Now we may be able to dispense altogether with the huge expense in time and money of placement testing, while maintaining the benefits of placement. Such a promise needs careful examination and we now have a rich source to launch serious inquiry.

INTRODUCTION

FAQ

Daniel J. Royer
Roger Gilles

Soon after the publication of "Directed Self-Placement: An Attitude of Orientation" in *College Composition and Communication*, we began receiving e-mail. Faculty at colleges big and small were asking us questions: Do you think this could work at our school? What did you do to convince administrators to let you try this? Are you sure this works? We plan to try this next semester, can you give us some advice about talking to students? We heard from Research I universities and community colleges. We heard from schools right down the road and we heard from places as far away as Israel. We knew from the reaction stirred on the WPA-L listserv prior to publication that directed self-placement (DSP) was a provocative idea people were ready to engage, and 3 years later we are still corresponding with faculty and continue to hear from those who are taking up the issue fresh.

This volume is really a first response to some of the questions we have received, and the authors here raise many new questions of their own. As readers will quickly understand, this volume does not offer a final response to every placement question that DSP raises. However, it will give those schools considering alternatives to traditional placement a place to begin and, we hope, supply them with important principles and practices on which to build.

What exactly is directed self-placement?

As the chapters in this volume show, there is no single DSP method. But we would say that DSP can be any placement method that both offers students information and advice about their placement options (that's the "directed" part) and places the ultimate placement decision in the students' hands (that's the "self-placement" part).

At our own institution, Grand Valley State University (GVSU), the *direction* we offer to students has taken three main forms, although we continue to adjust what we do as we learn more about our students and their decision making—and about our curriculum. First, we send to all admitted students a letter and brochure that describe our courses and the placement decision they will need to make in order to register for classes at summer orientation. The brochure includes a brief self-inventory that asks students to consider their experience and expertise as writers. The letter urges students to consult with parents, teachers, and counselors as they consider this important decision prior to orientation. Second, we address students during the orientation itself, basically reviewing the same information about our courses and impressing on students the importance of their decision. We also share with them some information about past students' performance in our courses. And finally, we ask students to fill out a formal "choice card" that reports on their self-inventory and indicates which course they feel is right for them. We ask students to show this choice card to their assigned orientation adviser prior to registering formally for classes. If students have questions or concerns, we encourage them to discuss their situation with their orientation adviser or with a member of the writing program.

As the chapters in Part II show, however, other schools have created other ways to direct the students' placement decision. Kutztown University, for example, asks students to detail their specific reading and writing experiences over the past 1 or 2 years (see chap. 6 by Chernekoff). Belmont University provides brief reading and writing samples to illustrate its program expectations, and even asks students to produce and self-evaluate a brief writing sample of their own as part of the placement process (see chap. 5 by Sims and Pinter). There are many possible variations, and obviously any schools interested in DSP need to consider their own students and courses in order to determine exactly what kind of direction will help their students the most.

Where did the idea of DSP come from?

The idea of *self-placement* has been around for some time. And people have had different experiences with it—many negative. Edward M. White writes on the WPA-L:

> Some years back, a student of mine gathered substantial data on self-placement vs. test placement in six California community colleges. About half of the students placed themselves differently than the test (a pretty good one, the Cal State U EPT) would have placed them.

White doesn't at this point question the validity of test placement as a standard by which to judge self-placement, nor does he distinguish in this context *self-placement* from *directed* self-placement (we do both). But more to the point, in May 1998, Mary Barkley writes in this same thread:

> I used to coordinate placement testing for comp courses at the University of Tulsa. The test included a sentence combining exercise and essay. On a separate sheet, the students indicated for which section—basic, comp 1, or advanced—they were testing. Of course, evaluators did not see this sheet, but I did as I was compiling results and making final placements. I was struck by the frequency with which students placed themselves appropriately. Only a handful each year placed themselves inappropriately, always future comp 1 students who thought they belonged in advanced.
>
> A second observation: incoming students were making this *judgment without much information about the courses*, only a written description. With more information and the implicit commitment of their own choices, their self-placements may have been more accurate than ours. We didn't track those who selected advanced but were placed in comp 1. (italics added)

Again, the question about what is "appropriate" placement is not discussed here. It is assumed that teachers reading timed essays are the *creators* of appropriate placement. But, again, although the notion of self-placement is not novel, the term *directed self-placement* is our own coinage, and the idea of *directing* self-placement has precedents in common sense. For example, Doug Hesse relates this anecdote, also on the WPA-L list:

> The comments about directed self-placement remind me of an experience I had 20 years ago this summer. I was attending a German lan-

guage and culture program at the University of Vienna with a diverse group of people from around the world. The first morning they had all of us (maybe 200) meet in a large auditorium for purposes of placement. There were six levels of courses.

The placement test consisted of slides full of text projected onto the screen at the front of the auditorium. The texts got progressively more sophisticated in terms of vocabulary and syntax and, even, cultural context. We were to decide, individually, whether we could read and understand the passages. At various intervals the placement folks would ask those who felt they'd reached their limit to leave the room and out of them would form classes at that particular level. We thus placed ourselves. While I have no idea how valid or reliable the test was, I remember feeling appropriately placed in my level four course, and I remember the whole process as festive and congenial and refreshingly in contrast with my preconceptions about a German-speaking university. But then this was Vienna and not Heidelberg.

It's interesting even here how—in the face of what seems so obvious—the concern for validity and reliability still pesters Hesse's recollection of the event. In chapter 2, Blakesley provides a thoughtful analysis of why and how the reigning institutional practices grip our imaginations and prevent us from reshaping programmatic change.

Cornell and Newton (chap. 7) describe the 4-year placement study at DePauw University, including their work with DSP. In 1995 they began writing letters to students that *recommended* and, later, asked at-risk students to *choose* course placement. Their study describes data on students with different readiness predictors, gender, and ethnicity. They track success and retention of several subgroups of students that were either mainstreamed or chose or chose not to take a two-course writing sequence. This is a detailed study with hard data that confirms the sense others in this volume report that real student needs have been grossly out of step with our curricula, pedagogy, and placement practices. The tail has been wagging the dog until, like at DePauw, Belmont, and other programs described in the following pages, we began to see curriculum and placement practices do an about face, now serving the exigencies of actual practice and student need instead of an essentialist *ideal* of student ability categories and paper curriculums. Much still needs to change and improve, but the DePauw study argues strongly that as long as we remain wed to placement practices that mask problems in our grading, curriculum, or pedagogy, we will commit the fallacy of misplaced attention to the instruments of placement when we should be looking at our programs, coursework, and classroom practice.

In 1998, Cornell and Newton modified their letter to students a little more along the lines of what we at GVSU had begun calling *directed self-placement*. The origins of DSP at GVSU are narrated in the 1998 *CCC* article and need not be repeated here. Chapter 3 explains more fully the pragmatist roots of DSP. Our own concern, it seems, has been more motivated by the psychological and practical dynamics of decision making and their consequences than by a concern for quantified proofs. In the pragmatist tradition of James, Dewey, and Peirce we have found insight for deeper development of our simple notion of DSP, and we discover there as well the "attitude of orientation" that perhaps permitted the various factors and players in our situation at GVSU to give rise to the notion of DSP the way they did. Perhaps it is because, as "nonexperts" in the placement business, we were not so deeply wed to the rhetoric of prevailing practice that we were unable to imagine possibilities outside the existing structural boundaries. More important than the question, "Where did the idea of DSP come from?" is, "Where is it going?" All of the following chapters have something to say about that.

What is the relation of assessment to placement, and how does DSP fit into larger issues of mainstreaming and university standards and requirements?

The inertia of bureaucracies in motion often protect the inert ideas that fuel them and keep us from seeing the web of connections that link one aspect of what we do with another. The insistence on the strict independence of ideas is precisely what creates inert ideas, and to some extent, it is what a number of the authors in this volume believe is wrong with current placement practices. Elbow (chap. 1) addresses this point most directly. He points out that assessment and placement are closely related, and that learning and growth are additional factors that cannot be left out of the equation.

Even though DSP is clearly a form of placement, it probably has more in common with mainstreaming than it does with other forms of placement. The connection lies in our shared eagerness to get all students into the curriculum—to give them a chance to get started, to begin the process of learning about and becoming a part of the university discourse community they have joined. Mainstreaming seeks to place students side by side in a given curriculum, and then to give the necessary support to students who need it—peer tutoring, extra conferencing, library-skills help, or whatever. The idea is that time alone is not the main factor in helping students develop their writing abilities, so adding *courses* is not the only way to conceive of developmental instruction. DSP also invites all students to enter the curriculum at the same point; that is, it *requires* no one to take an extra course. But it does provide an extra course for those who feel that more *time* is precisely what they need as developing writers.

Is DSP anti-assessment—that is, an argument against our ability as faculty to assess student writing fairly and accurately?

DSP argues against our ability as faculty to assess student writing fairly and accurately—during the placement process. Fair and accurate forms of authentic assessment are certainly within our reach, and we wholeheartedly endorse them as part of classroom and program assessment. Indeed, our own commitment to a program-wide portfolio grading at GVSU, a program portfolio system in which final student portfolios are team-graded by teachers at the end of each semester, convinces us of the impracticality of replicating such authentic assessment measures as part of the placement process. As we argue in chapter 3, we would much rather put our admittedly limited time and energy into providing authentic assessment to students at the end of our first-year composition program, when the students have had a chance to get to know the university and its culture, to see and understand the writing expectations of our program, to draft a range of papers in response to a range of assignments, to give and receive feedback from other student writers, to work closely with a teacher for at least one full semester, to revise and edit their papers, and finally to select their very best work for submission for grading. Far from being anti-assessment, then, DSP seems to us to be strongly in favor of assessment—so much so that we insist on doing it only when we can do it well.

Is DSP just a cheap substitute for better, more resource-intensive forms of placement?

We note in chapter 3 that authentic inquiry begins with real doubt. Real and serious doubt is what finally goads inquirers to action, not cost savings. The cheapest form of placement uses a static index such as ACT-English score to place students. But those schools that have begun experimenting with DSP have not been motivated by mere efficiency. Kutztown University is a good example of the more common reason for looking into to DSP, namely, doubt. Chernekoff describes a not uncommon placement program, one involving ACT scores and direct writing assessment. She also describes a "lack of belief" in the placement system. For no blatantly obvious reason, deep suspicion and lack of confidence grew up around a placement program that gradually became viewed as "arbitrary, subjective, and punitive" by both students and parents (130). The situation there was no different (in some ways better) than many other placement programs, yet even without validity and reliability statistics to back them up, everyone had an intuitive sense that nobody really believed in what they were doing. Readers of Chernekoff's chapter will learn how DSP has changed things at Kutztown and that "resource intensive" does not equal better placement.

Money is often easier to come by than enthusiasm, belief, and commitment. Blakesley reminds readers that DSP is far from a cheap, self-regulating, autopilot placement system. Furthermore, Tompkins (chap. 9) notes that DSP leverages some of its potency through the Hawthorne effect. He writes, "I can assure you that when I stood before those students who were taking placement tests, they responded very well to me in large measure because for perhaps the first time in their academic lives, and certainly the first time during their placement test experience at JTCC, someone took a few moments to explain the procedures and the rationale for them, to inform them about what they might expect from JTCC writing courses, and most importantly, to allow them the rare opportunity to make their own choices about their academic future" (200). The challenge for those using DSP, as Tompkins points out, is to maintain this level of attentiveness and concern, invoking the Hawthorne effect for each incoming student, thus taking advantage of the positive consequences that showing a serious interest in students affords.

Placement should be related to curriculum and pedagogy. This is why many schools have been trying to use portfolio placement. How does DSP relate to curriculum and pedagogy?

Several of the chapters in this volume comment on the relation of DSP to pedagogy and curriculum. But in their chapter, Sims and Pinter show how far short a well-run, timed essay—carefully monitored and meticulously scored—can be from the ideals involving "sharing power, forming relationships, fostering reflection," as the subtitle of their chapter forecasts. At Belmont University, DSP replaced an exam placement program because the faculty wanted to align the placement process with the writing program's philosophy, pedagogy, and practices. Even contemplating DSP shifted focus and discussion among faculty to students' perceived needs and current course offerings. DSP was adopted with a 1-hour companion course that students might choose to take. And in a wonderful shift, "the placement *test* now became the placement *process*" (110) as the time that used to be spent testing was replaced by time spent communicating program standards and expectations to students who were now invited to take responsibility for much of this new placement process.

If a school's placement method serves as an indicator of what it values about writing, and indeed how the school conceives of writing in the first place, what kind of a message about writing does DSP send to high school students, their parents, and other tax-paying citizens?

In chapter 8, Frus writes that DSP "seemed to offer us some of the pedagogical and other benefits of portfolio placement, such as the ability to communicate the kinds of writing we expected students to have done in high school . . . administrators and faculty also looked forward to fewer appeals of placement decisions, a less-resistant population of students in the developmental writing course, and an entering class with morale improved by having been given the privilege of as well as the responsibility for making an important choice" (182).

And, as we point out in chapter 3, DSP sends an important message about the importance of self-assessment in writing generally. If the old message sent by the direct assessment of writing during placement was, "At the university, we value good writing," we now add "and students' ability to assess their own needs and abilities as writers." With DSP, we continue to say "we value good writing" by highlighting the place of writing in our curriculum and sharing the expectations of the first-year writing program; we say "we also value students' ability to assess their own needs and abilities as writers" by asking them to assess their own needs and abilities as writers!

Moreover, in recent discussions about DSP, the concern is sometimes raised that DSP sends the message that writing teachers cannot distinguish between good and bad writing. Indeed, the field of writing studies often seems not nearly so interested in talking about how to assess student writing at the end of the term as it does how to place students based on a single piece of writing or a portfolio at the beginning of the term before much at all is known about the students' writing ability. The purpose of placement should be about determining how ready a student is to enter a given curriculum given a student's readiness factors such as writing skill, motivation, grade expectations in the course, the difficulty of the course, and the student's attitude toward the work. Unfortunately, no matter how expert faculty become at reading and scoring placement essays, these readiness factors are very difficult to divine from a portfolio of writing, let alone a single placement essay. For, again, the task is not so simple as merely determining the quality of a particular essay (is it good or bad writing?) but rather the task is to project—without knowing anything about or even laying eyes on the student—where that student should begin in a curriculum in order to eventually pass the regular, required course. Faculty "reading the leaves" in portfolios or student placement essays will undoubtedly, after such effort, believe they are sorting students properly, but there is little evidence that trained readers can do more than predict who will excel and who might fail a course while giving no attention at all to these other readiness factors. Indeed, those who argue about the accuracy of a placement method generally minimize the importance of final grades, preferring instead to survey teachers about their students' placement a certain number of weeks into a course. Too many variables go into final grades, they argue, to consider them an indicator of the accuracy of a placement decision. This is precisely our point: If the standard of "accurate" placement is a teacher's view of the student's ability to write that is somehow purified of these other readiness factors we mention previously, then we end up with a very reductive view of students as learners. These "too many variables" are precisely what we believe must be anticipated in the *directing* aspect of self-placement. Of our own school's experience, we write in chapter 3, "trained, timed-essay graders of a 2-hour exam could not place students in such a way that gave them any particular advantage or disadvantage in *passing* with a C or better the regular first-year writing course." Note the emphasis on "passing." We have yet to see any evidence to the contrary at any other school. Students, parents, and taxpayers are less impressed with interrater reliability among essay readers than they are seeing students get started in the curriculum where is most appropriate for each student.

Aren't the least capable students—students who need basic writing—the very students who are least capable of choosing the right course? And don't placement decisions based on student self-perception create biases against certain populations—women, for example, or minorities?

In fact, there is convincing research demonstrating that self-efficacy (task-specific confidence) has a positive correlation with actual writing ability. In chapter 4, Reynolds synthesizes that research and notes also that students who are highly apprehensive (lack confidence) also report weak self-efficacy. Her summary of research indicates that writing apprehension is predictive of what students will attempt with regard to writing to begin with. This finding supports the idea that students with high writing apprehension will be less likely to enroll in an upperlevel writing course.

Furthermore, Reynolds reports that

> Dale Schunk addresses this phenomenon in "Self-Efficacy and Academic Motivation," pointing out that self-concept, which incorporates self-esteem and self-confidence, is "hierarchically organized, with a general self-concept at the top and subarea self-concepts at the base" (212). He maintains, based on Bandura's social cognitive learning theory, that of self-concept's various dimensions, self-confidence seems the

most akin to self-efficacy and that "in the hierarchy, self-efficacy judgments would lie at low levels because they are generally construed to be domain specific," that is, Algebra or Geometry (212). In other words, even within an academic area, a high self-concept does not imply that students feel highly confident about their abilities in all academic areas, or necessarily confident in general. (91)

Studies she cites say that females have more positive attitudes about writing, whereas males have less positive attitudes and experience more apprehension. This research supports the evidence reported by several programs using DSP that males place themselves in basic writing courses at a higher rate than do females. In that one of the goals of a basic writing course is to improve skills and confidence, this is certainly an appropriate placement.

The research Reynolds reports helps us to understand how student apprehension, confidence, and gender factor in to the dynamics of DSP.

Doesn't DSP change the basic writing population—and thus change the basic writing course itself?

Indeed DSP can upset the status quo of our programs and curriculum. With students participating in the placement decision, it becomes more important to respond to students' real and perceived needs. DSP caused us at GVSU to face the fact that if nearly all students could pass the regular, required first-year writing course, then we—as administrators and faculty—faced an unwelcome ethical dilemma if we told them that our placement will not allow them to take this course—one we knew they were very likely to pass. Rather than face the real problem (e.g., grade inflation, weak curriculum, a freshman class with such a high profile that a basic writing course is simply not needed), some programs may be asking students to shoulder the burden of our own administrative confusion or inability to fix other problems with our programs. Is it easier just to keep placing students in basic writing courses than it is to create standards for passing the course that in fact make a basic writing course a real necessity instead of a theoretical given? Has our basic writing course become such an economic necessity that eliminating it or radically changing it to respond to the "reality therapy" of DSP is more difficult than simply insisting that a certain percentage of students take the course?

The Writing Center at the University of Michigan (UM) faced a number of these difficult dilemmas. The 7% to 8% that they were placing in the practicum course, according to DSP, was much higher than needed. The freshman profile at UM is quite impressive, and students arriving on campus had a very difficult time viewing themselves as writers in need of extra help.

The chapter by Frus boldly faces many of these tough questions raised by DSP.

Finally, DSP asks the question: What helps and what hurts students? If students pass the regular class, and if they do so happily, confidently, and without trauma, then they did not need a basic writing course. Now if they pass the course but still can't write well, then we don't have a *placement* problem, we have a *curriculum* or *teaching* or *grading* problem. It is precisely the strength of DSP that it points us toward these real problems and keeps us from making our students shoulder what are really our problems as faculty and administrators. It is an ethical issue. The last thing we want DSP to do is prop up basic writing courses that students don't need. This would be self-serving. The students at UM, by all objective standards, are the cream of the large school crop (97% have a high school GPA of 3.0 or higher, an ACT of 26–30, and report very high self-confidence). It would not be surprising if very few of these students needed a basic writing course. Furthermore, if there are no obvious drawbacks to having students go right into first-year writing courses, it is very difficult justify a traditional basic writing course. It may often be the case that DSP forces us to shift our overconcern with getting more students to take the basic writing course, and refocus it on how can we design a companion course that meets real needs students have so that they will be knocking on our door, not us on theirs.

The chapters by Sims and Pinter on Belmont College and Cornell and Newton at Depauw illustrate how this dynamic can quickly change a curriculum. Cornell and Newton write: "But the more data we collect, the clearer it becomes that mandatory placement of such students in our first course is not justified. For that reason, directed self-placement has become for us not an accommodation but a matter of principle" (149). The chapter by Frus shows that when writing centers are involved, DSP causes us to examine honestly the kind of services we offer and, given what is needed to do well enough to pass the regular first-year course (in a way that pleases students, not placement experts, for many students will happily risk a C grade before they will take an extra course—a risk many of our prevailing placement programs blatantly ignore in their limitation of targeting only the very good and the very bad), causes us to reevaluate the kinds of programs we offer and the reasons for doing so.

What if students choose the wrong course? Haven't we failed in our job of placing them into the course they really need?

To us, this is similar to asking, "What if students choose the wrong major during their freshman year, and then end up switching to another major later? Haven't we failed in our job of helping them set themselves on a productive career path?" Switching majors seems to be a part of the learning or growing process of many college students. It can sometimes set students back, perhaps by requiring additional coursework or by adding new grade point average requirements. But to call the first declared major a "mistake" would be to deny the process that students often undergo as they arrive at their life's work—or at least their initial life's work. It would also assume that every student has a "true major" that is only to be found, preferably very early on. This view simply does not square with experience.

Likewise, questions about the "wrong course" or "improper placement" assume some kind of "true placement" against which a placement method must measure itself. Proper placement—being in the "right" course—is a complex matter of deep context that includes not merely the student's writing ability at the beginning of the semester, but more importantly the student's opportunity for success in the course, a prediction that is very difficult to make accurately based on a single piece of writing or even a whole portfolio of writing no matter how much expertise and training we give our faculty. For example, what does a whole portfolio of writing tell us about the motivation and interest level of a student who enrolls with the thought that he or she intends to put all of his or her energy this semester into his or her calculus class and just "get by" in everything else? Perhaps for such a student the "right" class is a basic writing class as a gentle alternative to the rigors of the regular class. We will never know if we rely only on faculty reading essay exams or portfolios of student work. A multitude of other examples could be given.

So does DSP work? Does it place students correctly?

This of course is the bottom line. This is the question that itself raises so many important questions. What is "correct" placement? What do we mean by "works"? The DePauw study in this volume supplies a 4-year study of the academic success and persistence at DePauw of their at-risk first-year students, some of whom chose a basic writing course and some of whom chose to move directly into the regular, required course. These students were also compared with a cohort that were mainstreamed. Chapter 10 also provides data indicating how DSP has "worked" on the Southern Illinois-Carbondale campus—as do several others. But all of the chapters ultimately address this key question, even those that seek to expand or revise our notion of what it means for a placement method to work. So there is no simple answer. Our collection of answers follows.

I

PRINCIPLES

1

DIRECTED SELF-PLACEMENT IN RELATION TO ASSESSMENT

Shifting the Crunch From Entrance to Exit

Peter Elbow
University of Massachusetts–Amherst

Does directed self-placement (DSP) get rid of assessment? Yes and no. There's no less assessment in DSP—perhaps more—but it's all being done by students themselves. What DSP gets rid of is *formal, institutional* assessment, and that's a big event in any larger story of assessment. I start by looking at DSP in relation to this larger, historically based picture; and then turn more specifically to DSP and issues of assessment in first-year writing courses.

WHERE IS THE CRUNCH?—AT THE ENTRANCE OR THE EXIT?

Most educational institutions create gateways where students may get messages like these: "We will not admit you." "You may go no further." "You flunk." "You get no diploma." I call these *crunch points* to highlight the fact that they are not just matters of negative evaluation or bad grades; they are places where students can be stopped or excluded. They are most commonly placed at admission and graduation—at entrance and exit. Almost every institution creates crunch points, and it is useful to notice how many are created and where they are placed.

Crunch at the Point of Exit

This could be called the *traditional model* in higher education as it evolved in Europe from the Middle Ages onward. Many ancient universities put relatively few barriers at entrance. Contemporary observers described hordes of students attending lectures and taking exams, but few passing. Admittedly, these hordes were often greatly restricted: Students often had to pass through some earlier gateway created by some other institution. But I'm interested in how institutions or programs create their own crunch points. The central fact is that some universities allowed many more students in than they would ever allow out. The paradigm example of this model is the scene at the Sorbonne: mobbed lecture halls where "all" could attend, exams were conducted only at the very end, and only a minority passed and were awarded a degree. This model enacts the principle from the gospel parable: "For many are called but few are chosen."

Crunch at the Entrance

Interestingly, the most highly selective U.S. colleges and universities turn this venerable European model on its head: They narrow the gate at entrance and pretty well skip any crunch at the end. They make a big deal—perhaps the biggest deal of all—about deciding which students to admit. Thus the frantic preoccupation about college admissions seen in so many middle- and upper-class families. Yet once students are accepted to these high prestige schools, they don't face any *major* yes/no gateway. They only have to negotiate the many smaller gateways involved in passing individual courses. If they fail one of these courses, they can make it up by passing a different one (occasionally having to pass the same one later).

"It's virtually impossible to flunk out of Harvard." This is a much repeated saying, and I gather it's not far from the truth. You can quit or be intimidated or humiliated out; you can commit suicide. But the institution itself almost never tells a student, "You're out." The institution puts great faith in its admissions process, and it makes a remarkably strong commitment to those it has chosen. In this situation, the college almost never gives up trying to find ways to salvage students who are struggling or even failing.

Crunches at Both Entrance and Exit

The traditional European model sometimes evolved to the situation we see at Oxford where there's a tough gateway at both ends: not only a highly selective admissions process but also the standard "European" battery of exams at the end—and virtually no assessments in the middle.

A few selective US colleges (not any universities that I know of) imitate this system of double crunching. I had chance to take part in an American Association of Colleges 1988 study of colleges using comprehensive exit examinations in the major—and some of these colleges were difficult to get into. Swarthmore is one of our most selective colleges, but we saw them also insisting on a tough final graduation oral exam in the major, conducted entirely by faculty from outside institutions. More commonly, it is only honors students who get this kind of exit hurdle. The premise here is that simply passing courses is not good enough. A number of states have been exploring exit exams for their state colleges and universities.

No Real Crunch at Either End—Many Little Hurdles Along the Way

This is the typical model in U.S. primary and secondary schools. It is not that public schools have never given large-scale assessments (e.g., the "California" this or that test we all grew up with). But these tests were not gateways; there was no crunch. They were intended as formative (and perhaps only for the school) rather than summative. No-gateway is also the model for nonselective colleges and universities: easy entrance, easy exit—as long as you pass lots of courses along the way. If you flunk some courses you can pass others. Admittedly, most colleges and universities have a kind of "probation" structure: if you persist in flunking too many courses, you can be kicked out.

But we have recently seen our culture hurrying away from this no-crunch reliance only on small assessment hurdles (grades). We've seen a mushrooming distrust of teacher assessment and rush to large-scale, higher stakes assessments devised and administered by outside companies. Boards of trustees, boards of education, and whole states are beginning to insist that students cannot graduate from high school or college without passing some gateway exit test. Even the federal government is trying to get in on this act.

Absolutely No Crunch at All—Not Even a Minor Gateway

This is the assessment system typically used by lone teachers who hang out their own shingle (e.g., for cooking or violin classes) and by small informal organizations offering classes in parenting, painting, or acting. Of course some of these lone teachers are picky in choosing students, but many invite almost any student to "enter" or "exit" more or less at will. Significantly, these courses are not for credit. It's the awarding of official and sometimes state-sanctioned credit that tends to spawn gateways and crunches. ("It would be irresponsible for us to award you our official credits if we didn't have a way of ensuring that you have 'earned' them.") Nevertheless, plenty of community colleges and university extension divisions give courses for credit where there is virtually no entrance or exit crunch: In many courses, attendance and doing the work are all that's required, and there is no final exam.

Having no gateways at all is also common in many early elementary grades—and it's not so very uncommon in upper grades: In this situation, nothing stops students from moving on to the next grade. Indeed, compulsory education presents schools with a dilemma. It's not so easy to say to children, "You must go through these grades under pain of law—but we won't give you credit for having done so unless you do well on a test" (especially if the test is structured so that some students must fail). Of course, we now see a headlong rush in the opposite direction. For example, Massachusetts gives a statewide exam to students in most grades. The alleged goal is to help students who are not learning rather than to prevent them from moving forward.

FIRST YEAR WRITING: SHIFTING THE CRUNCH FROM EXIT TO ENTRANCE

In the early and mid-20th century, many large U.S. universities admitted large numbers of students (sometimes all who applied), but counted on attrition during the first year to cut down the entering class to a size that the rest of the university could handle. This system for culling led to a primal scene that is often described in other settings, too: A gentleman stands at the front of a large assembled group and says, "Look to the persons on your left and right. Ten weeks from now, one of them will not be here." Jill Ker Conway describes an Australian instance of this situation from the 1950s: ". . . the University authorities admitted all who qualified, but expected more than a third to fail or drop out during the freshman year" (155).

This was a classic reliance on crunch at exit rather than at entrance, but the crunch came early—during the first year. Sometimes it kicked in even before the end of the semester because students who got consistently failing grades on essays often slipped away early. Sink or swim. Many are called. Institutions were frank to acknowledge what they were doing, but the motivation seemed defensible and consistent with the mission of land-grant universities: Give all students a chance to prove themselves. Interestingly for readers of this book, this approach to assessment had no inherent or stated relationship to writing; it was just that first-year writing courses seemed to be the most helpful tool for weeding out surplus students. (Am I too cynical? Perhaps some of them said, "Writing *should be* the gateway since writing is the main skill needed for success in every other course.")

It was this approach to assessment that gave such a bad name to the system of easy entrance and crunch at exit. Despite defensible motivation, these mid-century institutions were understandably judged irresponsible: "You invited in lots of poorly prepared students and gave them no help and thereby ensured that many of them would fail." (I wonder whether some of the institutions might be getting a bum rap. Did any of them provide more help than we hear about?) This is an approach to assessment that Marxist commentators rightly enough call "education as cooling out": Schools function to give the illusion of opportunity to all—and then trick those who never had a chance in the first place into feeling that their exclusion was their own fault. Education thus serves dominant classes and institutions by getting an unfair social and economic system off the hook and keeping the majority of the people from seeing how rigged things are against them.

Clearly, there is a historical link here to the placement process now common in first-year writing programs. Today's widespread placement testing is a humane response to an earlier inhumane reliance on exit rather than entrance crunches. The argument for placement testing is obvious: "It's unfair to accept students who are poorly prepared and just let them fall by the wayside. We must figure out which students need help and give them a remedial course so that they won't flunk out." We see this most graphically in the extreme case: the City University of New York (CUNY) decreed open admissions in the 1960s and—knowing that many students would be poorly prepared—also decreed a vast battery of placement tests to identify which students needed extra preparatory instruction to get them ready for the regular courses.

The scale of this reaction against exit crunching has been huge. In all of higher education, there is more placement testing than *any other kind* of assessment (except, of course, classroom grading). (This is the finding of three research reports: CCCC Committee on Assessment; Greenberg, Wiener, and Donovan; Lederman, Ryzewic, and Ribaudo). When a procedure gets this large and bureaucratized, it's not surprising to see many critiques. I have found it useful to try to sort them out.

First came critiques of how the assessing or measuring is done. The earliest placements were often based on scores from SATs or other large-scale, short-answer tests; sometimes they were based on high school grades. It's a testament to the rhetorical skill of people in composition that these temptingly cheap and simple methods have so often given way to the much more expensive placement exams where students must actually write essays and graders must actually read and score them.

But this more sophisticated assessment has also been easy to criticize. Even when programs work hard to achieve reliability among readers (and many do not), these tests have damning flaws in validity. That is, placements are usually based on just *one* short sample of *unrevised writing* on an *unknown topic* produced under *exam conditions*. (I've been one of many making this point—see both my "Writing Assessment" essays.) Yet for various reasons, this system is still perhaps the most common form of placement testing. Portfolio assessment is a big improvement and a few universities have gone this route, but portfolio assessment is expensive (the University of Michigan abandoned it). Most programs go along with the defense of placement essay tests by Ed White, who takes a kind of "realist," "let's face it" stance, and argues that these tests are not so flawed, they're good *enough,* and after all, the stakes are not so high.

The next critique is interesting: "It's not just that you are measuring badly. You're measuring the wrong thing. You're trying to measure whether a *piece of writing* is weak or strong instead of measuring whether a *writer* is weak or strong." (See William Smith for an approach to scoring placement essays that focuses on the student's ability behind the text—not just the quality of the sample essay. See Richard Haswell for a useful developmental perspective on writing ability.)

But I want to continue the critique. Even if placement tests *could* validly and reliably identify writers who are actually weak, it would still be wrong-headed. It's not really *weak writers* we need to identify but rather *writers who won't succeed or benefit in the regular course*—or not succeed without help. For every teacher knows that some very weak writers succeed and even prosper in the regular course—whereas many strong ones do not.

So this leads to an obvious question: What factors lead students not to benefit from the regular course? The fact is that lack of writing skill is often trumped by other factors like these: not being willing to try hard; not believing you can make it because you have been convinced you are unintelligent, unprepared, or developmentally retarded; being too afraid; having no sense of your agency; having no good sources of support from peers and community—or not being able to use the ones that are there. (I'd like to patent an assessment instrument to identify which students cannot handle alcohol or being away from home—and whose parents will divorce or whose best friend die).

When we stand back in this way and look at the real goals of the assessment process, some embarrassing bulbs light up. For it turns out that the placement process can foster exactly those factors that undermine success in learning—sending problematic messages like these: "You are not fit to make a valid decision for yourself as to whether or not you need extra help. But we are experts and we can assure you that you haven't got what it takes to succeed in the regular course." Often there's also a subliminal message to these students that they are lacking in intelligence or ability. Perhaps most important of all, the process wrests all agency and control out of their hands. When students fail the placement test (writing programs try to avoid this word, but it's inevitable) and are forced to take a basic writing course, they are segregated away from all the more confident, stronger, and more willing writers and surrounded by students whose main relationship to writing is likely to be negative.

These problems have not escaped notice. For example, Peter Dow Adams did some research at his urban community college that alarmed him. He noted that the goal of the basic writing system was to increase the chances that poorly prepared students would move forward through 101 and the rest of the college. But when he computed dropouts over many semesters, he couldn't help wonder whether the whole structure of placement testing and basic writing might be decreasing their chances. His essay was published in a special issue of *The Journal of Basic Writing* devoted to misgivings about basic writing. See also Bartholomae; Benesch; Elbow ("Writing Assessment: Do It Better"); Greenberg; Jones; and Kidda, Turner, and Porter. Karen Greenberg resigned her high-level leadership position in the CUNY testing hierarchy because she concluded that even though the extensive placement and testing process had been designed to open the door to less privileged students, these tests had, in the end, been used to exclude them.

This line of critique has led to some powerful new approaches to placement, such as the Writer's Studio program at the University of South Carolina (Grego and Thompson). In that program, all students join the regular course, but teachers spend a week getting to know them and their writing and only then do they try to decide which students will need supplementary help. (In this shrewdly sophisticated kind of assessment, teachers are not so much trying to identify that abstract mythical beast, "the basic writer." Rather, they are trying to decide, "Which of my students has problems with writing that I don't think I can handle well?" Teachers differ as to what problems they feel they'll have trouble handling and thus which kinds of students they send to the Writer's Studio.) Students designated as needing help stay in the regular course but they are obliged to spend two extra hours a week in the Writer's Studio in groups of four—getting the short-term pragmatic help they need to prosper with course assignments, but also lots of long term help designed to help them psych out the politics and psychology of teachers and institutions and being a student. So the crunch doesn't segregate weaker students from stronger ones and force them to do all their writing with others who have been picked out as needing help. And the supplemental help increases these students' chance of staying with their cohort rather than being delayed. The success of Writer's Studio students has been notable.

Other institutions have developed other ways to make obligatory help take the form of supplement rather than segregation. The University of Hawai'i requires targeted students to get weekly supplemental help both individually and in a group. Washington State University and Cal State Chico were among the first to put obligatory help in the form of short-term, one-credit supplemental courses or workshops that students must take if they are judged to need extra help. (I haven't been able to keep up with all these developments, but I gather that the institutions are pleased and that these approaches are being imitated. See Rodby, Wyche-Smith and Haswell.)

DSP SHIFTS THE CRUNCH BACK FROM ENTRANCE TO EXIT

This last group of institutions (University of South Carolina and others) started by recognizing problems with the way the entrance crunch has tended to be enacted in first-year writing programs: the impossibility of making trustworthy decisions ahead of time about who will prosper and who will need help; and the bad effects of both the placement test process itself and the compulsory segregation of the writers who do badly on the placement test away from the regular classes. These not-so-new experiments retain the crunch at entrance, but they struggle in interesting ways to make the consequences of that crunch do the least harm and the most good. Thus, I've been telling a story of how the entrance crunch can grow more sophisticated and less harmful.

In one sense, DSP is a continuation of this process; it grew from the same dissatisfactions with placement testing. In another sense—because it moves the crunch from entrance to exit—it represents a complete change of direction. DSP says to students, "We know that some of you will need extra help in order to pass the regular course, but we think you are in a better position than we are to decide whether you are one of those persons." Help is still being offered to poorly prepared or unconfident students on the basis of a "placement process," but that process is no longer an institutional assessment or crunch at all; control, agency, and decision making are returned entirely to the student.

It seems as though a crunch is likely to pop up at exit if you take it away from the entrance. (Is there a law of the conservation of crunch?) I'm curious as to whether all the DSP programs have an exit crunch, but at Grand Valley State University (GVSU), it takes the form of an exit portfolio assessment (like the one that Pat Belanoff and I inaugurated at State University of New York Stony Brook). Students cannot pass the regular course unless their portfolios are judged adequate by teachers who have had no prior contact with them—teachers who read with the cold eye of external examiners. The student's own teacher cannot grant credit. (Note the reappearance here of a form of the traditional "European" model that *separates* the two educational functions of teaching and assessing. See my "Shall We Teach or Give Credit?")

What interests me here is to notice the distribution of crunch. In programs with an entrance crunch (placement-testing-and-segregative-basic-writing), there is often little or no exit crunch. Once students enter the regular course, they can count on a passing grade at the end if they are good citizens—if they come to class, do all the work, and put in adequate effort—even if they still write badly. Writing teachers inevitably develop sympathy and respect (and even gratitude) for any student who is a good citizen over 14 weeks. Not many teachers have the heart actually to *flunk* students who do this but still write badly. The grade of D will usually suffice. An entrance crunch provides a kind of justification for this absence of exit crunch: "If we admit only 'suitably skilled' students to the course, and if these students come to class and do all the work, they will surely end up competent enough to merit credit—even if their actual essays at the end are pretty discouraging." But when GSVU instituted DSP and relinquished the crunch at entrance, it also relinquished any assurance that all the students in the regular course would be "suitably skilled."

Of course there is sometimes a crunch at *both* ends (as in the Oxford model). That is, some writing programs retain a strong entrance placement crunch and also set up some kind of exit crunch to get around teachers' reluctance to flunk good citizens who write poorly. I know three kinds of exit crunch that are sometimes used along with the conventional entrance crunch: the final program-wide portfolio system I just described; a program-wide exam with "blind" grading; or a requirement that students get the grade of C in order to pass on (thus teachers can give a passing D to good citizens yet still require them to retake the course). In addition, of course, there are always a few hardy teachers who *do* have the heart to flunk students who have done all the work but who still write poorly at the

COMPARING ENTRANCE AND EXIT CRUNCHES TO SEE WHAT WE CAN CONCLUDE

Both exit and entrance crunches can be used in ungenerous ways that seem harmful to students who are less skilled or well prepared.

- The exit crunch can be deployed in such a way as to invite people in and then "cool them out"—instead of giving them the help they need.
- The entrance crunch can take the form of an intimidating placement test that feeds a segregating and delaying basic writing class and sends unhelpful messages to those who do poorly on the test.

Nevertheless, behind the use of entrance and exit crunches, I sense the presence of an essentially *generous* impulse or principle. Or rather, I sense two opposed or competing principles of virtue—competing rules of thumb for trying to treat all students well. We could call the first one the principle of *open door laissez faire virtue*: "If there is rejecting to be done, let's reject at exit rather than at entrance. We should give people a chance to show they can make it rather than trying to decide ahead of time that they won't make it—or can't or shouldn't. People deserve a chance to prove themselves." But in direct conflict with this is a contrary principle of (let's call it) *caretaking paternalistic virtue*: "It's immoral to accept people, lead them on, give them hope, when they don't have a chance. We have a duty to figure out which ones are too badly prepared to make it, and we must make them get enough help until they are ready—not only for their own sake but for the sake of others in the classrooms." In both principles, I sense a quintessentially "American" and egalitarian impulse: to open the door of higher education to more citizens than, to my knowledge, any other culture has attempted.

The caretaking, paternalistic principle seems well enacted at the University of South Carolina and the other institutions I mentioned: They impose an entrance crunch and compulsory help, but the help is designed in such a way as to do the least harm and the most good.

The open door laissez faire principle seems well enacted in DSP where the crunch is shifted to the exit. Strong help is explained and offered but not forced on people. DSP fosters one of the main factors that helps students learn: their sense of agency and control. The basic writing course is utterly transformed by the fact that everyone enrolled is there by conscious, informed choice.

This analysis leads me to seek experiments that combine these two desirable deployments of the virtuous principle. That is, DSP (as I know it) offers only one form of help: a segregated and delaying basic writing class. This is good; this is just the right course for students who want it. But students could *also* be offered the option of *supplemental* help such as we see in the Writer's Studio, tutorials, and one-credit supplemental seminars.

MODIFYING DSP: AN EXIT CRUNCH WITH A DIFFERENCE

I just mentioned one modification. For another more counterintuitive one, I need to turn away briefly from the U.S. egalitarian ideal and look at a highly elitist entrance crunch. Let's go back to Harvard. (I've never forgotten a 1950s *New Yorker* cartoon where a comfortably affluent family sits around its suburban backyard barbecue and the mother says to her son, "Why don't you give Harvard a second chance, dear?") I am not a Harvard fan. After studying at Oxford and Harvard, I've concluded that institutions are inevitably tainted with elitism and snobbery when they think they are the best in the world. (I was not happy at either place, so of course my view is biased.)

But interestingly enough—and linked directly to its elitist entrance crunch—Harvard enacts what may be the most powerfully beneficial principle there is for improving student learning. Harvard may be rife with competition and one-upsmanship games, but the institution says to all its students, "We know you are smart. We know you can make it. We'll never give up on you. No matter how badly you screw up, we will try over and over again to find ways to help you succeed." Admittedly, Harvard has a couple of other advantages, such as the ability to accept only extraordinarily strong and achievement-oriented students—not to mention the second largest endowment in the world (behind Kamehameha School for native Hawai'ians). But I argue that their stance of belief in, commitment to, and support for students is the real secret of Harvard's success.

For I see the biggest boost for learning when people hear exactly this message from a strong and respected authority: "We know you are smart, we know you can make it, we will never give up on you." This is an old story: elite institutions set up precisely the conditions that *all* students need. Sadly, when people plan for poorly prepared students, they often set up unhelpful conditions. For example, basic courses and remedial tracks often give in to the temptation to stress drill-and-skill activities that can keep students from prospering as writers—activities which nevertheless "cool them out" because students must acknowledge that they've been given so much extra training and help.

But I want to end by suggesting how to modify the DSP approach to assessment by stealing from Harvard. DSP has already stolen something valuable from Harvard: It says, "We grant you more than usual control over your own educational decisions." (When I taught at MIT, the joke was that if students wanted control over whether to take humanities courses, they should transfer to Harvard and escape the paternal meddling.) But there's something else to steal from Harvard that's even more valuable: its almost unconditional faith, commitment, and support for students. I know it sounds impossible to reconcile these two approaches: It is the exit crunch that's essential to DSP, and it is the entrance crunch that's essential to the Harvard virtue I want to steal. After all, the only reason Harvard is willing to believe so deeply in its students is that it weeds out ahead of time any students it might not want to believe in. It chooses *only* students deemed *worthy* of this more or less unconditional faith, commitment, and support. When DSP moves the crunch to exit, it has to send exactly the opposite message—the message I am trying to avoid: "We're *not* sure you can make it. There's a final crunch coming and you may fail. Be on guard. Don't relax or trust yourself. You have to prove yourself." Roger Gilles acknowledged this to me: "We do want our students to 'be on guard' as they proceed through our curriculum. You make it sound mean, of course, but I think we can put it in much more positive terms" (e-mail 7/19/00). Certainly the on-guard stance toward students (*en garde!*) is sweeping the country with the mushrooming of high-stakes assessments at all levels.

Could one ever reconcile these opposed messages that come from entrance and exit crunching?—Harvard's "We believe in your excellence because we've chosen you so carefully" and DSP's "We'll accept you without your having to prove yourself." Parents certainly do it all the time. Parenthood is an open admissions process—you take what comes. Yet many parents say to their children: "We know you are smart, we are committed to you, we'll never give up on you." (And even those who don't say it or those who even belittle their children tend, in fact, to believe it deep down.)

But I'll argue that these conflicting stances can be reconciled even in an educational setting (about reconciling opposites, see my "Embracing" and "Binary Thinking"; about considering all students smart, see my "Illiteracy" 11-14). The key here is to look more closely at *crunch* itself as a concept. *Crunch* contains two different meanings or dimensions: (a) rejecting or excluding students; (b) insisting that students meet high standards. DSP could make a crunch with a difference by insisting on the high standards part, but not on the rejecting part. If we gave voice to this modified crunch, it would say two things to students: "We know you can make it, we are committed to you, and we'll never give up on you"; but also, "We won't let you pass or get credit till you do good work." But this still doesn't solve the problem. How can a program be so generous yet so demanding to students who have not been vetted by a stringent entrance crunch?

It will require breaking out of the default model of assessment—shifting from a norm-referenced model to a criterion-referenced model. In the norm-based model, what's constant is the time dimension, and the accomplishments vary: Everyone gets 1 hour or one semester, but accomplishments and scores are spread out (ideally on a bell curve). In criterion-based assessment, what's constant is the accomplishment—everyone has to meet a strong standard—while time is allowed to vary. Some people learn fast, some take longer. This could be called crunch-as-delay rather than crunch-as-exclusion. (For the classic essay on criterion-based assessment, see McClelland.)

At this point, someone might say, "This is just Jesuitical hair splitting. You're just calling for what already goes on in the standard placement process and in DSP. For when the standard placement system forces some students to take basic writing, it is simply delaying students in order to insure they meet high standards. DSP is doing the same thing to students who take and fail the regular course and must take it again."

Putting aside the fact that I admire DSP but not the standard placement system, my main response here is to insist that there is a large pedagogical difference between two ways of handling students who take longer—between saying: "You fail the placement test and must take a course for the needy"—or similarly—"You fail the course and must retake it" and "You aren't done yet."

This distinction might look Jesuitical to teachers or administrators, but it is not usually experienced that way by students, and the difference has a big effect on learning.[1]

So when I talk about a form of DSP exit crunch where strong performance is the constant and time is the variable, I am not satisfied with just adding a euphemistic spin. What I am seeking would involve structural experiments that are beyond the scope of this chapter—experiments that would require shrewd strategies for adjusting the rigid time structures in most curricula. I just mention three illustrative examples:

---

[1] Still, this analysis of a crunch-with-a-difference helps me see why some versions of placement-test-plus-obligatory-basic-writing seem better than others. That is, the best basic writing classes I've seen are suffused with the spirit of, "We trust you, we know you are smart, we know you can make it." I see this spirit in the University of Massachusetts basic writing program. (I say this in all modesty because I had nothing to do with it; it was entirely designed by Marcia Curtis and Anne Herrington and is run by Curtis.) But it's *harder* to say, "We trust you and know you're smart" when we didn't trust you in the placement decision and decided you couldn't survive the regular course.

1. The idea of a "stretch course" for first-year writing is a limited attempt to move in this direction *without* disturbing the default time structures: giving students a two-semester option to the one semester course instead of saying, "You failed the placement test."
2. Various "competence-based" experiments and programs are based much more squarely on this principle of holding all students to the same standards of "mastery" but letting time be a variable. The insight of the extensive competence movement is that it's easier to hold everyone to high standards if you specify those standards concretely in some detail—rather than leaving them mysterious as is the case with most grading—so that students can understand them better and can meet them in stages rather than having to meet them all at once (see Grant et al.).
3. I've suggested elsewhere the idea of a "yogurt model" for first year writing (see "Writing Assessment in the Twenty-First" 95-98). In this structure, students exit the course when they have met the necessary standards or criteria; the classroom has a gradually shifting population such that new raw students are always joining an ongoing living writing culture (thus the yogurt metaphor). If this sounds weird, consider the fact that it is exactly the situation in most writing groups, clubs, committees, and organizations (not to mention the famous "Burkean parlour" [Burke 45]): the culture remains, while members gradually enter and exit. New members always get to see and learn from the skilled members they find around them.

To conclude, I should summarize my long journey. I have looked at DSP as an important event in the history of assessment. This led me to explore the implications of entrance and exit crunching—and of different enactments of a crunch. This analysis led me to admire DSP with its exit crunch as well as the sophisticated deployments of an entrance crunch by the University of South Carolina and the other programs I mentioned with them. And it led me finally to imagine two ways to experiment with modifying DSP.

1. DSP could offer students not just the normal basic writing course but also some of the supplementary forms of help pioneered at South Carolina and the others—help that doesn't segregate or delay the students.

2. Finally, it would be useful to see some experiments to explore whether DSP could harness the exit crunch in a richer, more complicated and human way: not only to demand that students meet tough standards but also to demonstrate a stronger faith in the capabilities of students and a greater commitment to sticking by them. The only way I can imagine working this out is to be more flexible about time—but perhaps others can figure out other possibilities.

REFERENCES

Adams, Peter Dow. "Basic Writing Reconsidered." *Journal of Basic Writing* 12.1 (Spring 1993). Special Issue: 4th National Basic Writing Conference Plenaries: 22-36.

Bartholomae, David. "The Tidy House: Basic Writing in the American Curriculum." *Journal of Basic Writing* 12.1 (Spring 1993). Special Issue: 4th National Basic Writing Conference Plenaries: 4-21.

Benesch, Sarah. "Ending Remediation: Linking ESL and Content in Higher Education." Wash DC: TESOL, 1988.

Burke, Kenneth. *Rhetoric of Motives*. Berkeley, CA: U Cal P, 1950.

CCCC Committee on Assessment. *Post-secondary Writing Assessment: An Update on Practices and Procedures*. (Spring 1988). Report to the Executive Committee of the Conference on College Composition and Communication.

Conway, Jill Ker. *The Road From Coorain*. Knopf, 1989.

Elbow, Peter. "Embracing Contraries in the Teaching Process." *College English* 45 (1983): 327-39. Reprinted in *Embracing Contraries*. NY: Oxford UP, 1986.

———. "Shall We Teach or Give Credit? A Model for Higher Education." *Soundings* 54.3 (Fall 1971).

———. "Illiteracy at Oxford and Harvard: Reflections on the Inability to Write." *Everyone Can Write: Essays Toward a Hopeful Theory of Writing and Teaching Writing*. NY: Oxford University Press, 2000.

———. "The Uses of Binary Thinking." *Journal of Advanced Composition* 13.1 (Winter 1993): 51-78. Reprinted in *Everyone Can Write*

———. "Writing Assessment: Do It Better, Do It Less." *The Politics and Practices of Assessment in Writing*. Eds. William Lutz, Edward White and Sandra Kamusikiri. New York: Modern Language Association, 1997. 120-34.

———. "Writing Assessment in the Twenty-first Century: A Utopian View." *Composition in the 21st Century: Crisis and Change*. Eds. Lynn Bloom, Don Daiker, and Ed White. Carbondale: Southern Illinois UP, 1996. 83-100.

Elbow, Peter and Pat Belanoff. (With Pat Belanoff) "State University of New York: Portfolio-Based Evaluation Program." *New Methods in College Writing Programs: Theory into Practice*. Eds. Paul Connolly and Teresa Vilardi. New York: Modern Language Association, 1986. Reprinted in *Portfolios: Process and Product.* Eds. Pat Belanoff and Marcia Dickson. Portsmouth NH: Heinemann, Boynton/Cook, 1991.

Grant, Gerald et al. *On Competence: A Critical Analysis of Competence-Based Reforms in Higher Education.* San Francisco: Jossey-Bass, 1979.

Grego, Rhonda and Nancy Thompson. "Repositioning Remediation: Renegotiating Composition's Work in the Academy." *College Composition and Communication* 46 (Feb 1996): 62-84.

Greenberg, Karen. "The Politics of Basic Writing." *Journal of Basic Writing* 12.1 (Spring 1993). Special Issue: 4th National Basic Writing Conference Plenaries: 64-71.

Greenberg, Karen, Harvey Wiener, and Richard Donovan. "Preface." *Writing Assessment: Issues and Strategies.* Eds. Karen Greenberg, Harvey Wiener, and Richard Donovan. NY: Longman, 1986. xi-xvii.

Haswell, Richard. *Gaining Ground in College Writing: Tales of Development and Interpretation.* Dallas: Southern Methodist UP, 1991.

Jones, William. "Basic Writing: Pushing Against Racism." *Journal of Basic Writing* 12.1 (Spring 1993). Special Issue: 4th National Basic Writing Conference Plenaries: 72-80.

Kidda, Michael, Joseph Turner, and Frank E. Parker. "There Is an Alternative to Remedial Education." *Metropolitan Universities* 3.3 (Spring 1993): 16-25.

Lederman, Marie Jean, Susan Ryzewic, and Michael Ribaudo. *Assessment and Improvement of the Academic Skills of Entering Freshmen: A National Survey.* NY: CUNY Instructional Resource Center, 1983.

McClelland, D.C. "Testing for Competence Rather than for Intelligence." *American Psychologist* 28 (1973): 1-14.

Rodby, Judith. "Testing Our Ideas of Literacy." Unpublished MS. Department of English, California SU, Chico.

Smith, William. "The Importance of Teacher Knowledge in College Composition Placement Testing." *Reading Empirical Research Studies: A Rhetoric of Research.* Ed. John R. Hayes et al. Hillsdale, NJ: Lawrence Erlbaum, 1992.

White, Edward. "An Apologia for the Timed Impromptu Essay Test," *College Composition and Communication* 46.1 (February 1995): 30-45.

Wyche-Smith, Susan, and Richard Haswell. "Adventuring into Writing Assessment." *College Composition and Communication* 45 (May 1994): 220-36.

2

DIRECTED SELF-PLACEMENT IN THE UNIVERSITY

David Blakesley
Purdue University

When the institutions make classifications for us, we seem to lose some independence that we might conceivably have otherwise had. This thought is one that we have every reason, as individuals, to resist. Living together, we take individual responsibility and lay it upon one another. We take responsibility for our deeds, but even more voluntarily for our thoughts. Our social interaction consists very much in telling one another what right thinking is and passing blame on wrong thinking. This is indeed how we build the institutions, squeezing each other's ideas into a common shape so that we can prove rightness by sheer numbers of independent assent.

—Mary Douglas (91)

In whatever form it takes, the placement of students in composition courses in the university is fundamentally an act of socialization. As such, and as Douglas suggests, placement or classification (i.e., *being* placed or classified) naturally breeds resistance. On the one hand, placement itself is the most social of acts whereby individuals accommodate themselves to the values and judgment of the group with which they identify or aspire to join, all in the interest of social harmony. On the other hand, individuals sacrifice some aspect of individual responsibility or identity in making such accommodations, whether these accommodations are prompted by self-knowledge or by the institution that has the power to confer such group identity. Even as we are, in Kenneth Burke's words, "goaded by the spirit of hierarchy" (*Language* 15) that perpetuates and rationalizes social groups, we sacrifice allegiance to self-determination, a value at odds with the normalizing function (or desire) of the institution.

In the broadest sense, placement is a fundamental and familiar process of socialization, a communal act of identification. We may have no choice but to act together, for as Burke writes in *A Rhetoric of Motives*, identity itself is contingent on what he calls *consubstantiality:* "A doctrine of *consubstantiality,* either explicit or implicit, may be necessary to any way of life. For substance [i.e., *identity*], in the old philosophies, was an *act*; and a way of life is an *acting-together;* and in acting together, [people] have common sensations, concepts, images, ideas, attitudes that make them *consubstantial*" (21). Although we might naturally resist *being* placed—*identified by the other*—we also find ourselves implicitly identified with the group by virtue of our active involvement in the social and ethical process of communicating and acting together. We choose and yet are chosen to act, from our first words to our last implicated in a give-and-take of identities. Our identifications—our shared substance or consubstantiality—are marked by the rhetorical power of naming and placement, by our answers to questions like "Who am I?" and "Who are you?" and "Who are we?"

I have invoked Douglas and Burke at this early stage because I believe that on the whole, composition studies has underestimated the ethical and moral complexity of writing placement, even as it has done much to show the value of ensuring that students take the course that will best help them become successful writers in the university and beyond. As Sharon Crowley argues in *Composition in the University*, we may have also underestimated the degree to which first-year composition itself functions culturally, and thus hegemonically, to preserve the status quo with regard to both institutional practice and politics, as well as attitudes toward literate practice (see especially "A Personal Essay on Freshman English" 228-249). Initially, as least, we might not anticipate that writing placement itself could carry with it such wide-reaching questions about identity, the role of the individual in society, or the function of institutions. After all, it is but one dimension of writing programs, which typically also involve questions of content or curriculum, pedagogy, instructor training, disciplinary status, and more, each of them complex problems of their own. Nevertheless, in my mind, the question of writing placement stands out as unique in that although, as I argue, it shares with these other questions a tendency to involve social forces and practices beyond the writing program itself, we spend much of our time detailing how existing methods of writing placement might function better or more accurately (setting aside momentarily the ambiguity of "accurate"). We ask whether, for instance, an ACT score alone (or in combination with a placement test) provides the best way to slot students in first-year composition courses, or whether placement itself is even necessary. We wonder if mainstreaming is the answer to the questions of logistical and economic feasibility as well as predictive validity that attend the politics of remediation. There are always alternatives. Whichever way we go, the ideological forces, or lines of power, that attend the more general concept of placement itself fade into the background as we grapple with the need to justify our means of placement, or even curriculum, with empirical evidence, expert opinion, and rational argument. We get caught up in solving the persistent problems of the moment and rarely have time to see the broader patterns of force, or even the imaginative possibilities, that contain our day-to-day adjustments to conditions.

Although it is true that in the past decade, composition scholars have paid increasing attention to the politics of writing instruction generally, we have yet to formulate a systematic approach to the question of how our disciplinary and pedagogical practices and the rhetoric we use to validate them function in the wider context of institutional practice, and thus, ideological contexts. Consider the well-publicized events surrounding the actions of the Board of Trustees for the City University of New York, who in May 1998 approved a resolution to refuse admission to senior status of all students who had not passed skills assessment tests in reading, writing, and math. In "Evaluating Writing Programs in Real Time: The Politics of Remediation," Barbara Gleason reports her discovery that "[t]he empirically verifiable account that we were striving for in this evaluation [of remediation efforts] was fatally compromised by the socio-political forces that had gathered around the issue of remediation" (582). We continue to underestimate how these forces of power regulate and forestall change, as well as how they compromise the forms of rhetoric we rely on to support change or rationalize our successes. As James E. Porter, Patricia Sullivan, Stuart Blythe, Jeffrey T. Grabill, and Libby Miles argue, we need to develop a methodology of institutional critique that would ground itself as "an unabashedly rhetorical practice mediating macro-level structures and micro-level actions rooted in particular space and time" (612). I won't be reiterating the methodology for institutional critique that these authors propose, but I do hope to show how our efforts to introduce directed self-placement (DSP) at my former university was from the start an "unabashedly" rhetorical enterprise and rooted in a context that, although perhaps unique in its particularity, will also be familiar to many writing program administrators (WPAs).

Unfortunately, when I first approached the question of writing placement in my role as the WPA at Southern Illinois University Carbondale (SIUC), I, too, underestimated the degree to which placement itself (and thus any changes I might instigate) functioned in the wider institutional context as the expression of power and a symptom of the institution's normalizing desire. And thus my discussion here is sleight-of-hand, or what Burke would call "prophesying after the event," a phenomenon whereby we substitute logical priority for a temporal sequence (*Language* 85). In retrospect, it is now easy for me to see how a seemingly innocuous and initially well-supported change could ultimately expose the institutional forces that not only govern what is possible in writing program administration but also reveal the function of institutions as static patterns of value. All of which is to say that DSP in the university raises more than just questions of validity, programmatic goals, and curricular integrity. In considering the merits of DSP, we find ourselves cast into a net of conflicting values that force us to re-examine writing placement itself as an institutional practice, and placement generally as a fundamentally rhetorical and thus social act. Therein, I believe, is one of DSP's unintended but delightful consequences. With the emergence of DSP as an alternative means of placement, we will find ourselves revisiting fundamental questions about the role of composition in the university, the function of the university as an institution, and the cult of individuality that runs deep in American culture.

I intend in this chapter, then, to articulate the ways that DSP might function to reshape institutional contexts and conversations, what types and sources of resistance WPAs will likely face at the university and among students, strategies for understanding them and (perhaps) overcoming them, and finally, how DSP itself can potentially and fundamentally affect every facet of a writing program. In the end, I believe, a writing program that successfully implements DSP will find its effects showing up in instructor training, instructor–student relations, instructor and student attitudes, and, of course, in student performance. The consequences of our placement methods run far deeper than we might initially presume.

I began this chapter from the top down by first considering "the institution" as an entity, not an individual with motives of its own, but as the abstract set of principles around which social groups form. I next move to "the university" to consider the ways in which my university manifested itself as an institution, with stress on the ways in which it conceives and expresses its mission as an educational institution and how this mission shapes the operative rhetorical dynamic (a dynamic that will sound familiar to many). In this context, I then examine the writing program itself to show how its institutional status as an agent of change impacted the move toward DSP. Finally, and perhaps most important of all, I consider the stakeholders, those groups of people who ultimately had vested interests in the writing program, including mid-level administrators, campus advisors, instructors, and, of course, the students themselves. How, finally, did the prospect and realization of DSP affect them?

The chapter by Erin Harvey, Erica J. Reynolds and I (chap. 10) in this volume speaks more directly to programmatic details and issues of student performance than I intend to here. I want to note, however, that it is critical that we come to the table with empirical evidence and specific plans to support such a programmatic initiative as DSP. But at the institutional level, such evidence usually does not carry the persuasive force that we and other WPAs might attach to it, and so I focus more here on the rhetorical dynamic at the level of the bureaucracy and hope that I can provide other WPAs with a better understanding of what's involved when we say what we are doing (or want to do) and why we are doing it. At the bureaucratic, institutional level, WPAs often find that empirical evidence, expert opinion, and (even) rational argument fail to produce good results. And yet I still believe that the rhetoric we use to reach disciplinary consensus can play a role in fostering institutional change, provided the institution will confer authority to those who proffer it and that the WPA can show it is warranted. In the end, disciplinary knowledge functions ethically rather than logically, establishing the intellectual integrity of the WPA more than it might rationalize or justify specific programmatic change.

THE UNIVERSITY

At the university level, the status quo has great momentum, designed as it is to preserve the values of the institution that it represents. Momentum never ends, it just changes directions, more often ever so slightly than in great shifts. Consider the following representative anecdote, which has circulated widely on the Internet and that I have adapted for the sake of illustration:

> The US standard railroad gauge (width between the two rails) is 4 feet, 8.5 inches. Why was that gauge used? Because that's the way they built railroads in England, and the US railroads were built by English expatriates. Why did the English build them like that? Because the first rail lines were built by the same people who built the pre-railroad tramways, and that's the gauge they used. Why did they use that gauge then? Because the people who built the tramways used the same jigs and tools that they used for building the wagons that used that wheel spacing. So why did the wagons have that particular odd wheel spacing? Well, if they tried to use any other spacing, the wagon wheels

would break on some of the old, long distance roads in England because of the spacing of the wheel ruts.

Who built those old rutted roads? The first long distance roads in Europe (and England) were built by Imperial Rome for their legions. The roads have been used ever since. And the ruts in the roads? Roman war chariots first formed the initial ruts, which everyone else had to match for fear of destroying their wagon wheels. Since the chariots were made for (or by) Imperial Rome, they were all alike in the matter of wheel spacing. The United States standard railroad gauge of 4 feet, 8.5 inches derives from the original specification for an Imperial Roman war chariot. The Imperial Roman war chariots were made just wide enough to accommodate the rear-ends of two war horses.

As a complex system, a university naturally resists change, especially the more its tendrils reach into the tidy wilderness of cultural ideology. It is easiest for a university bureaucracy to lumber on, to continue to do things as they have always been done, its dormancy often shored up by nostalgia for a bogus past or for "economic necessities." But on occasion and (sometimes) at watershed moments, people arise to question the status quo either because old ways no longer seem to be working or because material conditions force (or allow) them to question it. The actors in such a drama at first tend to perceive their efforts as revolutionary, but functionally speaking, such efforts often merely provide the university and its constituents the opportunity to reassert principles that have withstood such tests countless times. (I should note here that whether DSP precipitated any sort of revolution at my university remains to be seen.)

I see two ways of understanding how and why the university as an institution might resist DSP conceptually, if not practically. To explain the first, I borrow again from Burke. His phrase "bureaucratization of the imaginative" names the phenomenon whereby amid a myriad of imaginative possibilities, we lean toward just one. The "imaginative" is a world of possibilities; bureaucratization, the carrying out of but one of them. As Burke sees it, the phrase itself names a fundamental process of history, or even dying, and is as "bungling as the situation it would characterize" (*Attitudes Toward History* 225). Unfortunately, the imaginative possibilities of the idea of a university were reduced to few in number long before any of us arrived. One of those possibilities concerns the educational mission of the university, which in the most general sense is charged with the rather schizophrenic task of preserving and disseminating collective knowledge even as it (ideally) prepares students to question that knowledge and perhaps reassemble it for future generations. Operatively speaking, the former possibility usually takes precedence so that in order to rationalize its existence, the university must identify students initially as outsiders, as the great unwashed or as empty, narrow-necked vessels, waiting to be cleansed or filled up with the wisdom of the academy. It is the lingering hegemony of this identification that rationalizes what Paulo Freire describes as the banking model of education in *Pedagogy of the Oppressed* (passim) and that trickles down to the earliest years of schooling. The status quo has been that the institution should make decisions for the students, even when students might be better served to make those decisions for themselves.

By the time they reach the university, most students in the United States have grown accustomed to being identified as empty vessels, and so there is normally little resistance to the drudgery of college entrance exams, writing placement tests, or any of the other battery of tests that serve to identify just how empty students might be. (Ironically, some resistance will likely show up among students when a university *does not* begin with the presumption that students are too irresponsible to judge themselves.) Much of this sorting goes on outside the immediate sphere of university faculty, having been bureaucratized as the means by which the university selects or accepts students into the system. It is normally a charge carried out by testing and placement offices, recruiting officers, and other people who set and administer admissions policy, a realm most faculty and perhaps even most WPAs either avoid or recognize as beyond their sphere of influence. Because it is also an expression of institutional ideology with deep roots in cultural presumptions about education, the means by which we place students at the university is very resistant to change. There are already complex mechanisms in place that make it work (well or not) and at a large university, often hundreds of people involved, each of whom has some stake in the process, even though there may be few opportunities for asserting it. An act as seemingly innocuous as changing the writing placement method to DSP thus requires changing the culture of the institution and rediscovering the imaginative possibilities of higher education. We have to re-bureaucratize them so that we can live with ourselves.

The second reason why the university might resist DSP results from the magnitude of the change and the number of people needed to make it work. At my former university, like many others, the normal avenue for implementing curricular change followed a fairly standard pattern. At first, a select few faculty devise strategies for improving courses or programs, build support for them by discussing their merits with other faculty and (sometimes) students, then garner support from a wider body of policymaking units, such as a faculty senate or council. Recommendations for change are passed to the people who grant the final seal of approval, such as academic deans or provosts, and then the new policy is enacted. When the change is largely content-based or curricular in nature, the process usually runs smoothly, with those not directly affected deferring to the authority and sovereignty of those who are. Problems only arise when changes in one area are likely to impact another.

Implicit in this process is an ideal of shared governance, which asserts that change be the result of compromise and discussion across all levels of administration and not just enacted from the top down (e.g., by decree of a dean or some other academic officer). People generally recognize that real change needs to occur from the bottom up, with all stakeholders involved from the beginning. As Gleason and her colleagues at the City University of New York learned, it is extremely difficult to involve all stakeholders in decision making from the outset. Attempting to do so can actually paralyze the process of change. The WPA does, after all, need to make decisions that disciplinary knowledge and immediate contexts warrant. If writing programs were autonomous units, it wouldn't be so difficult to involve all stakeholders—students and teachers—in decision making. But writing programs, for better or worse, serve the university also when they are charged with preparing students for the rigors of academic writing. And they serve the larger community as well, representing perhaps the last hope of ensuring a literate citizenry. (Whether or not WPAs see the writing program as "serving" in such a way is irrelevant except when changing that perception is the goal.) Involving all stakeholders in the decision-making process thus is a great challenge for the WPA, who must try to balance the demands of theory with the practical need for support from those outside who may not share the same disciplinary knowledge and who may imagine different goals for the writing program. It is a kairotic moment, with the WPA feeling the need to improve the program even as he or she needs to recognize that the circumstances, some of which may be beyond direct influence, significantly affect the rhetorical dynamic necessary to implement change. In such circumstances, and as Aristotle long ago reminded us, the truth alone may not be enough to persuade.

When arguing for the implementation of DSP, I recognized from the outset that stakeholders needed to be involved, but I significantly underestimated the degree of that involvement, as well as the time it would take to foster it. My philosophy from the outset was that the status quo did have great momentum and that in order for DSP to work as it should, it would need to become the status quo itself. I also believed that if the "official" constituencies supported it, we could make it work. As most WPAs know (or learn), however, even official acceptance is no guarantee of cooperation. The residual status quo can reassert itself in beguiling and unanticipated ways.

Before I describe more specifically how my attempts to re-bureaucratize the imaginative worked (or didn't), I should say that for the most part, DSP has been a great success at the university and a model for other programs in the university to emulate. And yet, whatever its successes, it has a tenuous future because while it may "work" for the time being, it is a high-maintenance change. Additionally, the forces beyond the writing program that might question it may have been appeased, but they have not been silenced. There may be little hope that the residual ideology that "imposes universal subjectivity" (Crowley 9) on students has been extinguished.

THE STAKEHOLDERS IN THE UNIVERSITY

We first had to persuade higher level administrators that we could make DSP work and that we would not be simply turning over to students the responsibility for making decisions that many presumed we were more qualified to make. Initially, people failed to appreciate the degree to which the "directed" part of DSP played a role. To some, it seemed "counterintuitive" that students would self-place accurately or honestly. At the time, we didn't have data to prove that they would. We used the articles by Gregory Glau and a draft of the Dan Royer and Roger Gilles *CCC* article on DSP to help us make the case, and those articles did have a positive influence, even though I now believe it was really the gesture of pointing to existing scholarship that was persuasive, not the substance of the articles themselves. At the administrative level, we actually spent very little time discussing these other models, and it seemed fairly clear to me that the people with whom I worked hadn't considered them too much. So, while I introduced existing scholarship to help make the case and to shape the discussion, that scholarship had a greater role as a demonstration that I had done my homework and that DSP and *Stretch* were not some hare-brained ideas I had invented. That approach seemed to work well to build ethos. Still, however, to appease the dean and provost, we suggested that we would provide a "safeguard" in the form of a diagnostic essay that would be administered to all students during the first week of either course (English 100—Basic Writing or 101—Composition I) and that students would be given a second chance to select the proper course using their results for further guidance. The diagnostic essay thus functioned as a trump card that we played to make doubters realize essentially that they (and, of course, the students) had nothing to lose by going along with the experiment. That strategy also worked, and the diagnostic essay became an important rejoinder to charges from the administration or anyone else that the English department was abdicating its responsibility. However, the diagnostic essay functioned as an adjustment, one of those unintended by-products of the imaginative, a necessity of our invention given the need to persuade others that the new program could work.

Conducting a blind, multiple reading of 2,700 essays and distributing the results in 2 days was manageable, but barely, with the cost being its intrusiveness at the start of each semester and the implicit message to students that we might not trust their judgment as much as we say we do.

In order to ensure that our plan would be accepted, I also promised to provide the university administration with the hard data showing that we had indeed achieved what we predicted we would. Using data from the Arizona State model, I had said that we would see students who started with English 101 ultimately achieve higher GPAs in English 102 (Composition II) than did their peers who started with English 100. I promised that students would indeed choose English 100 in the first place, even though it meant they would have to take an additional three credit hours in composition. (At the time, I estimated that 15%-20% of the students would choose English 100.) I promised that we would see retention in writing courses from semester to semester increase as a result of the changes (something also predicted by the Arizona State model). In summary, I had committed to making the introduction of DSP and the other changes to the program a safe bet for the administration. Perhaps inadvertently, I had also committed myself and writing program staff to an undertaking in statistical compilation that would require enormous expenditures of time and resources. I didn't realize at the time that no one at the university had ever generated such statistics measuring individual student performance and retention across a range of courses, despite the obvious benefits of doing so.

Our situation was somewhat different than it was at Grand Valley State University (GSVU), where it is possible for writing program representatives to meet directly with students during summer orientation programs. Our students enrolled in courses off-site, by phone, or in one-on-one meetings with campus advisors. Campus advising was de-centralized, meaning that each college (e.g., Liberal Arts, Education, Science, etc.) was responsible for advising the students who had chosen to major in a field within the particular college. We had no presemester orientation program. And thus our first task was to make sure that campus advisors were well-informed about DSP and that they in turn could help us ensure that their students were well-informed.

This aspect of the implementation has turned out to be the most difficult to manage for several reasons. As we spread the responsibility for ensuring that students were well-informed about their choices, we also created opportunities for people to assert their influence on those choices. Ideally, students would carefully consider the options we presented them, perhaps with parents, teachers, and guidance counselors, then make their choice. We prepared brochures for students to review, established a Web site with more information, and invited them to contact me or a placement coordinator if they were uncertain. Logistically, simply getting this information to the students proved to be difficult. (On our first presemester survey, only about half of the students said they had heard of DSP.) To make sure that campus advisors—who would be the lead contacts with students—were well-informed, I and the placement coordinators met with each advising unit multiple times, speaking to more than 100 advisors in all about the change. Most were very enthusiastic. And yet, over time, we saw that we had also created the opportunity for people to intervene by assuming perhaps too much of the "directing" in the space we had created when we asserted that we were not advocating self-placement, but *directed* self-placement. This tendency, I believe, proved to be the biggest challenge to overcome, in large part due to the material conditions that prevented our direct contact with students and the ideological insistence that allowing students to choose was counterintuitive. It is an issue over which the stakeholders themselves still felt conflicted, even if DSP itself had become "official policy."

In principle, it would seem most efficient for the WPA to be the chief overseer of the writing program and thus responsible for formulating and enacting policy, standards, or guidelines, with stakeholders involved only to the extent that they would support and learn to implement such directives effectively. Of course, everyone knows that good teaching and good administration are not merely matters of formulating and enacting policy, of being efficient. With the healthy state of scholarship in composition studies, it is fairly easy to design programs and curricula with sound rationale and theoretical support. It is much more challenging to make a program work as intended. Stakeholders need to feel a sense of ownership and that comes only with their active involvement at the conceptualization stage, when the future is a tangled wilderness of possibilities. And so we are better off sacrificing efficiency in the early going, on the promise that our programs in the long run will be much better because of our efforts to involve stakeholders at every stage. As I mentioned earlier, there are more stakeholders on the periphery of a writing program than one might imagine initially. There are the teachers and students, of course. But aside from them, who are they? And what do they think? What motivates them to have a stake in the first place?

On our campus, advisors are the ones charged with making sure students take the right courses and thus make good progress in their degree programs. They function as the interpreters of academic policy and thus play an important role in ensuring that it works as it should. They are also often the first point of human contact a new student has with the university. For these reasons, I knew that I would need to appeal to them for help, because the dynamic of DSP would work best when their contact with students went well.

Initially, the advisors were highly skeptical of the initiative, not so much because they disagreed with DSP in principle, but because it would change the nature of their interaction with students. As I saw it, I was simply asking them to distribute information to students and then to advise them when the students had questions. Previously, placement was predetermined before they would ever see a student. So DSP upset a mechanism that functioned daily to make their work with students run more smoothly. Previously, placement was merely a matter of reading the student's transcript on a computer screen.

My first meeting with the group of chief academic advisors came 9 months before the Fall 1998 semester, which would mark the time when the policy would be fully implemented. They were a tough bunch and in the end proved to be more concerned about ensuring success for students than any of the other constituencies I met with, with the exception of our instructors. We discussed—argued in fact—what students should be learning in our courses, whether our instructors were well trained, whether it was a wise idea to focus the courses themselves on process and rhetoric rather than grammar, and so on. They recognized fairly early that I had not fully anticipated how complex a problem was posed by the need to prepare students for their first advising appointment. They also knew that it would be very difficult to allow students to move back and forth between English 100 and 101 during the first 2 weeks of the semester, when both the advisors and students were already overburdened with managing schedules. By the time we had finished debating the mechanism itself, I had promised them I would make their work as easy as possible. That meant that I and writing program staff would manage all student movement during the first 2 weeks of the semester, that I would provide them with all the information they needed to keep their records straight, and that we would generally do everything possible to make their task simply one of informing students about DSP and answering questions as they arose. By the end of this first meeting and in the days that followed, it seemed I had garnered their support.

I learned later that one reason I had "persuaded" them was that I had simply met with them in the first place. Because DSP reached well beyond the writing program itself, it was absolutely necessary for me to meet with them. Nevertheless, our campus advisors are normally left out of the loop, with little say in the formulation of curricular policy. Although much of the policy had been formed already, the advisors felt in this case as if their stake was being measured and appreciated. For the next 2 years, as DSP took hold, the campus advising units, with one notable exception, proved to be the initiative's most vocal proponents.

Unfortunately, we had significant problems garnering the support of the university's Center for Basic Skills, the advising and support unit responsible for ensuring that at-risk students made the adjustment to academic life successfully. These special admission students, comprising approximately 20% of the incoming freshman class, were the ones who had previously been tested for writing ability and slotted either in the English 101 or 101-Restricted course depending on their performance, the writing test itself complementing whatever indications of ability their ACT scores provided. They were also the students we believed had been short-changed under the previous two-tiered system, with clear statistical evidence that their first course was not preparing them to do well in English 102. Early in the process of implementing DSP, we discovered that *all* special admissions students had been automatically placed into English 101 and were not given the choice of starting with English 100 in the new *Stretch* sequence. That came as a great surprise to us because several meetings with the the unit's director and chief academic advisor led us to believe that they would support the plan. As we did with the other advising units, we had periodically checked with them to ask if they needed our assistance. We were assured that everything was going smoothly. In fact, it wasn't going at all. There had been apparent agreement with the plan, but it was disingenuous. Not only were all 450 special admission students placed in English 101, I knew that many of them would likely have chosen English 100 had they been given the choice, so I had planned the course offerings based on my projections. But because these students had been placed (rather than placing themselves), all of our scheduling of courses and instructors would have to be revised because enrollment in English 100 was not meeting our projections.

Suffice it to say there was substantial discussion of our alternatives. When things don't go according to plan in an academic bureaucracy, the war of words can be fierce, even if on the grand scheme of things the issue may seem rather trivial. Push came to shove, with even our provost issuing an executive order that the Center for Basic Skills cooperate with the dictates of DSP. That order went unheeded, of course, in part because the unit was not perceived as an academic one and the director himself reported to the chancellor, who was one step higher up in the administrative hierarchy. (At the time, we had only an interim chancellor who was in the midst of leaving office.) We chose to contact all special admission students directly to let them know of their opportunity to choose their course. Forty percent of the students who responded to our letter chose to move to English 100 (and thus, to drop the English 101 course into which they had been placed). We had averted the crisis in the short term. By the start of the first semester of DSP and *Stretch*, 275 students, or approximately 12% of the incoming class, had chosen to take English 100, including 90 special admission students.

The rhetorical dynamic that ultimately resulted in this breakdown was clear from the beginning, but no one noticed it. One way of avoiding action is to argue details, with the resulting particularity of the argument distracting attention from the urgency of moving forward, even when there's a fairly widely accepted mandate to do so. Even if one misunderstands the details, simply questioning them works to obstruct the intended action. It is a tactic that those skilled in deliberative rhetoric know well. At the outset, the director of the Center for Basic Skills had said, "Just because [DSP] worked at Grand Valley State, that doesn't mean it's going to work here." We spent little time discussing how the previous system hurt the students or how the new one would benefit them. Whenever I would try to begin that discussion, a new detail would be introduced, so that there was never resolution or agreement on any individual point. This sort of exchange went on for more than a year, well past the time when DSP had been accepted by the rest of the campus community as a matter of policy. Eventually, the new status quo exerted enough pressure to make DSP work, but in patchwork form.

I am often asked what "reason" was given for this lack of cooperation, but there remain no clear-cut answers. Certainly, none were ever offered. I believe now that we were witness to the enactment of an ideology that said students were unable to make good judgments about their writing readiness *because* they weren't good writers. They needed to be led with a firm hand by those who were able to judge them, even if those judgments were unsupported by research and by the record of actual student performance. It is an ideology that transcends our particular circumstances. We have seen in other cases that some advisors will insist on making choices for the students because, perhaps, that's simply how it's always been done. But there is also the possibility that some students would rather not make a decision about their placement, feeling it to be too risky a decision. Our surveys of student attitudes, however, show that students overwhelmingly value their right to choose their writing course (see chap. 10 in this volume), so it's more likely that where there was ambiguity, some people seized the opportunity to force choice in a particular direction.

Other advising units took to DSP eagerly. Another of our at-risk populations—students deemed "pre-major"—enrolled in English 100 at about a 25% rate, well above the rate for other students. Pre-major advisors had been the most enthusiastic about the change in placement procedures and had worked the hardest to make sure their students were well-informed. By the second year, we discovered that these students had also made the biggest turnaround in terms of their performance throughout the composition sequence, with their overall GPA in the courses higher than all other groups, whereas in past years, it had been well below. (See chap. 10, this volume, for specific details on these gains.)

As an exercise in consensus building, our implementation of DSP had unintended byproducts that have served the writing program well. Our campus advisors, because they have a prominent role in placement, know what we do in our courses and why we do it. They have been able to see that their efforts make a difference. It is important for a writing program to have allies beyond its borders, as WPAs know. In the next 2 years, the usual complaints from faculty and the administration about students who can't write diminished substantially, so that we were left to make improvements to the program without always feeling the need to defend ourselves or the integrity of our curriculum. Perhaps ironically, those of us who have fought on behalf of DSP have found ourselves cast into a net somewhat like the one we lay for students when we place them by any means. We saw the ways that the institution asserted its hierarchical system of ordering as we debated the legislative function of academic policy. But we also emerged from the process with a new spirit of cooperation, a feeling among many that we each had a stake, that we had changed the status quo, if slightly, and that its momentum could be influenced in directions that we chose, not ones chosen for us by necessity or conveniences of the past.

Instructors in our writing program became much more involved in the placement process. No longer did students magically appear in their courses, with the knowledge of how they got there a mystery to the students and the instructors. The instructors play a vital role in disseminating information about DSP in the first 2 weeks of the semester. Each has to be a spokesperson capable of answering questions for the students. When they read diagnostic essays by students written in other classes, instructors must base their reading not merely on the evidence in front of them but on their conception of the composition sequence, the differences between English 100 and 101, and the goals of the program on the whole. Instructors of English 100 had the opportunity to rethink their approach to teaching writing on the knowledge that they would have their students for a full year rather than merely a 15-week semester. Sequencing of assignments becomes more a matter of scripting writing growth than it does of simply squeezing 6 (or however many) essay assignments into the calendar. As I see it, these are each positive results and directly attributable to DSP and the *Stretch* model.

For these reasons, I see DSP as a superior method of placement to the standard way writing placement used to operate on our campus, with students forced on the sly to simply accept the decree of administrators long ago who determined that an ACT score would be a good way to sift students by writing ability. That original act, even as it tidily reinforced the university's position as the guarded gateway to higher learning, also placed many students in great peril from the start by virtue of naming them using standards no one quite understood, appreciated, or even, when put to the test, trusted very much. As DSP takes hold, I believe we will also see dramatic changes in the culture of the classroom, if not just the academic culture that supports it. The simple act of providing students some stake in exercising personal agency in such an explicit way can begin the process of achieving that more noble goal of higher education: to prepare a citizenry to write its own future by deliberating on its past. DSP is an act of restoration, not preservation, to the extent that it asks students to learn from the past to make decisions about their future. I think it will be very exciting and interesting to see whether the institution can withstand relinquishing to its subjects at least some of its power to name and place.

ACKNOWLEDGMENTS

An early draft of this chapter was presented as a paper at the Conference on College Composition and Communication in Minneapolis, MN, on April 16, 2000.

I acknowledge some of the people who graciously contributed time and resources to this project: Placement Coordinators Laura Ciancanelli, Todd Deam, Erin Harvey, Stacy Nicklow, Erica Reynolds, and Kristin Tracy; Dr. Gordon White, who provided all the data; advisors Virginia Rinella, Richard Oakey, and Wanda Oakey; and above all, Donna Vance, for her all-around diligent and expert help on behalf of DSP at the university.

REFERENCES

Blakesley, David. "Directed Self-Placement and the English 100/101 Stretch Program at Southern Illinois University Carbondale: A Report on Student Performance, Retention, and Satisfaction." Internal Report. Southern Illinois University Carbondale. Carbondale. 9 April 2000.

Burke, Kenneth. *Attitudes Toward History.* 1937. 3rd Rev. Ed. Berkeley: University of California Press, 1984.

——. *Language as Symbolic Action: Essays on Life, Literature, and Method.* Berkeley: U of California P, 1968.

——. *A Rhetoric of Motives.* 1950. Berkeley: U of California P, 1969.

Crowley, Sharon. *Composition in the University: Historical and Polemical Essays.* Pittsburgh, PA: U of Pittsburgh P, 1998.

Douglas, Mary. *How Institutions Think.* Syracuse, NY: Syracuse UP, 1986.

Freire, Paulo. *Pedagogy of the Oppressed.* 1970. Trans. Myra Bergman Ramos. New York: Continuum, 1990.

Glau, Gregory. "The 'Stretch Program': Arizona State University's New Model of University-Level Basic Writing Instruction." *WPA: Writing Program Administration* 20 (1996): 79-91.

Gleason, Barbara. "Evaluating Writing Programs in Real Time: The Politics of Remediation." *College Composition and Communication* 51.4 (June 2000): 560-88.

Porter, James E., Patricia Sullivan, Stuart Blythe, Jeffrey T. Grabill, and Libby Miles. "Institutional Critique: A Rhetorical Methodology for Change." *College Composition and Communication* 51.4 (June 2000): 610-42.

Royer, Daniel J. and Roger Gilles. "Directed Self-Placement: An Attitude of Orientation," *College Composition and Communication* 50.1 (September 1998): 54-70.

3

THE PRAGMATIST FOUNDATIONS OF DIRECTED SELF-PLACEMENT

Daniel J. Royer
Roger Gilles
Grand Valley State University

For several years now, writing assessment experts have been calling on those of us involved in writing program administration and the teaching of college writing to step back and take a longer look at the consequences of our assessment practices. The 1995 CCCC position statement on writing assessment, for example, urges the creation of forms of assessment that demonstrate "systemic validity"—that is, that connect to good classroom practice (432). In terms of evaluating the validity of various assessment options, Camp urges us to broaden our focus from the practicalities of testing measures and scoring devices to the larger personal and educational consequences of our assessments (61). Likewise, Brian Huot calls for assessment practices that "look beyond the assessment measures themselves . . . and have positive impact and consequences for the teaching and learning of writing" (551).

Kathleen Blake Yancey observes that one way to trace the history of writing assessment "is through its movement into the classroom" (484). The historical trend in assessment, according to Yancey, has developed from multiple-choice tests (outside the classroom and outside the curriculum) to direct writing assessment (often outside the classroom and curriculum—

e.g., exit exams) to portfolios developed inside the classroom. Two key directions of writing assessment, then, seem to be from narrow, statistically "valid" assessment practices to broader, more personally valid ones—and from external measures unconnected or only indirectly connected to actual curricula to internal measures closely tied to the students' present curricula.

Camp, Huot, Yancey, and others thus show a concern not just for assessment methods that lead to better grades and better retention rates, but also for methods that positively affect the larger social and academic life of the students—and we would add faculty—that are involved.

But what exactly are the positive consequences we should seek for students and faculty in college writing programs? Some, like test scores, student satisfaction data, or even grades in first-year writing courses, are easy to measure but perhaps still more indicative than consequential. The consequences of first-year writing courses go far beyond the courses themselves. But the broader the consequences we consider, the more difficult they are to measure in a way that would satisfy an educational statistician. Yancey asks, "Which self does any writing assessment permit? . . . which self does an assessment construct?" (484). These are wonderfully apt and important questions—questions that all educators should be asking. But once we as educators begin pursuing particular kinds of educated "selves," we have, of course, reached a level of abstraction that defies easy quantification in posttests or follow-up surveys. Nonetheless, we believe that placement—a kind of assessment that goes on at the beginning of a course of study—should not evade the questions raised by these writing assessment experts:

- How does our placement method connect with the curriculum it seeks to serve?
- Which self does our placement procedure permit or construct?
- What are the personal and educational consequences of our placement method?

Directed self-placement (DSP) is different from other placement methods—from the most simplistic use of standardized test scores to the most localized and sophisticated use of writing portfolios—in the way it attends to these three questions.

HOW DOES DSP CONNECT WITH THE CURRICULUM IT SEEKS TO SERVE?

In conventional placement methods, the relationship between the student and the curriculum is heavily mediated—primarily by the assessment tools themselves, which have become increasing complex as writing program administrators (WPAs) have sought to increase the validity and reliability of their methods. For good reason, assessment experts have urged us to "think about whether our assessments adequately represent writing as we understand it" (Camp 61). As our understanding of writing has deepened, our best assessment methods have become ever more context-rich and authentic (see, e.g., Hamp-Lyons and Condon). Indeed, as Edward M. White points out, if writing teachers had full control over writing assessment, "the ideal assessment would likely be an expanded version of classroom assessment—such as we now see in portfolios" (14).

Because of the good work of those who first championed direct-writing assessment and more recently portfolio assessment, it is now difficult to justify any assessment method that does not include authentic writing situations, process materials, writer reflections, multiple samples in multiple genres, clearly articulated performance expectations rooted in particular contexts, and so on. As responsible WPAs seek to create increasingly honest and fair forms of placement assessment, they spend more and more of their time and energy on placement—and perhaps less on teaching and teacher-preparation and on other forms of assessment, including grading and program evaluation. As we create "an expanded version of classroom assessment" as a way to place students into our courses, we may have less and less time for classroom assessment itself. We reach the point, then, when we have to be reminded by assessment experts not to forget that our main work is not about placement, as such, but about developing curricula that positively affect our students' lives.

DSP creates a far more direct relationship between the student and the curriculum than do other forms of placement. It peels away an entire complex of concerns and activities—an entire industry, really—that discourages us from attending to the only really important variables: our students and our curriculum. With DSP, we do not have to be reminded about our students and our curriculum; they are our only concern.

Anyone who has been involved with college-level writing placement over the past two or three decades knows just how complex placement can be, primarily because of the twin concerns of *reliability* and *validity*. As Roger D. Cherry and Paul R. Meyer point out, reliability and validity are two of the most basic—and complex—concepts in assessment theory (110). Consider, for example, just three of the many variables that must be considered when we attempt to create *reliable* placement methods—and keep in mind that, as Cherry and Meyer say, "reliability is not as complex and therefore not as problematic as validity" (111):

- the variability of student performance from day to day, which makes single-shot writing samples problematic
- the relative difficulty of writing prompts or assignments, which makes it difficult to measure on a common scale writing produced in response to different prompts or in different contexts—even writing produced by a single writer
- the idiosyncratic nature of rating sessions and individual raters, which makes it difficult to compare ratings between sessions and between raters—and even between a single rater at different times during a single session. (112)

As the result of the important and productive work of measurement theorists and placement experts over the years, placement has indeed become a very complex process. Some larger schools have composition boards whose primary job is to coordinate the writing program's year-round placement efforts. The largest schools place several thousand students per year in first-year writing classes. This is big business. Figure 3.1, below, illustrates the range of variables that typically come into play in the placement business.

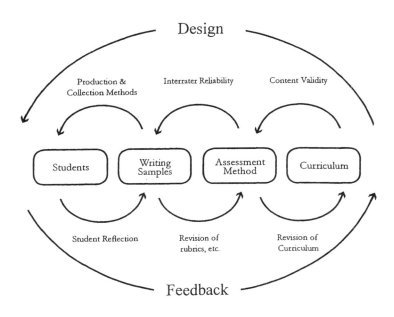

Fig. 3.1. Effective conventional placement requires a complex design-feedback loop.

As Figure 3.1 suggests, there is a "design–feedback loop" in all placement approaches that begins with the initial design of the assessment method—a design that ideally takes into account the particular curriculum into which students are being placed. Assessment methods include determining placement by scoring a timed writing sample or, at a few schools, some kind of entrance portfolio. Many schools use ACT-English, SAT-Verbal scores, or high school GPA in combination with timed writing samples or portfolios. Whether the writing sample includes a single essay or a full portfolio, those in charge of placement must design prompts or portfolio submission guidelines, recruit and train (and retrain) readers, arrange for the actual student writing to be written (perhaps on a particular word processing program in campus computer labs, perhaps in blue books in large lecture halls) or collected (as part of the application packet, as a separate mailed or e-mailed submission, or during orientation sessions), conduct scoring sessions, and process and report the results to students. All of these processes must be *designed*, and of course there are books, journals, conferences, and consulting services devoted to helping schools design and implement effective placement programs.

And then the feedback begins. Responsible placement designers must ask students (and the high school teachers and administrators who might be affected by student placement results) to reflect on the placement process and make suggestions; they must consider and experiment with the effects of word processed versus hand written student writing, of single-shot writing samples versus multisample portfolios, of various writing modes (narrative, expository, persuasive) on rater response; they must assess their own training methods and track interrater reliability and make necessary adjustments; they must experiment with various writing prompts and assignments and tweak the ones that work best; and they must always consider ways in which the placement process affects the curriculum itself—either positively by preparing students for the kinds of writing they'll be asked to do in their courses or by guiding teachers to a deeper understanding of program goals and expectations, or negatively by creating angry or frustrated students, or defensive or confused teachers. All of this must be taken into account as the placement administrators assess their own assessment practices. It is indeed a complex business.

As Figure 3.2 illustrates, DSP simplifies the design–feedback loop of the placement process. The only method is to explain to students the courses in the curriculum and the placement options available to them. If student feedback indicates that the explanations are not clear enough, we need to do a better job of it. Then, once students are underway in the curriculum, we need to ask whether they are getting what they need out of the courses they enrolled in. If they are not, we need to adjust the courses—and then share those adjustments with future students so that they in turn can make the placement decisions that are best for them. The only two variables, then, are the students and the curriculum.

Certainly, there are materials and activities that need to be designed: as the chapter in Part II indicate, various schools have designed explanatory letters, informational brochures, orientation speeches, small-group workshops, written surveys and inventories, and so on, as part of the DSP process. Here, however, we wish to emphasize that all of these materials have only two things in mind: explaining the curriculum to students, and helping students find their place in that curriculum. It's all very direct.

But conventional placement methods are almost wholly *indirect*. There is the student, and there is the curriculum—and in the middle is the placement method. A prompt designed to elicit a timed writing sample is at best an indirect approximation of the kind of writing that gets done in an actual first-year writing course. A trained essay or portfolio rater is at best a *representative* of the performance expectations of teachers in the actual curriculum. Indeed, William L. Smith urges us to use actual teachers from the program as the best representatives of the teaching and expectations of a program for placement purposes (173-74). So even ideally, all we can do is

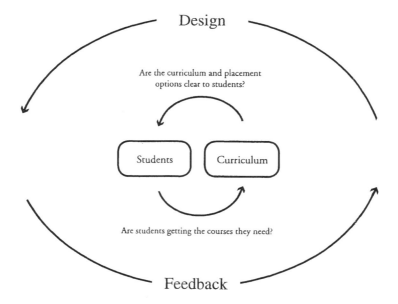

Fig. 3.2. DSP simplifies the design–feedback loop of the placement process.

replicate the values and practices of the program in our placement methods: writing prompts *just like* real assignments being read by people *just like* real teachers using standards *just like* real course expectations. At some point we have to wonder why we don't just offer *classes* over the summer as a way to place students.

Others try to connect the placement process to the curriculum by, for example, making the placement essay part of the first classroom assignment. But the placement process is never really a part of the curriculum. Placement happens before classes begin, or during the first week of classes during the safety of the drop/add period. Our point is that in their quest for authenticity, placement methods have become every bit as complex and involved as the courses themselves. Most current placement systems, or at least the ones we call good, require energies—and resources—that might otherwise go directly into the curriculum.

And as we all know, these energies and resources are precious and limited. We believe it is far better to commit our resources to the curriculum itself. As we say, every aspect of a conventional placement system has its analogue in the actual curriculum: in the actual curriculum, we design writing courses and writing assignments (rather than placement methods and writing prompts); in the actual curriculum, we design performance standards and grading criteria (rather than scoring rubrics); in the actual curriculum, we meet to discuss student writing and grading practices (rather than conduct training and scoring sessions). Indeed, our growing appreciation for the complexity of writing assessment has led people like Peter Elbow, for example, to urge us to "Do It Better, Do It Less." It's simply too hard—and too important—to do quickly, or at the wrong time. Do it better, do it less. This is precisely what DSP encourages. Rather than spend so much of our assessment energies and resources on placement, we prefer to spend it directly on teaching, grading, and program evaluation.

WHICH SELF DOES DSP PERMIT OR CONSTRUCT?

Although there has been little need to argue for the superiority of DSP over multiple-choice tests or static test scores, those invested in portfolio placement or timed essay exams have been eager to see the "evidence" that DSP "works." It's an interesting request. For what works, validity, and the nature of evidence can, according to the metrics of traditional placement systems, best be measured by those in charge of placement. This commitment among strong advocates of essay placement may not be entirely wrong, but it is limiting—and it is rarely questioned, but instead it reigns as the unbending standard of effectiveness by which all other placement must be judged. That is, the evidence such advocates call for is, in some cases, the very evidence DSP calls into question.

Every placement method must shoulder a burden of proof—and merely getting a writing sample or collecting a portfolio does not mean a placement method *works*. For example, our statistics indicated that trained, timed essay graders of a 2-hour exam could not place students in such a way that gave them any particular advantage or disadvantage in passing with a grade of C or better the regular first-year writing course. We were able to generate impressive interrater reliability among essay graders, and we were able to some degree to predict which students would do particularly well or particularly poorly in our classes, but there was no significant correlation between placement and a student's chances of *passing* the regular, required course. That is, although we were able to identify students who were more likely to do *well* in our regular course, we could not consistently identify those more likely to get *credit* for the course. Thus, we were uncomfortable telling students they *could not* take the regular course when we knew (as well as they apparently did for many slipped through and took the regular course anyway) that their chances of passing with a grade of C or better were as good as any other student. Those schools using exam placement should check these correlations for themselves.

So when people ask, "Does DSP work?" if they mean, "Do students choose the same course that we would have chosen for them had we used timed essay + ACT score or had we looked at a portfolio of the student's writing?" they are simply revealing a prior commitment to a particular standard of evidence—a standard that may be legitimate in some contexts but one that is certainly more narrow than it need be. We would not, for example, ask if timed placement essays "worked" and mean, "Does it place students the same way a multiple-choice grammar essay places them?" We wouldn't use the prior standard of evidence because we realize that essay exams or portfolio placement introduces a wider range of evidence, that it is not limited by a student's knowledge of subject–verb agreement, but rather it takes a broader view of what counts as "writing" and thus introduces new evidence. In the same way, DSP—as we suggested at the beginning of this chapter—introduces a fresh array and quality of evidence, evidence that permits and includes the student's own self as an essential component in the placement decision. This is evidence that is simply overlooked if we limit our standard of "what works" to the evidence generated by existing placement methods and ignore the consequences of the prevailing method of placement. DSP gives us new understanding of what counts as evidence that a placement method *works*.

What we should be asking is not whether DSP can replicate the placement decisions that caused our statistician to throw up his hands and exclaim, "They may as well be placing themselves!" but rather we should ask richer, more penetrating questions like the one asked by Yancey: What self does our writing assessment permit? This, of course, is just one question. But once we have admitted the student self into the placement process, we have to ask an entire web of interesting questions: How informed were students about the choice? How much guidance did they receive in their decision-making process? After several weeks, months in the class, how convinced are they that they made the right choice? What was the essential basis of their decision? what factors were most important in determining which course would be most helpful? After all, the question "Was the student placed properly?" cannot be answered without asking these questions. And research in social psychology on student self-efficacy, gender, and DSP promises to supply a kind of meta-criticism of DSP itself, a level of investigation that is largely ignored by the prevailing placement doctrines. "Proper placement" will, in most cases, have very little to do with the kinds of things that can be detected in a 1-hour placement essay exam. Of course, these questions don't make sense if the student is not involved in the placement decision.

PRAGMATISM, INQUIRY, AND THE STUDENT SELF

These are all interesting questions, and they are addressed throughout this book. For now, it is important to note that a unique feature of DSP is that it permits the construction of a self within a community because it fosters agency, choice, and self-determination. The educational self that DSP encourages is one that develops through the tensions presented by choice and consequence. American pragmatism has charted much of this territory in books and essays on education, thinking, learning, and psychology. From Charles Sanders Peirce's "The Fixation of Belief" to Dewey's *How We Think, Democracy and Education*, and many essays on the nature of learning and inquiry, these thinkers have sought to make room for the living self that is too often eclipsed by positivistic assumptions or stubborn commitments to received traditions.

American philosophic pragmatism might be said to have been inaugurated in Peirce's 1878 article, "How to Make our Ideas Clear." The pragmatic procedures he discussed in this essay emphasizes that *meaning* is always understood as a function of consequences. William James developed Peirce's notions of reasoning and mentality, in part, against the prevailing *correspondence* view of mind that held it to be a disembodied mirror of things external. James insists that we cannot leave the full range of human experience out of the equation when we think about *mentality*:

> Mental interests, hypotheses, postulates, so far as they are bases for human action—action which to a great extent transforms the world—help to *make* the truth which they declare. In other words, there belongs to mind, from its birth upward, a spontaneity, a vote. It is in the game, and not a mere looker-on. (67)

Interests, hypotheses, and postulates are forecasts about meaning in the world by one who is experiencing. Pragmatism is an extension of historical empiricism (James spoke of "radical empiricism"), but it conceived of experience in a much richer way than the English empiricism from which it departed. Most importantly, it focuses on the future not the past, on consequences and possibilities, not on antecedents, precedents, and prerequisites. Dewey said that "one will understand the philosophy of James better if one considers it in its totality as a revision of English empiricism, a revision which replaces the value of past experience, of what is already given, by the future, by that which is as yet mere possibility" ("Development" 34).

Both Dewey and James offered a great number of examples of these principles properly at work in the business of philosophy and education. The pragmatist outlook—what James called an "attitude of orientation," "the attitude of looking away from first things, principles, 'categories,' supposed necessities; and of looking toward last things, fruits, consequences, facts"—permeated Dewey's many volumes on inquiry, learning, and education. And when we examine the conceptual framework that has guided our own development of DSP, we can point out in particular several important developments of these pragmatist foundations. The first has to do with the nature of inquiry.

Dewey describes successful inquiry as that which begins with an "indeterminate situation," a situation that is uncertain, unsettled, disturbed. Accordingly, *inquiry* is the process whereby such a situation is transformed through interaction with the social environment into one that is *determinate* or settled. In other words, inquiry traffics in the productive realm of uncertainty. Peirce makes a similar point in "The Fixation of Belief": "Belief," he says, "does not make us act at once, but puts us into such a condition that we behave in a certain way when the occasion arises. Doubt has not the least effect of this sort, but stimulates us to action until it is destroyed" (67). DSP provides just such an educative situation. Students may come to orientation sessions with a particular belief. That is, they may be settled and satisfied with a particular view of themselves as writers. Yet, the aim of our short talk with students is to create some dissonance, to help stimulate—if even for just a few moments in their experience—an "indeterminate situation" that will promote inquiry. In this way, doubt may displace belief long enough for students to consider fresh the new situation they are about to encounter as writers in our program.

Peirce says that it is a mere tautology that we think each one of our beliefs to be true. Thus, it is not "true opinion" about a matter that the inquirer strives for, but rather the settlement of doubt. As we discuss later in this chapter, there is no "true" placement to haggle over, only better and worse decisions to make. The point here is about the Peircian method of "fixing belief." It's not merely antecedent "facts" such as ACT score that guide our students; it's not the authority of directors of composition that can finally fix belief; it's not the *a priori* belief in one's self as a "good" or "bad" writer. These precedents in experience can be factors, but finally it is the prospect of success in one class or the other that secures this particular doubt in our students in this particular situation.

A premise of DSP is that the doubt about which we venture inquiry is about a student's ability to do satisfactory work in a class. We have no business inquiring after the phantom essentialist understanding of a writer's ability, for such an ability is highly contextual and, more importantly, even if there were such a thing, it's not a real and living doubt in the student's experience. The real, living doubt that we help create for the student has to do with his or her ability to do well enough in a particular class to learn and, with some effort, get a good grade. And again, the importance of inquiry in such a situation is directly related to questions about what kind of self our placement procedures permit. When James says that mental interests, hypotheses, postulates "help to *make* the truth which they declare," he means that there are not essentialist structures that simply play out in an individual's future. Our job as educators is much more complex than this. Future experience is the consequence of a "vote," making actual in experience what was only mere possibility. And where placement is concerned, it's what students are going to do—what they could do and might do—not what they have done, that is most important. It really is a choice between emphasizing students as active, inquiring agents on the one hand, or in emphasizing the passive, static, essentialist limitations of past experience on the other.

Pragmatism ferrets out many pseudo-problems through its claim that meaning is coupled with thought and action and that the only real philosophic problems are those that arise out of real experience (not hypothetical or feigned experience). There is a scholastic sickness, not unfamiliar in our own field of study, whereby *theories* themselves become answers to problems. We might see, for example, the name (or ethos really) of Bourdieu or Giroux invoked as a *solution* to problems. But theories, James tells us, should become *instruments,* not answers to enigmas in which we can rest. In like manner, James says that pragmatism—as a method, an attitude, an orientation toward practical and philosophic problems—is really a program for further work, not a solution that stops investigative activity as it settles in, comfortable with its essentialist understanding.

On the contrary, we have been saying that agency, choice, and self-determination are the kinds of consequences DSP wants to foster in our placement procedures. Such consequences may sound naïve to a Bourdieuian intent on the ways that educational practices replicate culture and privilege in a particular way, but if such is the view we hold, then we really have no "placement problem" to begin with. What we would have in this case is the theoretical difficulty or ethical paradox of trying to extricate ourselves from the infinite regress of participating in and fostering vicious educational structures that replicate a prevailing practice that, presumably, we believe needs changing. This is why it is so important to stay oriented by the original problems that prompt inquiry, for we can easily spend all our time pondering problems that our theories have created, instead of solving the problems that confront our students.

But surely solutions have implications beyond the immediate problems we encounter. And DSP, as a solution to the placement problem, has consequences that take us beyond the immediacy of the original placement problem. But as the scope of consequence widens, we should not allow subsequent problems to distract us or become substitutes for the original problems that prompt inquiry and problem solving. We should keep looking back and reminding ourselves what real problem we are trying to solve. When *theories* become *solutions* we get sidetracked from living inquiry and our solutions are in danger of becoming ends in themselves.

This principle applies especially to WPAs. In the philosophic ground clearing of early 20th-century American philosophy, Dewey lamented the "epistemology industry," the philosophic preoccupation that had lost sight of the original problems in lived experience that had prompted questions about "how we know" in the first place. We must be careful we don't allow "supposed necessities" to cause us to lament as well the placement industry. When we consider the problem of placement in first-year composition, what pragmatism does for us is orient us in a particular way toward certain problems and guide us in our work and understanding of their solutions.

A second important development of these pragmatist foundations has to do with the individual and community. Dewey tells us that democracy is fundamentally a "mode of associated living, a conjoint communicated experience" (*Democracy* 101)—in other words, a way of living together. The ideal of community life, Dewey insists, involves *association, connection, and dependence*. But we have also been stressing the values of *agency, choice, and self-determination.* DSP plays across an important tension here: Students are given individual freedom of choice, while at the same time they are being guided through deliberation—they are allowed agency, choice, and self-determination, but it only works to their advantage so long as there is association, connection, and dependence with established members of the community. Navigating this balance is itself a Deweyian kind of response to the extremes of freedom and autonomy on the one hand and institutional control on the other. The point is really Dewey's: Proper connection with community increases freedom and opportunities for growth. Dewey held with other process philosophers that "association in the sense of connection and combination is a 'law' of everything known to exist. Singular things act, but they act together. Nothing has been discovered which acts in entire isolation" ("Public" 250). Our autonomy is something of a mirage and as an "ideal" it doesn't promote freedom or growth. As Dewey notes, "No man and no mind was ever emancipated merely by being left alone" ("Public" 340). And, of course, nobody was ever emancipated by merely being told what to do.

The premise at work in this discussion of community is that the university is in fact a kind of community, that all our professional talk about our classrooms and "discourse communities" is not just talk. At student orientation, we talk about joining a learning community and we say or imply that a community is more than mere association. Dewey has much to say about this topic, but the following will perhaps make the point well enough:

> Associated or joint activity is a condition of the creation of community. But association itself is physical and organic, while communal life is moral, that is emotionally, intellectually, consciously sustained. . . . For beings who observe and think, and whose ideas are absorbed by impulses and become sentiments and interests, "we" is as inevitable as "I." . . . But participation in activities and sharing in results are additive concerns. They demand *communication* as a prerequisite. ("Public" 330)

Admittedly, our talk with students about choices in first-year composition is just a small step toward this kind of communication and community building. But given the problem at hand—how to find a way for students to begin first-year composition in a course that matches their abilities and psychological readiness—it is a step that is guided by the same pragmatist principles that we hope will guide other important moments in the students' educational lives at our university. The ideal we should strive for is *agency, choice, and self-determination* coupled with *association, connection, and dependence*—in short, the ideal of a democratic community. When students gather at our orientation sessions, listen to our 10-minute talk

"Which Course is Right for You," they begin to participate in the community life of our university and, in turn, engage this pragmatist ideal.

The best learning stems from authentic inquiry. Ultimately, the inquiry in which writers become involved isn't "settled" until the end of the first-year writing program—or, in some schools, the end of the 4-year writing program. By that time the writers have had one, two, or perhaps several semesters to work on their writing. Our hope is that these writers have pursued their work with the "internal control through identity of interest and understanding" that Dewey describes as a hallmark of joining a community. But, of course, we must invite them into this community by allowing their participation in important decision-making moments.

WHAT ARE THE PERSONAL AND EDUCATIONAL CONSEQUENCES OF DSP?

The essential consequence of all other placement methods is that students are told where to go; they are told what course to take. Even the term *placement*, reveals the long-accepted systemic relationship implied by all other placement methods: Teachers and administrators, as agents of the university, "place" students where the students supposedly belong. Teachers are active, students are passive. Teachers know, students do not. So no matter how "accurate" the placement—and no matter how well the students end up doing in their first and subsequent courses—the first consequence of placement is always the same: The students' agency is denied. And this at the very doorstep of the college or university, typically during summer orientation or the first day of class. As an introduction to college life, traditional course placement sends a message oddly discordant with the basic educational values of agency, choice, and self-determination.

But of course the consequences of any placement method go beyond the initial moment of decision making. Consequences range from the way students feel about the placement method to the curricular adjustments we make based on feedback from everyone who participates in the process.

TRANSFORMED MOMENTS: THREE CONSEQUENCES OF DSP

If the college experience can be viewed as a connected series of educational moments that begin with the student's first look at the school's admissions brochure or first visit to the school Web site or campus, then to assess the impact of DSP we might consider the potential it has to transform several well-known moments in the lives of those involved with first-year composition. Here we focus on three such moments. We highlight the way these moments broaden rather than narrow what counts as "evidence" of proper placement for student writers, and we also emphasize that in good pragmatist fashion, writing placement can become an integral part of the educational process: Students can be woven into the educational fabric, committed to the educational decision at hand, no longer an alien object in our placement procedures.

Consequence 1—Summer Orientation

The role of writing faculty at summer orientation has for the past several decades been an odd one. In the midst of welcoming speeches by deans of students and coordinators of academic services, the writing faculty show up—usually through a back door—to administer and evaluate the dreaded placement test. Students in sandals move from a cheerful campus tour to a crowded lecture hall with cramped writing trays to write cramped essays in crowded blue books. Then they're released for lunch, and 2 hours later they receive a slip of paper or a hushed report from an orientation group leader: "You've been placed in ENG 101"—or 100, as the case may be. Or, more recently in a few select schools, students are spared the timed writing exercise because they've already submitted a portfolio of their high school writing, so after lunch the portfolios appear with a slip of paper inside: "You've been placed in ENG 100." That old high school question—"What'd you get?"—works through the room. New friends compare slips and rejoice or commiserate, as the case may be. The sorting has begun.

Before DSP, then, orientation day was a testing day, a sorting day. Students started the day with a question—"Which class will I take?"—and they left with an answer. It was the banking concept of first-year composition. Advisors like tellers read test scores or placement results off computer screens angled for privacy. Students asked, faculty answered. Student uncertainty was met with faculty certainty: "We know where you belong."

But with DSP, orientation day is a problem-posing day, a day for faculty to answer a question with a question: "Given what you now know about the year-end expectations of the academic writing community you've decided to join, with which course would you like to begin?" Faculty are still knowers, of course, but what they know is their own program—the courses and the community standards for success in those courses. But now, the students are knowers as well. They know their own histories and their experiences with writing. They know their own abilities, and their own needs. What we can offer them is what Dewey pressed for in *Democracy and Education*: direction and guidance. There is often an unconscious assumption that students act only from individualistic or selfish motives. "But," Dewey notes, "they are also interested, and chiefly interested upon the whole, in entering into the activities of others and taking part in conjoint and cooperative doings. Otherwise, no such thing as a community would be possible" (29). What Dewey describes as the "environment as directive" gives us alternatives to external modes of controlling students. By establishing a common understanding with students, DSP makes possible the kind of educational activity that Dewey describes as "intrinsic to the disposition of the person, not external and coercive." Moreover, he adds, "to achieve this internal control through identity of interest and understanding is the business of education" (47).

Although faculty still play an important role as guiding experts, students are given full control over this crucial first-year decision. We think this is particularly important for basic writers. Just because they may struggle with certain aspects of writing, we need not assume that they cannot be thoughtful about their own experiences and abilities and act responsibly in their own best interests. In fact, Erica Reynolds' research (see chap. 4, this volume) surveys a range of studies that indicate that self-efficacy, which is expressed as a situation- and subject-specific personal confidence in one's ability to successfully perform tasks at a given level, is a strong predictor of actual ability. And might skewed self-confidence (low or high) be a particular stumbling block for basic writers? Reynolds further points out:

> Daly and Wilson point out that although the "magnitude of relationship" between writing apprehension and self-esteem was "uniformly small, the consistency across two measures of self-esteem" was present (330). They explain this finding by stating that "general self-esteem, since it is a very broad construct, might not be expected to have a large relationship with any highly specific construct like apprehension" (331). Dale Schunk addresses this phenomenon in "Self-Efficacy and Academic Motivation," pointing out that self-concept, which incorporates self-esteem and self-confidence, is "hierarchically organized, with a general self-concept at the top and subarea self-concepts at the base" (212). He maintains, based on Bandura's social cognitive learning theory, that of self-concept's various dimensions, self-confidence seems the most akin to self-efficacy and that "in the hierarchy, self-efficacy judgments would lie at low levels because they are generally construed to be domain specific," i.e., Algebra or Geometry (212). In other words, even within an academic area, a high self-concept does not imply that students feel highly confident about their abilities in all academic areas, or necessarily confident in general. (91)

Students who choose to begin with the basic writing course signal to us a desire to take things slowly, to test the waters of college writing before jumping into the standard course. Students who choose to begin with the standard course—including those who might previously have been labeled *basic writers*—signal to us a desire to dive right in. This eagerness, we believe, can go a long way in helping a basic writer to make great strides in the standard writing course. If all of our students begin their first writing course thinking, "This is the course I want," we feel we are in an ideal educational position.

Consequence Two: The Placement Complaint

Before DSP, if WPAs talked to students about placement at all, we might have said something like this: "If you have any questions about your placement, please come see me in my office." And students did come—although rarely with questions. Rather, they took the "certainty" we'd handed them at orientation and challenged it, and sometimes we argued back. Our message was, "You may think you know, but we know best." We defended our placement methods as reliable and valid, even when we had suspicions ourselves. We agreed to look again at the placement essay or portfolio, and as we scanned the pages we searched for weaknesses—anything that would justify the placement that had already been so confidently handed down. Sometimes, even as we said "I can see why you weren't placed in 101," we wondered to ourselves who among the faculty could possibly have scored the essay so low!

If we were stubborn, the students would finally leave, still angry but perhaps a bit less confident about the grounds for their resistance. At best, the students would see that not just two, but now three writing faculty thought they were "basic" or "developmental" or "remedial" writers. At worst, they would seethe with the conviction that they'd been misunderstood, overlooked, ignored.

Perhaps more often, we were honest with ourselves and admitted that the placement method wasn't perfect, that we did indeed make mistakes. Then the students would leave knowing that the "certainty" they'd been handed hadn't been certain after all—that when faculty first say "We know best," they sometimes mean "We *think* we know best." Educationally, what is at stake is nothing less than the status of knowledge itself. Because of our hastily made claims of certainty—which are later challenged and occasionally shown to be false—we call into question our ability to make any claims at all. We create skeptical students, which ultimately is not a bad thing, but we portray ourselves as simple believers in truths that we cannot always support. The students earn their skepticism at our expense.

With DSP, placement complaints simply don't happen. *Because* the placement decision is the students' own, they have no one to complain to. WPAs might, however, still invite students to visit the office if they have questions. But now we really mean it: come see us if you have questions. During their visits, students may express their own uncertainty about the course that is right for them—and our role is to help them work toward a more certain position. First of all, then, we are guides, not judges, which is consistent with the kind of pedagogical stance most of us have been trying to take in the classroom these past few decades. But also, we model in these discussions a far better educational practice than we had before: Without certain knowledge, the students and faculty work together to explore the variables and reach a satisfactory, although still tentative, conclusion. In the end, we protect the students' agency, but we show the students that good decisions must be made in a rich context of knowledge and understanding. Michael Williamson says, "Tests don't have validity; *decisions* have validity." We are helping the students reach a valid decision.

Regardless of the students' final decision, however, we never have to leave the uncomfortably productive realm of uncertainty. The best the student can say is, "I think I now know the best course for me." This is a solid educational goal, to help students generate hypotheses and then to test them—for Dewey, this is the fundamental pattern of educative inquiry. We'd prefer to have our entering students *thinking* rather than *knowing,* testing their uncertainties rather than challenging our certainties. In the past, it was only after crisis and argument that uncertainty was allowed to creep in. The pose was certainty, but the reality was uncertainty. Now the reality from beginning to *end* is uncertainty. There is no "true" placement to haggle over, only better and worse decisions to make.

In our embracing of uncertainty, however, we do not disavow knowledge about writing. We know our own program, and the kinds of writing that succeed in our program. After a semester of work and interaction with particular students, we can know the difference between an "A" and a "C" course portfolio. Confident judgments about student writing can be made when faculty collaborate on establishing program goals and standards and meet regularly to discuss student papers in the context of the program— and when students produce their work within the rich context of such a fully articulated program. As faculty, we do know a lot about writing and how to assess it in context. What we don't know is the entering students' writing— which has, after all, been produced outside the context of our program and institution. The key is that we don't pretend to know what we cannot know. We thus affirm our ability to make knowledgeable claims about student writing—but only when the time comes. We affirm that the time for faculty to make knowledgeable claims about student writing is at the end of a course or sequence of courses, in a rich programmatic context, not at the beginning.

At the same time, we affirm the value of our students' past experiences as writers. Students do not come to us from a vacuum. They come to us from high schools and high school teachers, from reading and writing lives that deserve to be taken seriously. The implication of a one-shot placement mechanism is that we, the college faculty, can learn more about the students as writers in a single day than the students (and their teachers) have managed to learn in 12 or 13 years of writing in school. Assessing their "place" within our own program does make sense, of course, but we believe it makes more sense to add in a one-shot fashion information about our program to the students' extensive knowledge about their own writing experiences and abilities than it does to add in a one-shot fashion our assessment of students' writing abilities to our extensive knowledge about our program. In other words, we prefer to weight the balance toward the students' experiences and abilities rather than toward the quirks and details of our program, that, in time, will be as familiar to the students as they are to us, but that often seem confusing or even overwhelming to a new member of the academic community. At orientation, students own experiences and abilities are far more familiar to them than are the details of our program. Again, Dewey's insistence that our roles as teachers and members of the community is "to select the influences which shall affect the [student] and to assist him in properly responding to these influences" and to recognize that all education—from infancy on—"proceeds by the participation of the individual in the social consciousness" of the community (*Pedagogic* 432).

Consequence 3: The First-Day Writing Sample

Different schools handle this differently, of course, but in many programs faculty are asked to collect samples of student writing on the first day of class, or during the first week of class. The purpose is to make sure that students have been placed properly. If teachers see that some students in a basic writing class write with fluency and purpose, they might recommend shifting these students into the standard class. Or if teachers see that some students in the standard class struggle on what appears to be a fairly basic level, they might recommend shifting the students into these basic writing class. The choice is typically made by the teacher in consultation with the WPA; the students may be consulted, but the final decision is not theirs.

Because of the utter conventionality of this process, it sounds reasonable. But on second thought, we can see that it undermines the initial placement decision that had been given with such certainty and authority. At orientation we say, "We know which course you need," and then on the first day of class—the very next time we see the students—we say, "We need to check your placement." Students thus discover that we aren't so certain after all. And yet we meet that newly admitted uncertainty with another "certain" decision: "You actually belong over here." If the students trusted our decision the first time around, many of them have to start wondering after the second. Is it any wonder that students so often challenge our grading at course's end? We show them in our placement processes that we often *don't* know how to assess writing well or fairly.

And the students whose placements we change are in effect being singled out as "difficult to place" students. Despite the lack of agency students have with traditional placement methods, at least they have the comfort of being placed in a course with others presumably much like themselves. Then during the first week we change our minds and place them with other, different students. It's not surprising that even students initially placed in developmental courses sometimes resist changing after the first day. They just want to settle in. The question that must linger in the minds of students whose placement has been changed is, "What is it about me that makes me difficult to place in a writing class?" Of course, some students are relieved to make the switch, or they feel vindicated after having questioned the initial placement in the first place; either way, the lesson they learn about the writing program is not a flattering one.

Also important is the way we respond to the first-day writing samples of students we do *not* want to move. When the school or program makes the placement decisions, our initial teacher response to student writing is likely to some degree to justify each student's particular placement. So when we respond to student writing in the developmental classes, our comments might at least *partly* be aimed at confirming that the student is indeed a basic writer: "You're in the right place," we need to assure them. Justifying the placement decision, however unintentionally, pulls us away from the central task, which is simply to help students improve their writing.

With DSP, a first-day writing sample is an opportunity for the teacher and student to "test" the student's admittedly "uncertain" placement decision. Based on what he or she sees in the student's writing sample, the teacher can provide some direction or feedback on how the student compares to others in the class, or on how the student's writing matches up against end-of-semester standards for the course or program. This is really an extension of the placement process, similar in a way to the use of first-day samples in traditional placement methods, but now it is the *student's* hypothesis ("I think I belong in this class") that is being investigated, rather than the teacher's thesis ("You belong in this class"). The whole process is an open-ended inquiry—again, much more conducive to the larger "environment as directive" (Dewey, *Democracy* 28) that most of us hope the college campus embodies.

Moreover, the first-day writing sample is an opportunity for the teacher to begin articulating a learning strategy for each student. If a student in the standard composition class appears to struggle with development, the teacher can emphasize the need for that student to work extra hard on development strategies during the course. If a student in the standard class appears to struggle with mechanics, the teacher can emphasize the need for that student to work extra hard on editing strategies. The point is that it's the student's choice to be there in the course, and we as teachers can let each student know what he or she will likely have to do in order to succeed in the course. For some, it may be quite a bit. But what traditional placement methods fail to take into account is the *motivation* of individual students—or other personal variables that might affect a student's ability to do well in a course, such as part- or full-time work, domestic responsibilities, and the like. Raw writing ability alone is not the sole factor in student success. If a writer with marginal ability is willing to write extra drafts, visit the writing center religiously, practice regularly at a good OWL Web site, and so on, he or she can undoubtedly accomplish more in a given semester than another student of higher ability with no motivation at all. As we talk with students about their first-day writing samples, we can gauge with them what it is they will have to do and whether or not they are willing to do it.

And finally, the teacher's responses to the student writing do not need to justify the students' placement. The responses can be fully authentic responses to the students' situations as writers looking for ways to improve and ultimately to meet the expectations of the first-year composition program.

We present these three "consequences" of DSP not to suggest that they are necessarily the most important consequences for all placement methods to strive for, or indeed the only consequences that follow from DSP as a placement method. Our main goal in this chapter is to point out that if consequences are really to become our central measure of the *validity* of a placement method, then we must put students in a position to weigh and act upon those consequences themselves. Pragmatism and Dewey's educational philosophy offer a convincing case for placing the student at the center of the learning process, and this means allowing students to become authentic inquirers and problem-solvers.

In summary, then, we can say that DSP works by taking three things very seriously:

- Agency—by giving students information about our program and inviting them to assess their own writing abilities and then to place themselves within our curriculum, we signal to incoming students that their college education will be an active one; they will be in charge.

- Articulation—by asking students to think back on their earlier experiences with writing, and even to consult with their parents, high school teachers, and counselors, we signal to the students and to the high schools that we acknowledge the emphasis placed on writing in the high school curriculum and expect students to draw on the knowledge and experience gained by it.
- Assessment—by choosing not to engage in any kind of one-shot assessment of writing produced even before the students' first day in a college classroom, we confirm our commitment to authentic writing assessment done within the context of our own university, within the curriculum, within the classroom, at the end of the program rather than at the beginning.

ACKNOWLEDGEMENTS

An earlier version of this chapter was published as "Basic Writing and Directed Self-Placement." Basic Writing E-Journal. http://www.asu.edu/clas/english/composition/cbw/summer_2000_V2N2.htm>. (2000).

REFERENCES

Camp, Roberta. "Changing the Model for Direct Assessment of Writing." *Validating Holistic Scoring for Writing Assessment: Theoretical and Empirical Foundations*. Ed. Michael M. Williamson and Brian A. Huot. Cresskill, NJ: Hampton, 1993. 45-78.

Cherry, Roger D., and Paul R. Meyer. "Reliability Issues in Holistic Assessment." *Validating Holistic Scoring for Writing Assessment: Theoretical and Empirical Foundations*. Ed. Michael M. Williamson and Brian A. Huot. Cresskill, NJ: Hampton, 1993. 109-41.

Dewey, John. "My Pedagogic Creed." 1897. Rpt. in John Dewey on Education. Ed. Reginald D. Archambault. Chicago: U of Chicago P. 1964. 427-39.

———. *Democracy and Education*. 1916. New York: Macmillan, 1923.

———. *How We Think*. Rev. ed. 1933. Lexington: Heath, 1960.

———. "The Development of American Pragmatism." *Thayer* 23-47.

———. "The Public and Its Problems." Rpt. in *The Later Works*, v.2 1925-1953. Ed. Jo Ann Boydston. Carbondale : Southern Illinois UP. c1981-c1990.

Elbow, Peter. "Writing Assessment: Do It Better, Do It Less." *Assessment of Writing: Politics, Policies, Practices*. Ed. Edward M. White, William D. Lutz, and Sandra Kamusikiri. New York: MLA, 1996. 120-34.

Hamp-Lyons, Liz, and William Condon. *Assessing the Portfolio: Principles for Practice, Theory, and Research*. Cresskill, NJ: Hampton, 2000.

Huot, Brian. "Toward a New Theory of Writing Assessment." *College Composition and Communication* 47 (1996): 549-66.

James, William. "Remarks on Spencer's Definition of Mind as Correspondence." *Journal of Speculative Philosophy* 12 (1878): 1-18. Rpt. in Collected Essays and Reviews. New York, 1920. 43-68.

Peirce, Charles Sanders. "The Fixation of Belief." *Thayer* 61-78.

———. "How to Make Our Ideas Clear." *Thayer* 79-100.

Smith, William L. "Assessing the Reliability and Adequacy of Using Holistic Scoring of Essays as a College Composition Placement Technique." *Validating Holistic Scoring for Writing Assessment: Theoretical and Empirical Foundation.* Ed. Michael M. Williamson and Brian A. Huot. Cresskill, NJ: Hampton, 1993. 142–205.

Thayer, H.S. *Pragmatism: The Classic Writings.* Indianapolis: Hackett. 1982

White, Edward M. "Power and Agenda Setting in Writing Assessment." *Assessment of Writing: Politics, Policies, Practices.* Ed. Edward M. White, William D. Lutz, and Sandra Kamusikiri. New York: MLA, 1996. 9–24.

Williamson, Michael. "Assessing Students, Assessing Ourselves." Presented at the Fifty-first Annual Conference on College Composition and Communication. April 12, Minneapolis, 2000.

Yancey, Kathleen Blake. "Looking Back as We Look Forward: Historicizing Writing Assessment." *College Composition and Communication* 50 (1999): 483-503.

4

THE ROLE OF SELF-EFFICACY IN WRITING AND DIRECTED SELF-PLACEMENT

Erica J. Reynolds
University of Arizona

> *A student might know what is expected in an effective piece of writing and might even know the steps necessary to produce such a piece . . . but if the person lacks the belief that he or she can achieve the desired outcome, then effective behavior will likely not result.*
>
> —McCarthy, Meier, and Rinderer (466)

Amid the early interest and excitement generated by the concept of directed self-placement (DSP), assessment expert Edward White posted the question on the WPA Internet Discussion List of whether DSP was more a measure of confidence than of actual writing ability. Although direct extrapolation of the findings from the studies that have been conducted to any DSP Program is not possible due to a multitude of factors, the research clearly suggests that students who accurately assess themselves as strong writers perform well and, likewise, students who assess themselves as poor writers perform as such. In light of this information and what we know about the inaccuracy, cost, and time requirements inherent in other means of placement, DSP must be considered a justifiable agency for placement because there are very definite theoretical bases for its utilization—students can reliably assess their writing skills and, one would presume, accurately place themselves accordingly.

Questioning a student's ability to assess him or herself accurately in terms of writing skill, and therefore to make an appropriate self-placement decision, may actually be questioning the student's self-efficacy. A term originally coined in 1977 by social cognitive learning theorist, Albert Bandura, and later more thoroughly defined in his 1986 publication, *Social Foundations of Thought and Action: A Social Cognitive Theory*, *self-efficacy* refers to "people's judgments of their capabilities to organize and execute courses of action required to attain designated types of performances" (391). Furthermore, because efficacy "can affect what behavior people will attempt in the first place and how long they will persist in the face of obstacles," its potential role in a student's writing placement decision deserves consideration (McCarthy, Meier, and Rinderer 466).

In "Confidence and Competence in Writing: The Role of Self-Efficacy, Outcome Expectancy, and Apprehension," Margaret J. Johnson and Frank Pajares report that self-efficacy, for Bandura, is regarded as not the only, but perhaps "the most influential arbiter in human agency and helps explain why people's behavior may differ markedly even when they have similar knowledge and skills" (313). In other words, "what people do is often predicted by their beliefs about their capabilities rather than by measures of what they are actually capable of accomplishing" (313). Research in this area has provided substantive evidence suggesting that an individual's sense of self-efficacy is a valid predictor in a diverse variety of outcomes, ranging from smoking cessation to career choice. Perhaps it is not so surprising, then, that self-efficacy has been found to play an influential role in academic performance and even persistence in relation to writing. In "Self-Efficacy and Writing: A Different View of Self Evaluation," Patricia McCarthy, Scott Meier, and Regina Rinderer explain this phenomenon as it relates to writing by stating that "a student might know what is expected in an effective piece of writing and might even know the steps necessary to produce such a piece . . . but if the person lacks the belief that he or she can achieve the desired outcome, then effective behavior will likely not result" (466). Research focusing on self-efficacy's role in relation to student writing suggests that confidence in one's ability to write well and actual writing ability have been shown to possess a high degree of correlation.

Although self-efficacy has been studied in relation to many areas of academic performance, unfortunately there have been relatively few studies analyzing its specific role in writing outcome expectancy. I have included a brief synopsis of three research studies and their findings because they specifically address self-efficacy, outcome expectancy, and undergraduate student writers. Although none of the studies deals with DSP explicitly, they are relevant in that they address many of the questions that DSP has generated among writing program administrators (WPAs) and writing instructors.

One study that addresses self-efficacy and outcome expectancy with consideration given to reading skills has been included because of the inherently interrelated components manifest in both reading and writing and because the DSP's battery of statements for consideration at most institutions includes self-assessment concerning reading (i.e., "Generally, I only read when it's required," and "I enjoy reading newspapers, magazines and books"). Essentially, however, the research presented is intended to illuminate the role self-efficacy plays in undergraduate student writing and is followed by an analysis of how that role relates to DSP.

STUDY 1: SELF-EFFICACY AND WRITING: A DIFFERENT VIEW OF SELF-EVALUATION (1985)

McCarthy, Meier, and Rinderer, guided by Bandura's theory of self-efficacy, studied undergraduate students' efficacy expectations in relation to their writing ability. The researchers' primary purpose in conducting this study was to determine whether high levels of efficacy expectations were related to "quality" writing. Their secondary purpose was to "provide a more complete picture of the psychological variables related to effective writing" (466). Therefore, in conjunction with self-efficacy, the researchers also explored students' anxiety, locus of control, and cognitive processing of information. In two separate studies McCarthy, Meier, and Rinderer tested the following hypotheses:

1. Students who evaluate themselves as capable of performing various writing tasks and feel fairly certain about their self-evaluation, that is, those with strong efficacy, will be better writers than students with weak efficacy (467).
2. Students who experience less anxiety will be better writers than students who are highly anxious (467).
3. Students who are more inclined to believe that their locus of control is internal will be better writers than students who are more inclined to believe that control is external (467-68).
4. Students who are deep information processors will be better writers than students who are shallow processors (468).

The students were provided with a prompt and instructed to write a 20-minute expository essay during the first week of the term and again at the end of the term. At the time the expository essays were administered, students were asked to fill out questionnaires: a Self-Assessment of Writing Measure that requires students to evaluate their ability to perform several specific writing skills and report their degree of certainty relating to each skill; an anxiety measure, in which students report emotive feelings about their writing; a locus of control questionnaire; and finally, an inventory designed to assess their cognitive processing levels. Psychological variables, such as apprehension, confidence, and gender, are widely believed to affect an individual's sense of self-efficacy and are discussed in more detail in a subsequent section.

The measure designed to aid students in assessing their writing abilities consisted of 19 questions that addressed those skills that the researchers admit were the "most mechanical" and "perhaps most easily measurable of writing skills" (468). Examples of such questions included the following: "Can you write an essay without run-on sentences?" "Can you write sentences in which the subjects and verbs are in agreement?" "Can you write an essay in which the ideas are clearly expressed?" After students had completed questionnaires and written the expository essays, four experienced raters from the English Department holistically scored student papers based on the criteria established by the 19-part Self-Assessment of Writing Measure.

The results indicated that the only statistically significant effect in the analysis of the four possible predictors of writing performance (strength of perceived efficacy, perceived locus of control, anxiety, and cognitive processing) was that of strength of perceived efficacy. In other words, those students with a strong sense of self-efficacy were perceived by experienced raters as also being the better writers. Although strength of efficacy proved to be the most highly correlative factor with writing ability, the study revealed that those students who were less anxious at the time of the pretest also proved to be better writers, furthering McCarthy, Meier, and Rinderer's hypothesis that psychological variables affect, at least to a degree, strength of perceived efficacy. Interestingly, locus of control, which would have explained from where students attributed their success to have been derived, internally or externally, was not a significant factor in the results of this study, thereby giving greater credence to self-efficacy than to outcome expectancy. In other words, those students who believed they had the necessary skills to perform well did so and this sense of confidence was not contingent on outcome expectancies that are related to the construct of locus of control or to "causal attribution patterns" (Bruning, Murphy, and Shell 91).

STUDY 2: SELF-EFFICACY AND OUTCOME EXPECTANCY MECHANISMS IN READING AND WRITING ACHIEVEMENT

Roger Bruning, Carolyn Murphy, and Duane Shell, in order to explore the relation between self-efficacy and outcome expectancy beliefs and achievement in reading and writing, examined 153 White, middle-class undergraduate students in a teacher preparation program at a midwestern state university. Building on the research of McCarthy, Meier, and Rinderer, Bruning, Murphy, and Shell questioned whether self-efficacy's effect on writing performance, like reading performance, increases as component skills are mastered. They reasoned that self-efficacy should become increasingly important to achievement in reading and writing ability as the "cognitive and behavioral skills necessary for proficient reading or writing are developed" (91). Their specific concerns in this study focused on whether the developmental trend in terms of reading, established by other studies, continues for students at the high school and college levels.

Beyond establishing developmental self-efficacy trends in both reading and writing, Bruning, Murphy, and Shell questioned the way in which outcome expectancy and self-efficacy interact. It appears that when outcome expectations are examined in conjunction with self-efficacy, outcome expectations have little correlation with actual performance. This lack of correlation between outcome expectancy and actual performance was also shown by McCarthy, Meier, and Rinderer. However, studies have shown that when outcome expectancy is examined in isolation it bears significant influence. Perhaps this is because, as Bruning, Murphy, and Shell surmise, "beliefs about the likely outcomes of successful behavior assume importance only after persons believe that they can do the behavior successfully" (92). Finally, because reading and writing are considered related domains, Bruning, Murphy, and Shell hypothesized that self-efficacy and outcome expectancy beliefs about these skills may also be related and therefore generalized. Specifically, the researchers hypothesized the following:

1. Beliefs would account for significant variance in reading and writing performance with self-efficacy accounting for a larger share of variance than outcome expectancy (92).
2. Self-efficacy and outcome expectancy for one domain would account for significant variance in the other domain (i.e., reading beliefs would account for significant variance in writing performance and vice versa), but generalized beliefs would account for less variance than direct, within domain beliefs (92).
3. There would be significant underlying relation linking beliefs and performance in both domains with self-efficacy being a stronger contributor to this relation than outcome expectancy (92).

As the researchers had hypothesized, the results showed that for reading and writing, beliefs were significantly related to performance. In the reading domain, the developmental trend correlating self-efficacy and outcome expectancy had progressed and bore a stronger relationship in the mature, skilled readers examined in this study than in previous studies conducted with second and fifth graders. Because no prior studies had been conducted on children that might have examined the relationship between self-efficacy and outcome expectancy in terms of writing, no conclusions could be drawn as to whether there is a developmental trend for this skill. Overall, the results for writing were less clear.

Although a significant relationship was found between self-efficacy and writing performance, it was "considerably lower than the magnitude of explained reading variance" (Bruning 96). However, the relationship was consistent with the findings obtained by McCarthy, Meier, and Rinderer. In other words, although the correlation between self-efficacy and writing was shown to be significant in terms of this study, it still bore a relatively moderate relationship when compared to the relationship between self-efficacy and reading achievement, suggesting that there may be "a difference in the development trends for beliefs and skill between writing and reading" (96). As was the case in earlier studies, self-efficacy beliefs were more strongly related to achievement than to outcome expectancy for both reading and writing which, like McCarthy, Meier, and Rinderer's study, led researchers to assert that "perceptions of competency are more strongly related to performance than perceptions of contingency relations between performance and outcomes" (96). Finally, in terms of cross-domain generalization, it was found that self-efficacy in reading produced both higher achievement in reading and writing, indicating, at least to these researchers, that self-efficacious reading beliefs may be "stronger predictors of either reading or writing achievement than writing beliefs" (96). Bruning, Murphy, and Shell suggest that these findings may have resulted because college students are more proficient and experienced readers than they are writers or, more likely, because of reliability difficulties they encountered in the scoring of the writing samples.

STUDY 3: CONFIDENCE AND COMPETENCE IN WRITING: THE ROLE OF SELF-EFFICACY, OUTCOME EXPECTANCY, AND APPREHENSION

Acknowledging Bandura's theories regarding self-efficacy and the research studies conducted by both McCarthy, Meier, and Rinderer and Bruning,

Murphy, and Shell, Johnson and Pajares set out to investigate the relationships among self-confidence about writing, expected outcomes, writing apprehension, general self-confidence, and writing performance in 30 undergraduate preservice teachers over the course of one semester. As was the case in the two aforementioned studies, Johnson and Pajares's study was designed to explore the relationships among psychological variables in order to test whether these relationships were consistent with the tenets of social cognitive theory as presented by Bandura.

Of particular concern in this study were the ways in which the psychological variables related to writing skills and performance. The results yielded, as had been expected, that full-scale writing self-efficacy (which included both skills and task scales) was significantly related with writing performance, whereas outcome expectancy was related to performance only on the posttest administration. Interestingly, writing apprehension was not shown to be related to performance, although it was related to writing self-efficacy at the time of the pretest, which was also the case in the study conducted by McCarthy, Meier, and Rinderer. Although Bandura has suggested that apprehension is correlated with weak efficacy expectations and leads to poor performance, neither this study nor the McCarthy, Meier, and Rinderer study revealed such a relationship. Daly and Miller showed such a correlation in their research on writing and this is discussed more fully in a subsequent section.

The variable tested that surprised the researchers the most was that of general self-confidence. General self-confidence was related to all of the variables examined, with the only exception being that of the skills self-efficacy scale, which measured confidence in specific writing skills. This finding supports Bandura's assertion that general confidence is not likely to predict positive performance in a specific skill or task. This is a particularly important finding in that one of the criticisms directed at DSP supposes that students' general sense of self-confidence will dictate their ultimate placement decision. Clearly, this study negates that supposition.

Therefore, as was the case with two aforementioned studies, only writing self-efficacy was significant in prediction of writing performance, further supporting Bandura's social cognitive theory that relationships among confidence to accomplish writing tasks, outcome expectations, and general self-confidence were nonsignificant. In other words, because self-efficacy is subject- and situation-specific, it does not bear a relationship to general feelings of self-confidence nor can causal or attributional inferences be made.

RELEVANCE OF RESEARCH TO DSP

The studies conducted by all three sets of researchers clearly suggests that there is a very definite correlation between an individual's strength of perceived efficacy regarding writing skills and actual ability to perform those skills. In response to the question, often posed by WPAs, "Can students accurately assess their writing ability?" the answer appears to be "Yes." Furthermore, the research conducted indicates that students are able to accurately assess their reading ability and, significantly, reading assessment bears a cross-domain generalization for writing ability. However, outcome expectancy, in the cases of both reading and writing, seems to have little or no consequence in a student's ability to assess him or herself, at least in terms of the results yielded by the aforementioned studies.

When considering that there are so many factors and variables that differentiate the methodology used in conducting each of the research studies, how might we relate these findings to the DSP process? Clearly, the research has shown that students who feel confident that they can perform specified writing skills do so. But, as has been explained, assessment experts and others have questioned whether general self-confidence might not be a major factor in a student's placement decision. The research shows that general self-confidence was shown to have no direct influence on a student's confidence about writing skills or abilities, in particular. The battery of statements for consideration in DSP does not question students' general level of self-confidence. What it does ask them to consider is whether they perceive themselves to be "strong writer[s]," and "good reader[s] and writer[s]," and whether they are "unsure about the rules of writing." It is possible that these questions, if considered on a continuum, might be perceived as being closer to questions of general self-confidence in regard to writing than are the specific skills questionnaires administered in the research studies. This perception is important because in the studies writing performance was measured by the criterion established in the 19-part skills self-efficacy instruments. Students knew exactly those skills that were to be assessed in their actual writing samples. Perhaps both their sense of self-efficacy and writing performance were enhanced by this knowledge. Alternately, it is possible that knowledge of the criteria affected already apprehensive students' sense of self-efficacy. In order to make DSP an efficient and expedient vehicle for several hundred incoming university students, it may be necessary to provide more general and fewer questions than those asked for the purposes of the research studies. It is not difficult to imagine that some students might be more likely to dismiss a 19-part questionnaire than they would a brochure asking them to consider 10 statements designed to assess aptitude and confidence for writing and reading ability in general as is the case with the DSP battery.

The DSP statements, although more general than the questionnaires administered in the studies, must not be discounted. Research has shown that posing specific, skill-oriented writing statements as opposed to general writing statements does not aid in the prediction of a student's overall ability to write competently. In fact, the more general writing statements put forth by the Daly and Miller Writing Apprehension Measure that parallel those in the DSP battery of statements for consideration are equally likely to predict a student's writing skill competency and overall quality of writing as those posed in the specific writing self-efficacy measures. Furthermore, although student writing in the self-efficacy studies was assessed for competency in writing skills, researchers noted that the overall quality of the writing was superior among high self-efficacious writers.

Although there are clearly similarities in the questionnaires administered in the research studies and the DSP battery of statements for consideration, there are differences that must be pointed out as well. Take, for example, that the rating in the research studies was performed by no more than four individuals. English 100 and 101 students at many universities are dispersed to the classrooms of as many as 100 graduate teaching assistants, each of whom, it can be expected, has at best slightly different perceptions of that which constitutes "good" writing performance. Perhaps, given more specific examples of what constitutes "good" reading, "strong" writing, and "rules" for writing, it is possible that students would feel more confident about their ability to assess their own skills thereby encouraging more accurate placement. Another possibility, with consideration given to contemporary rhetorical focus, might be to adjust the DSP statements to include process-oriented abilities, for example, "I am able to formulate ideas and adapt the level of language to meet audience expectations," keeping in mind, however, that a correlation between writing process and self-efficacy has not yet been determined. Finally, given that strong self-efficacy beliefs about reading skills correlate with both strong reading and writing performance, it certainly seems prudent for the statements, "Generally, I only read when it's required," and "I enjoy reading newspapers, magazines, and books," to be incorporated in any DSP battery of statements for consideration.

Another important difference to consider between the writing skills self-efficacy measures and a DSP battery of statements is the timing of when they are administered. Because incoming students are oftentimes sent the DSP information through the mail, they are expected to assess their ability, and therefore place themselves in some instances months before they are actually expected to write. In the case of the research studies, however, students were questioned about their skills at the same time they were expected to perform those skills. It is possible that students are likely to be more accurate, or even honest, about their ability to perform writing skills at the time they are expected to write because they realize their work is going to be assessed in conjunction with the measurement of their self-efficacy claims. Bandura asserted that "self-efficacy and performance should be assessed in as close a temporal interval as possible" and that when researchers "allow time to pass between assessments of confidence and competence, they fail to take into account the confidence change that may take place during the interval" (cited in Johnson and Pajares 324-325). Wood and Locke, examining academic self-efficacy, found that when self-efficacy was measured 2 months prior to performance, it bore no significant influence. In terms of enrollment and class scheduling, it might be inexpedient or perhaps even impossible for the WPA to wait until all of the incoming freshman arrive on campus to administer the DSP battery of statements for consideration. However, it might be possible to ensure that students place themselves in as near a time as possible to the actual writing that will take place in the classroom, for instance, during a summer orientation workshop.

RESEARCH ON APPREHENSION, CONFIDENCE, AND WRITING

DSP relies on the premise, outlined by self-efficacy theory, that students are better able to assess their own writing and reading abilities and decide for themselves whether they should enroll in English 100 or English 101 than are traditional placement methods. Certainly, one would hope that each student, barring external factors such as monetary cost of an additional class or peer pressure, would choose the course that is most likely to serve her or him best based on a personal assessment of ability.

However, despite results that showed a significant correlation between strength of perceived efficacy in terms of writing and actual writing performance, McCarthy, Meier, and Rinderer urged researchers to question the possibility of whether "accurate assessment of self-efficacy predicts writing performance" and suggested that certain students are likely to either vastly overestimate or underestimate their writing performance which would naturally lead to inappropriate placement (468). For example, Johnson and Pajares explain in their article, "Confidence and Competence in Writing: The Role of Self-Efficacy," that in many cases, "inaccurate perception of mathematics ability, and not lack of skill, are responsible for avoidance of math-related courses" (328). They found that some students underestimated their competence (327). In addition, White suggested that, based on an unpublished research study conducted by one of his former students, females are more likely than are their male peers to place themselves in lower level writing courses. Such sentiments are paralleled in Susan McLeod's article, "Some Thoughts About Feelings: The Affective Domain and the Writing Process," in which she stresses that the activity of writing is as much an emotional as a cognitive activity and affective components influence all phases of the writing process. For WPAs who want to ensure that properly executed DSP does not exclude particular "types" of individuals, these concerns must be addressed. The following discussion of research and analysis addresses the ways that apprehension, confidence, and gender, as isolated and interrelated variables, affect an individual's willingness to attempt writing in the first place, actual writing performance, and strength of efficacy as it relates to writing confidence.

The study of what has come to be known as "writing apprehension," which is a situation- and subject-specific concern regarding "people's general tendencies to approach or avoid writing" was initiated by John Daly and Michael Miller in 1975 (Daly, "Writing" 10). Their articles, "The Empirical Development of an Instrument to Measure Writing Apprehension," and its follow-up, "Further Studies on Writing Apprehension: SAT Scores, Success Expectations, Willingness to Take Advanced Courses and Sex Differences," predated Bandura's seminal article on self-efficacy, "Self-Efficacy: Toward a Unifying Theory of Behavioral Change," by merely 2 years. Although they were contemporaries, it appears that Daly and Miller were not familiar with Bandura's work, nor vice versa. Daly and Miller published largely in educational and English journals, whereas Bandura's work found its way into the annals of psychology.

It was not until the study conducted by McCarthy, Meier, and Rinderer, then, that researchers began to consider that psychological variables like anxiety might be related to low self-efficacy in regard to writing. The results of the study by McCarthy, Meier, and Rinderer, described in the previous section, indicated that efficacy strength and "anxiety" were significantly related to performance at the time of the writing pretest, but that only efficacy strength was related to performance at the time of the post test. Although McCarthy, Meier, and Rinderer acknowledge the studies by Miller and Daly, they did not employ the Daly and Miller Writing Apprehension Test for the purposes of their study, opting instead for the "anxiety" measure, State-Trait Anxiety Inventory Manual. Nevertheless, McCarthy, Meier, and Rinderer concluded that students with strong efficacy were better writers; and less anxious students were better writers. In the study conducted by Johnson and Pajares, also outlined in the previous section, the Daly and Miller Writing Apprehension Test was administered. This time the results yielded, interestingly, that although writing apprehension was not related to writing performance, it did bear significant correlation to writing self-efficacy. In both the studies conducted by McCarthy, Meier, and Rinderer and Johnson and Pajares, the lack of a compelling relationship between apprehension and writing contradicts the earlier findings by Daly and Miller that, therefore, deserve closer attention.

Daly, a researcher originally interested in the role of apprehension in the field of speech communication, questioned whether there might "reasonably exist a general anxiety about writing as well" (Daly and Miller 244). Extrapolating from research conducted in speech communication, Daly and Miller contended that individuals with writing apprehension would be fearful of having their writing evaluated due to anticipation of negative ratings and, therefore, would avoid writing whenever possible. They also suggested that highly apprehensive writers would likely experience failure because they would tend to avoid situations that involve writing and therefore would not have opportunities to get additional practice. And, finally, they expected that individuals with high apprehension would "seldom enroll voluntarily in courses where writing is known to be demanded" (244). Daly and Miller were initially concerned with adults and occupational choices in relation to writing apprehension, but as their interest began to turn more toward a pedagogical focus, they examined whether writing apprehension measures correlated with SAT-Verbal scores as a possible predictor of success. They also considered whether writing apprehension might be related to the willingness of students to voluntarily take additional courses in writing and if placement in "remedial" as opposed to "normal" basic composition courses (i.e., English 100 and English 101), bore a correlation to writing apprehension.

Based on these presuppositions, Daly and Miller developed the 26-item Writing Apprehension Measure and administered it to a population of 246 university undergraduate students enrolled in either the basic composition course, the remedial composition course, or an advanced creative writing course. Students had been placed, based on their SAT-Verbal score, in either the remedial or normal writing course. Enrollment in the advanced creative writing course was entirely voluntary. In addition to the Writing Apprehension Measure, students were asked to self-report their SAT-Verbal scores. Furthermore, they were asked, "In the courses you have previously taken in high school or college where writing was a major requirement, how successful do you feel you were?" followed by two additional questions that essentially asked how likely they felt that they would take courses in the future which stress writing. Finally, because they were currently enrolled in a writing course, they were asked how successful they expected to be in that course.

The results yielded that although there was a statistically significant correlation between high apprehension and remedial students, it accounted for little shared variance. In other words, individuals in the remedial group did not differ significantly in terms of writing apprehension from those in the normal group. This finding, in light of what we know about the predictive success of standardized scores (i.e., ACT/SAT), is perhaps not surprising. At the time of Daly and Miller's research, the SAT-Verbal test did not include a writing component and instead addressed reading, vocabulary, and analysis. It was not expected that these skills would relate to either predispositions towards writing, or expectations of success in writing performance, and indeed the results indicated that they did not. Daly and Miller did find, however, that there was a significant correlation between low writing apprehension and perceived likelihood for success and a willingness to take voluntary courses which stressed writing. Conversely, individuals with high apprehension, compared to the general population examined, reported significantly lower expectations in terms of success and an unwillingness to take other courses in writing. Those students enrolled in the advanced creative writing course were significantly lower on apprehension than the general population enrolled in the basic course. Finally, students with high apprehension reported significantly lower success in past writing experiences and, perhaps most interesting, males reported significantly higher apprehension than did females, and that apprehension was related to self-reported previous success (or failure) in writing courses. This finding is important and is discussed further in the subsequent section.

The most important difference between Daly and Miller's 1975 study, and the studies by McCarthy, Meier, and Rinderer and Johnson and Pajares, is that although Daly and Miller were attempting to find a correlation between writing apprehension and a student's perceived likelihood of success, willingness to take additional courses in writing, and success in previous writing courses, McCarthy, Meier, and Rinderer and Johnson and Pajares were testing whether writing apprehension influenced writing performance. Considering the fact that writing self-efficacy and writing apprehension influence individuals in similar ways, it is curious that the studies by McCarthy, Meier, and Rinderer and Johnson and Pajares did not show writing apprehension to have a significant influence on students' writing performance. The research has shown that individuals with feelings of strong efficacy in regard to writing, like students with low writing apprehension, are more likely to feel confident about their ability to write well. And, like strength of writing self-efficacy, writing apprehension influences what writers will attempt in the first place (i.e., advanced writing courses, occupations that require writing, etc). Furthermore, highly self-efficacious writers are confident about their ability to perform writing skills and students with low apprehension respond positively to statements like "I feel confident in my ability to clearly express my ideas in writing" and "It's easy for me to write good compositions." Similarly, writers with weak self-efficacy lack confidence that they can perform writing skills and high apprehensive writers respond positively to statements such as "I never seem to be able to clearly write down my ideas" and "I'm no good at writing." It would certainly seem that highly self-efficacious writers would also be low apprehensive writers and likewise, that writers with low self-efficacy would be highly apprehensive writers and indeed research, presented later in this section, has shown this.

There are several plausible reasons why the study by McCarthy, Meier, and Rinderer only suggested a correlation with positive writing performance and low writing anxiety at the time of the pretest. The fact that McCarthy, Meier, and Rinderer did not employ the Daly and Miller Writing Apprehension Measure and opted instead for an alternative measure for anxiety may have altered results that otherwise might have shown anxiety to have a more significant correlation to writing performance. Another possibility is that when students were administered the unfamiliar anxiety inventory in the beginning of the semester, those students who might already have been apprehensive about having their writing tested, were naturally intimidated and therefore performed poorly. Additionally, some students may have simply been more cautious about reporting their degree of writing prowess because they were freshman undergraduate students and unsure about that which would be expected in terms of writing at the university level. That there was not a positive correlation between writing anxiety and writing performance at the end of the semester may be attributed to several variables as well. At the time of the posttest, students had spent an entire semester in the course and, presumably, had become better or at least more experienced (and perhaps more confident) writers, had received feedback from the instructor, and had a more accurate "feeling" for their standing among other college freshmen in terms of writing ability. Furthermore, students had taken the anxiety measure before and may have been less intimidated by the instrument itself.

The Johnson and Pajares study is more troubling. Although they reported that high self-efficacy was a predictor of strong writing performance and writing apprehension bore a correlation to self-efficacy, they maintain that writing apprehension and writing performance were not related. It is perplexing as to why this might be so and, unfortunately, Johnson and Pajares do not explain this lack of correlation. That apprehension was negatively related to self-efficacy beliefs, however, leads one to question what, exactly, the relationship is between self-efficacy and apprehension. Social cognitive theory suggests that "as confidence increases, apprehension should decrease" (Johnson and Pajares 318). It is possible that feelings of apprehension are the "antithesis" of feelings of self-efficacy, but that apprehension, like outcome expectancy, and anxiety, tested in the study by

McCarthy, Meier, and Rinderer, is not as decisive a predictor of performance as is strong self-efficacy. This makes sense based on Bandura's theories regarding self-efficacy as a subject- and situation-specific predictive construct. For instance, the Writing Apprehension Measure employed in this study measures more general writing concerns than does the self-efficacy measure. While the Writing Apprehension Measure asks students to consider whether or not they feel they are "good at writing," the writing self-efficacy measure asks students whether they are confident in their ability to use proper capitalization, for example.

In a follow-up study, reported in his article, "Writing Apprehension and Writing Competence," Daly did examine the relationship between writing apprehension and writing competency. Unlike the later studies by McCarthy, Meier, and Rinderer and Johnson and Pajares, Daly found that apprehension does indeed correlate with writing competence. Daly measured "competence" by selecting 12 skills from a 68-item, multiple-choice test that was constructed from a more comprehensive skills test originally compiled to accompany a composition textbook. The skills chosen were those most often identified by a set of experienced writing instructors as those most indicative of "good" or "competent" writing. Like the skills chosen as criteria in the studies by McCarthy, Meier, and Rinderer and Johnson and Pajares, Daly dealt with product-oriented, easily measured, mechanics (i.e., case, punctuation, capitalization, agreement, etc).

The respondents, 3,602 students, mostly first-semester undergraduates enrolled in a mandatory basic composition course, were administered both the Writing Apprehension Measure and the 12-part skills test. In this study, respondents were rated as high, low, or moderate apprehensives, based on their responses to the apprehension measure, in an attempt to establish that there is a continuum that correlates the degree of writing apprehension to the strength of performance. Daly's hypothesis, that students having low apprehension in terms of writing would perform significantly better than those with high apprehension, was substantiated by the results of the study. The writing performance of students with moderate apprehension, as had been hypothesized, "fell between high and low" apprehensive writers suggesting "the accuracy of a continuum ranging from low to high apprehension" (13).

This study is significant for several reasons. First of all, the findings paralleled those in the self-efficacy studies. Specifically, students who had strong self-efficacy about their ability to write well did write well. Likewise, those who felt confident (students with low apprehension) about their ability to write well performed well when administered the writing skills test. Furthermore, in both the self-efficacy accompanying skills tests and writing apprehension accompanying skills tests, students were questioned about their knowledge about specific, product-oriented skills (i.e., grammar and mechanics). In the case of the self-efficacy studies, however, students were required to employ those skills in expository essays, whereas in Daly's study, students were only tested for their knowledge of the skills. Nevertheless, a correlation between performance of low self-efficacious writers, and highly apprehensive writers, at least in terms of their knowledge of writing skills, can be made.

Although grammatical and mechanical skills are, for many, crucial to "competent" writing, Daly acknowledges that terms like competency and skill are "very limited" and that "many of the most important competencies and skills which contribute to writing (e.g., the ideas) are not, and indeed probably could not, be assessed through an objective testing procedure" (Daly 13). For this reason, Daly, in conjunction with Lester Faigley and Stephen Witte, examined the role of apprehension as it relates to standardized tests of writing skills (competency) and, most importantly, two essays of different types (performance), and reported their findings in the article, "The Role of Writing Apprehension in Writing Performance and Competence."

This study is unique because instead of examining relationships between writing self-efficacy or writing apprehension and specific writing skills, as a single measure, it examines both micro- and macrolevel writing performance in the context of an actual composition. It is important to point out that the major distinction between "performance" for McCarthy, Meier, Rinderer; Johnson and Pajares; and Daly, Faigley, and Witte, is that in the cases of the first two sets of researchers, performance relates only to the ability to employ grammatical/mechanical skills in a piece of writing, and in the case of the third set of researchers, performance relates to the overall "quality" of an essay, determined by "internal characteristics," number of total words, words per T-unit, words per clause, and the frequency of nonrestrictive modifiers (17). Daly, Faigley, and Witte chose the aforementioned syntactic characteristics based on their assertion that they are "widely used indices of writing development" (17).

For the purpose of this study, Daly, Faigley, and Witte administered the Daly and Miller Writing Apprehension Measure to 110 freshman undergraduate students, enrolled in 20 sections of a beginning composition course at a large southwestern university. Based on their responses, students were divided into categories of highly apprehensive students and low apprehension students. In order to assess competency, students completed eight standardized measures of writing competency prior to beginning classes. Among those items tested were the verbal and vocabulary subtests of the SAT, the Test of Standard Written English, the McGraw-Hill Writing Test, the McGraw-Hill Reading Test, and the English Composition Test. Students also wrote two essays. The first elicited narrative and descriptive characteristics, drawing heavily on the writers' personal experiences; the second elicited argumentative discourse. For the purpose of guiding students in their writing, prompts were supplied. Additionally, two trained judges were assigned to rate the overall quality of each essay and they were scored holistically.

Based on previous studies by other researchers, perhaps it is not surprising that for every standardized measure designed to assess writing competency, students with low writing apprehension scored higher than did the students with high levels of apprehension. It is compelling that the essays (utilized in this study to determine writing performance) written by low apprehensive students were longer in terms of total word count, had more words per T-unit, employed more words per clause, exhibited a higher ratio of words in the final nonrestrictive modifiers to the total number of words used, and were holistically scored higher on a four-point scale. Daly, Faigley, and Witte reported that "in every instance, the pattern was for the low apprehensives to perform better than the high apprehensives," suggesting that writers with high levels of apprehension have "less command over matters of usage and written conventions" than do writers with low apprehension (18-19). The fact that students with low apprehension produced longer essays and that those essays were more syntactically "mature," according to Daly, Faigley, and Witte, may indicate that less apprehensive writers employ different writing behaviors or even invention methods (19). Similarly, McCarthy, Meier, and Rinderer have questioned whether students with high self-efficacy in relation to writing "behave differently as writers" from those with weak self-efficacy, whether they take more "notable risks," or more control "over their planning" (469). The researchers maintain that students' written products suggest that they do.

In terms of the two separate essays that were required (narrative/descriptive and argumentative), there were also notable differences. Students with high apprehension, across all of the variables measured, scored lower than students with low apprehension on the narrative essay, which may be because high apprehensive writers are "more anxious about expressing their own feelings, attitudes, and experiences than they were about writing on a topic that demanded they argue objectively for a particular point of view" (20). As might be expected, the argumentative essays were more formal in style and in the cases of both low and high apprehensive student writers, were of greater complexity in terms of the characteristics examined than were the narrative essays (19). This finding indicates that the "types" of writing requirements assigned to low and high apprehensive writers may need to be tailored to ensure that students are given an optimal chance to exhibit performance. Narrative/descriptive assignments, in other words, may confound apprehension among certain types of student writers.

With regard to DSP information, further consideration might be given to the types of writing assignments described for each course. Currently, the description of English 100 at Southern Illinois University Carbondale (SIUC) (see chapters 2 and 10, this volume) informs students that they will be given practice in argumentation and analysis and that they will be writing about subjects that are familiar to them. The research indicates that high apprehensive students are better skilled at writing essays that are more formal and "removed" from them personally than they are about writing on personal subjects. It is possible that students would be comfortable writing argumentation and analysis essays, but if they perceive "familiar subjects" to indicate those of a personal nature, already apprehensive students may avoid English 100 and inaccurately place themselves in English 101. The description of English 101 informs students that it is assumed that they "can summarize and analyze published material from magazines, newspapers, books, and scholarly journals" and that they have had previous experience "writing a variety of essays in a variety of forms, including persuasive and analytical writing." Summary and persuasive (or argumentative) types of writing may appeal to those high apprehensive students who are not comfortable writing about their own experiences. However, narrative writing is a component in the English 100 curriculum and therefore needs to be included in the course description.

Precisely because much writing is "an exposure of self to others," Daly and Deborah A. Wilson question whether writing apprehension is related to a variety of measures of self-esteem, or general self-confidence (Daly and Wilson 329). Based largely on anecdotal evidence and social theories of self-esteem, Daly and Wilson hypothesized that a student's self-esteem should affect the way that they write and the way that they perceive writing. Daly and Wilson point out that "teachers indicate, for instance, that students who are apprehensive about writing (e.g., don't like writing, are uncomfortable when writing) also tend to feel comparatively less positive about themselves" (329). Daly and Wilson argue that an individual's apprehension about writing develops, and is maintained, at least in part from others' evaluations of his or her writing and that people receiving positive responses from others for their writing should be less apprehensive about the act than their counterparts who typically receive negative reactions (329).

In order to test their hypotheses, Daly and Wilson administered the Daly and Miller, 26-item Writing Apprehension Measure, and two general measures of self-esteem, one developed by Rosenberg and one created by Pervin and Lilly, to seventy-two undergraduate students enrolled in a basic writing course at a large midwestern university. A second sample of 292 undergraduate students at a large southern university were administered the Daly and Miller Writing Apprehension Measure and the Rosenberg instrument, alone. The results of this study, published in "Writing Apprehension, Self-Esteem, and Personality," suggested that writing apprehension and self-esteem are inversely related to one another. Daly and Wilson point out that although the "magnitude of relationship" between writing apprehension and self-esteem was "uniformly small, the consistency across two measures of self-esteem" was present (330). They explain this finding by stating that "general self-esteem, since it is a very broad construct, might not be expected to have a large relationship with any highly specific construct like apprehension" (331). Dale Schunk addresses this phenomenon in "Self-Efficacy and Academic Motivation," pointing out that self-concept, which incorporates self-esteem and self-confidence, is "hierarchically organized, with a general self-concept at the top and subarea self-concepts at the base" (212). He maintains, based on Bandura's social cognitive learning theory, that of self-concept's various dimensions, self-confidence seems the most akin to self-efficacy and that "in the hierarchy, self-efficacy judgments would lie at low levels because they are generally construed to be domain specific," that is, Algebra or Geometry (212). In other words, even within an academic area, a high self-concept does not imply that students feel highly confident about their abilities in all academic areas, or necessarily confident in general.

In establishing whether there is a stronger correlation between self-esteem about writing and writing apprehension, than writing apprehension and self-esteem in general, Daly and Wilson administered the 26-item Writing Apprehension Measure to 88 undergraduate students enrolled in a basic communication course at a large eastern university. In addition to the Writing Apprehension Measure, each student completed a measure designed to assess "naive" readers' reactions to writing. Specifically, respondents were asked to focus on a sample of their own writing and to determine the positive degree of 14 separate dimensions including, among others, "interest, tempo, forcefulness, and organization" present in their writing. The results of this study suggested that there is a "substantially larger" correlation between self-esteem about writing and writing apprehension than that of general self-esteem and writing apprehension, supporting social cognitive theory and earlier findings related to self-efficacy (333).

ANALYSIS OF THE RESEARCH

Clearly, the research shows a strong correlation between students' confidence about their abilities to write and their actual writing ability. Studies on self-efficacy show that students with high self-efficacy in relation to writing are indeed better writers than are their low self-efficacious peers. Likewise, students with low apprehension are better writers than are students with high apprehension. It is important, however, to point out that in the studies conducted on self-efficacy and writing, researchers were looking for writing skills, specifically those that are easily and objectively measured (i.e., product-oriented, mechanical, grammatical). Initially, studies on writing apprehension measured very similar types of writing skills (those skills that Daly referred to as exhibiting writing "competence") and although such skills are deemed important by most evaluators of writing, they are certainly not the only components considered in determining that which is "good" writing. Later studies on writing apprehension, however, were conducted to measure other indices of what experienced evaluators of writing consider necessary for "good" writing performance for instance, essay quality, words per T-unit, and total words per essay. Despite the fact that researchers were looking for writing ability beyond micro-level skills, they again found that low writing apprehension was correlated to "quality" writing. For example, Daly ("Writing") reported that even "the intensity of the language selected" by the low apprehensive writers was "superior" and furthermore, "messages written by high apprehensives tend to be evaluated significantly lower in quality than those encoded by low apprehensives" (11). This is not surprising given that the self-efficacy studies utilized to assess ability in terms of writing skills also showed that the essays written by students with high self-efficacy were different from those written by low self-efficacious peers in ways other than the specific skills being examined for the purpose of the studies. McCarthy, Meier, and Rinderer, referring to previous research conducted by such notables as Beach, Perl, Flower and Hayes, point out that this may be due to the fact that "weak writers do not take advantage of the full range of opportunities and choices available in composing or revising their work," or that writers who negatively evaluate themselves use "limited rhetorical strategies because they would not see themselves as being capable of anything complex" (469).

Daly suggests that individuals who fail to exhibit "appropriate and necessary" writing skills are unlikely to find success and therefore avoid writing activities" ("Writing" 13). Apprehension and low self-efficacy in conjunction with poor evaluations and avoidance techniques become cyclical for the writer and an unfortunate stasis, therefore, occurs. McCarthy, Meier, and Rinderer explain, in Bandura's terms, that "evaluations about one's abilities (efficacy expectations) develop as individuals attempt a behavior and receive feedback about the quality of their performance" (466). Certainly, this cyclical effect makes sense, but it does not illuminate a necessary causal inference. For example, it is difficult to say whether a student is a poor writer who has received legitimate negative feedback and is therefore apprehensive or low self-efficacious (and perhaps should be) as a result. It is possible that some students are more negatively affected by feedback, despite the fact that the evaluator did not intend the feedback to be perceived as such, or that some students have had the unfortunate experience of receiving feedback from less than sensitive evaluators. When exactly apprehension and self-efficacy develop, and how static those social cognitive constructs are, is also curious. For example, in the study conducted by Johnson and Pajares, students' writing anxiety remained unchanged "even as they grew in confidence and competence" (325). Nevertheless, confidence, as it is synthesized by both strength of self-efficacy and lack of apprehension, as long as it is being studied as a content- and subject-specific concept, is a strong predictor of writing performance and competency. As Roger Gilles and Daniel Royer point out, "Who knows exactly how this confidence has developed, but feedback from teachers and others is likely to have been a part of it, so it's reasonable to assume that the confidence is in many cases justified."

That writing performance and competency can both be predicted by self-efficacy strength and writing apprehension is crucial to the success of DSP. In order to ensure that the DSP process mirrors, as closely as possible for students, the results of the studies thus reviewed, several factors need to be examined. First of all, it must be determined what, exactly, the battery of statements for consideration on the DSP brochure is intended to assess. As has been pointed out, the pronouncements do not identify students' self-efficacy in regard to specific writing skills, but instead more closely parallel the attestations put forth on the Daly and Miller Writing Apprehension Measure. If the DSP Program is intended to direct students toward one class or the other based on their skill competency, one might suggest that the battery of statements for consideration would not be effectual in the realization of this task. There are no statements which ask students to consider, for example, if they are competent in subject–verb agreement. However, students are asked to consider whether they believe themselves to be "good reader[s] and writer[s]," which approximate statements proposed on the Writing Apprehension Measure like "It's easy for me to write good compositions." Bandura offers stern warnings that self-efficacy is not intended for generalization across domains and asking students about specific skills is not necessarily asking them to generalize about their writing abilities. Therefore, asking students to consider their ability to perform precise skills would be expected to yield higher correlative results.

However, the field of rhetoric and composition has evolved significantly since the 1970s and 1980s. More and more theorists and practitioners concerned with writing are de-emphasizing product-oriented, microlevel components in student writing and are more interested in process-oriented and macrolevel elements instead. As a result, most instructors are probably not as concerned with grammatical problems in student writing as they would be with organizational complications, or lack of clarity. At any rate, *directing* students into the most appropriate course should be about directing students into a specific curriculum and a specific course with specific outcome expectations. The orientation talks with students and printed program materials should communicate clearly those course goals and expectations whether they be up to date with current writing pedagogy or not. The point of DSP is to guide students into the most appropriate course for a specific curriculum.

GENDER AND DSP

As a result of their initial research on writing apprehension, Daly and Miller hypothesized that high apprehensive individuals would report significantly less success in previous writing courses than would low apprehensives and that male writers would have significantly higher scores on the Writing Apprehension Measure than would female writers. The impetus for their hypothesis that males would report higher levels of apprehension was based on research they had done that had "consistently shown that females tend to be rated significantly higher in composition writing than males" (252). Daly and Miller felt that it was reasonable to suggest that "positive reinforcement for writing, or the lack thereof, is crucial to level of apprehension" and that because males had generally been rated poorer than females in writing assignments, they would score higher on writing apprehension (252). The results of their study published in, "Further Studies on Writing Apprehension: SAT Score, Success Expectations, Willingness to Take Advanced Courses and Sex Differences," showed that indeed males "were significantly higher in writing apprehension than females" and that overall individuals with high apprehension felt significantly less successful in past writing courses than did those with low apprehension. Daly and Miller, apparently satisfied with validating their hypothesis that students who had experienced a lack of success in past writing courses would exhibit a higher level of apprehension about writing, never pursued this important gender issue in later research. However, it is curious as to why males reported less success in their previous writing endeavors and why, furthermore, they reported a heightened sense of apprehension. Like high apprehension, low self-efficacy is also suspected of being associated with past failures. In, "Self-Efficacy and Academic Motivation," Schunk states that "an individual's own performances offer the most reliable guides for assessing efficacy. . . . Successes raise efficacy, and failure lowers it" (208). It is important to point out, however, that neither writing apprehension nor writing self-efficacy has been studied and shown to determine, conclusively, whether failure necessarily precipitates apprehension or strength of efficacy or whether apprehension and strength of efficacy precipitate success or failure.

In "Development of A Writing Attitude Survey For Grades 9 to 12: Effects of Gender, Grade, and Ethnicity," Ruth Knudson reports that she has found, utilizing a writing-attitude survey, that "boys have less positive attitudes toward writing than girls" in all grades of school from as early as the first grade through the eighth grade. Knudson reports that this finding is consistent with other gender differences in attitudes toward reading and other language-related activities. Knudson, curious to assess whether this negative attitude toward writing is still present in males in Grades 9 through 12, administered a modified version of her original writing-attitude survey, based largely on Daly and Miller's Writing Apprehension Measure, to 870 high school students in Southern California. In addition, she examined effects for grade differences and ethnicity.

The results of her study indicated that there was no significant main effect for ethnicity, but that overall, students in Grade 12 had more positive attitudes toward writing than students in Grades 9, 10, or 11. Knudson suggests that this positive attitude in Grade 12 may be because less positive student writers, or less able writers, have already dropped out by the time of their senior year. Finally, like her earlier studies, Knudson also found that "girls had significantly more positive attitudes toward writing than boys across ethnicity and grade" (591). That Daly and Miller found that male students were more apprehensive and reported having had less success in their writing courses than females may be attributed to pedagogical practices or even social values deemed appropriate regarding academics at that time. It is important, however, that Knudson found, in 1993, nearly 20 years later, that males still report less positive attitudes toward writing. Knudson's student subjects were not questioned, as were Daly and Miller's, as to why they had negative attitudes toward writing and, therefore, one cannot conclude that it is a result of a lack of success in past writing experiences. Furthermore, it is somewhat difficult to imagine that the children surveyed in their early grade school years have had either a great deal of success or failure in terms of writing. However, according to Dianne McGuinness, "Education is almost a conspiracy against the aptitudes and inclinations of the schoolboy" (cited in Jessel and Moir 65). McGuinness maintains:

> In the early school years, children concentrate on reading and writing, skills that largely favour girls. As a result, boys fill remedial reading classes, don't learn to spell, and are classified as dyslexic or learning-disabled four times as often as girls. Had these punitive categories existed earlier they would have included Faraday, Edison and Einstein. (cited in Jessel and Moir 65)

It is likely that such early classroom experiences and specialized classifications greatly affect male self-efficacy, apprehension, confidence, and general overall attitudes toward writing. The National Assessment of Educational Progress (NAEP) reported in 1975 that as early as the age of nine, "female and male performances on achievement tests in mathematics, science, social studies, and citizenship are nearly equal, while females outperform males in reading, literature, writing, and music" (cited in Stitt 41). However, by the age of 13, females begin a decline in achievement, which continues through the age of 17 and into adulthood. By adulthood, however, "males outperform females in everything but writing and music" (cited in Stitt 41).

In a report prepared by the Wellesley College Center for Research on Women, presented in *How Schools Shortchange Girls*, it was noted that as recently as 1990 the Educational Testing Service found that although the gap between genders in many academic areas has lessened, "in all age groups, girls have consistently received higher test scores in reading and writing since the 1970s" (36). Furthermore, NAEP data from 1989 indicates that "girls consistently outperform boys on writing skills assessment[s]" (cited in *How Schools Shortchange Girls* 38).

A research study, conducted by Trudy Bers and Kerry Smith, "Assessing the Assessment Programs: The Theory and Practice of Examining Reliability and Validity of a Writing Placement Test" was designed to assess statistics on the placement of 4,284 two-year college students including ESL males, non-ESL males, ESL females, and non-ESL females. As is the case with many college composition placement programs, the students were administered a prompt and resulting essays were graded holistically. Based on their scores, students were placed in either the remedial or regular college English courses. The surprising preponderance of female non-ESL students who were placed in the regular English 101 course caused the researchers to question, "Do women have better verbal skills than men?" and "Are there other factors, related to gender, but unrelated to writing ability, that produced these differences?" (23).

It is difficult, if not impossible, to explain why males experience less success in areas like reading and writing, even at the early grade levels. Furthermore, one wonders why Deborah McGuinness refers to reading and writing as skills that "largely favour girls." Although a highly controversial subject, geneticist Anne Moir and her collaborator, David Jessel, address this issue in their book, *Brain Sex*. According to Jessel and Moir:

> what makes us better at one thing or another seems to be the degree to a which a particular area of the brain is specifically devoted to a particular activity—whether it is focused or diffuse. Men and women are better at the skills that are controlled by specific areas of the brain—but

different areas of their brain are focused for different things. This means that the male and female pattern of brain organisation has advantages and dis-advantages for both sexes. (44)

Furthermore, Jessel and Moir explain:

The superiority of women in verbal tests can . . . be explained by the difference in brain organisation. The language skills related to grammar, spelling and writing are all more specifically located in the left-hand side of the brain in a woman. In a man they are spread in the front and back of the brain, and so he will have to work harder than a woman to achieve these skills. (45)

Jessel and Moir do not explain exactly what constitutes a test of verbal ability in the aforementioned assertion and brain "mapping" is considered an abstruse science even to the most highly trained neurologists. In addition, to an egalitarian-conscious academic society that for the most part values equal treatment and opportunity for both genders, such scientific proposals may seem threatening. However, if there are indeed identifiable and calculable differences in male and female brains, in terms of verbal ability, it might explain both why males feel more apprehensive and less positive about their writing prowess. McGuinness warns that "hiding the knowledge concerning sex-specific aptitudes in learning has done far more harm than good. . . . It has caused a great deal of suffering in many boys who normally are slower to acquire reading skills when compared to girls" (65). In addition, it could explain why males report having experienced less success in their writing enterprises. In other words, the brain's organization, and neither apprehension nor failing grades, might be the actual reason explaining why males do poorly and thus develop such negative attitudes.

Of course, there are alternative and very plausible reasons which might answer Bers and Smith's question: "Are there other factors, related to gender, but unrelated to writing ability, that produced these differences?" Chase maintains that "The scoring of essays is a complex process, with many variables in multiple combination differentially influencing the reader. Only one of these variables is the content of the essay" (cited in Bers and Smith 19). It is possible that there are other factors that influence test-takers (e.g., gender), and the test situation (e.g., SAT-Verbal multiple choice questions) may affect students' test scores. For example, Bers and Smith point out that Chase has shown that raters of essay examinations, for instance, may award higher scores to exams written in better handwriting, or to exams that espouse values similar to those of the readers (25). Perhaps written work by female students encompasses and more closely reflects the values of teachers during grade school and high school years where the majority of teachers are female. And as Jessel and Moir explain, "even manual tasks, such as handwriting, suit the fine motor skills of the female, as opposed to the grosser mechanics of the boy" (65).

Early writing experiences involving failure, however, may not have as great an influence on males as one might think. A great deal of research has shown that males are not as responsive to the valence of academic evaluative feedback as are females. Roberts explains in "Gender and the Influence of Evaluations on Self-Assessments in Achievement Settings (1991)," that in academic situations "men allowed positive evaluative feedback to influence them more than negative feedback" and men were "less influenced overall by negative feedback than women" (299). Maccoby, and Jacklin referred to this self-promotional tendency in men as the "male selective filter," because it is characterized by an acknowledgement of successes but a denial of failures (Roberts 305). Based on Roberts' research, it seems that even if males do receive more negative feedback in regard to their writing, for example, they might not be as affected, because it is females who "tend to lower their expectancies for future success more than males after failure experiences" (300). However, research shows that individuals with low self-esteem or with low expectancies about their competence before performing a task are more influenced by others' evaluations than are those with high self-esteem (Roberts 300). Therefore, although males are less likely to be influenced by negative evaluative feedback in academic settings, it is possible that if they already experience a lack of confidence about a particular academic endeavor (i.e., reading or writing), they are more likely to be influenced by negative evaluative feedback than they normally would be.

White, in an initial comment on the DSP process, suggested that women might be more likely to place themselves in basic-level writing courses than would males and that this choice might be a result of a lower sense of self-confidence as opposed to ability. Although much research on self-efficacy theory has shown that one's strength of self-efficacy is subject- and situation-specific to the task at hand, his suggestion is not entirely unfounded. In "Highly Confident but Wrong: Gender Differences and Similarities in Confidence Judgments," Paul Fox, Mary Lundeberg, and Judith Puncochar, found that "lack of confidence is not necessarily indicative of low ability. Even when female students achieve as well or better than their male counterparts, they tend to underestimate themselves" (114). The study, consisting of 251 students enrolled in psychology courses, examined the differences between genders when asked to assess the degree of confidence they had in their ability to answer any particular test question. Specifically, Fox, Lundeberg, and Puncochar were interested in whether students would exhibit high confidence in their ability to correctly answer questions to which they indeed knew the answer and would report low self-confidence when they did not know the answer. They found that "Women . . . showed more accurate perceptions of their potentially incorrect answers than did men, who tended to show high degrees of confidence when wrong" (115). Furthermore, they reported that this finding was "particularly true of undergraduate men, who were especially overconfident when they were incorrect" (115). Fox, Lundeberg, and Puncochar reported that in general they found "scant evidence to support the notion that women have low confidence" and, as one would expect based on social cognitive efficacy theory, "any such finding . . . must be qualified by the particular course involved and by the domain-specific nature of the examination items" (119). It should be pointed out, however, that the aforementioned study did not address either the domain-specific academic category of either reading or writing, although it is possible that such extrapolations may be made in future research. Finally, Roberts asserts that most research in the area of gender and social behavior relies on a "model that assumes that where gender differences exist, men's behavior is normative and women's behavior therefore requires explanation as a deviation from that norm" (306). This view is echoed by Fox, Lundeberg, and Puncochar when they suggest that in their investigation "the problem may not be that women necessarily lack confidence but that, in some cases, men have too much confidence, especially when they are wrong!" Furthermore, in their study "unlike many situations in life" they "were able to use an objective standard of accuracy to judge confidence, which eliminates the problem of using men's level of confidence as the norm" (120).

It is difficult to say how males' general attitudes and apprehensions about writing might affect the DSP process. On the one hand, it would seem that the battery of statements for consideration, which closely resemble those in the Daly and Miller Writing Apprehension Measure, would serve in deterring males, who are more apprehensive about their writing, from taking English 101, and that females, who are less apprehensive in regard to writing, would be more likely take to English 101. On the other hand, it is possible, based on research examining confidence exhibited by males and females in academic situations, that males might be more confident about their ability to write than they are actually competent writers. The data, including attitudinal surveys, generated by SIUC for the purposes of tracking the DSP Program, indicates that women were indeed more likely to place themselves in English 101 although both males and females reported, to a very large degree, being confident about their decision either way.

It seems likely that students' placement decisions do, at least to a degree, reflect their level of self-efficacy and apprehension in relation to writing. Certainly the fact that female students consistently test higher on national examinations of reading and writing and have been shown to score higher on writing compositions, might explain why women may be more confident that they can succeed in the higher level writing course. Furthermore, it might be expected that males who traditionally score lower in writing and reading skills on national exams and have experienced less success with composition writing might not be as confident about enrolling in English 101 and would instead opt for English 100. Finally, both male and female students reported less confidence in their placement decision when the decision was to take English 100. This phenomena might reflect that because these students have less confidence in themselves as writers they also have less confidence in their writing placement decision.

CONCLUSION

Perhaps, ultimately, there is no "perfect" writing placement mechanism. ACT examinations do not mandate that students submit writing samples, and the verbal test employed by both ACT and SAT are often not valid predictors of writing per se. In addition, students do not exhibit equitable performance on standardized tests despite their ability levels. (The very recent introduction of the SAT writing component, however, may prove to mitigate some of the problems associated with traditional standardized test.) Some students work well under timed examinations and others do not. Similarly, some students are comfortable with multiple-choice tests while others prefer essay questions. Diagnostic essays, although they concentrate on writing, are graded en masse and often a 30-minute timed writing is not truly representative of a student's actual ability when he or she has been given time to research, discuss, and mull over ideas. Although portfolio submissions may exemplify a comprehensive picture of a student's writing ability they are often unwieldy, difficult to transport, and time- and cost-consuming in terms of their perusal.

DSP is concerned with students' reading and writing abilities and allows students the freedom to reflect on their experiences with reading and writing at their own pace. In addition, DSP is cost- and time-efficient. But most importantly, from a theoretical and empirical standpoint, DSP is quite possibly the best writing placement mechanism.

There are three essential reasons why DSP works. First, the battery of statements for consideration and the descriptions of the two courses are genuinely representative of the abilities and skills that students will need to utilize in order to succeed in each of the courses. Second, most students are more acutely aware of their own reading and writing abilities than can be measured by any of the traditional placement methods. And finally, the majority of students want to do what is best for them. By empowering students to place themselves we are doing them a favor. When we choose a writing course for students based on ACT scores or timed writing tests we are imposing a very important decision in their lives—a decision that may not even be the best for them.

If we place students in the basic writing course and they are not challenged, then we have done them a disservice. Conversely, if we place students in the regular writing course and they are not prepared, they will, almost inevitably, experience failure. In both scenarios we risk not only confounding apprehension but also lowering levels of self-efficacy in regard to writing. On the other hand, if we direct students in guiding themselves in their placement decisions we allow them to rely on their own knowledge of their individual strengths and weaknesses and we empower them. If students choose the basic writing course and are not challenged, then they will gain an important awareness about their self-efficacy as it relates to reading and writing. And if students choose the regular course and find it more challenging than they had anticipated then they, too, may gain insights about their writing self-efficacy. In addition, they may even be motivated to work harder in order to succeed. Either way, the research has shown that students are very capable of calibrating their own reading and writing skills and that the affective power of apprehension serves as both an indicator of skill level and a predictor of that which students are likely to attempt in the first place. Proof of this has been exhibited in a number of research studies among undergraduate student writers from diverse backgrounds, at many different types of universities, all over the country.

According to preliminary data generated at SIUC, students report that they value being given the right to choose which writing course they take and they report being confident about the decisions that they make. This is because, as the premise for DSP presumes, students are naturally the most acutely aware of their past reading and writing experiences. The majority of students surveyed reported that they indeed considered their writing background when making their placement decisions. In fact, students considered their writing background more than any other factor in their placement decisions including advice from advisors, parents, or peers. Certainly, beyond DSP, there are no alternative methods available that are capable of giving personal attention to hundreds and even thousands of reading and writing experiences in determining placement. And DSP encourages students to begin thinking about and assessing their reading and writing experiences before they even arrive at the University. DSP encourages what its originators call "the restoration of interpersonal agency."

It is likely that as research studies and data which support the idea of DSP accrue, it will not only be adopted by other university writing programs, but will be utilized for other core curriculum courses as well. Research has shown that in subjects ranging from geometry to psychology, students are distinctly aware of their abilities and if we are willing to trust and empower them, they can make appropriate placement decisions based on that awareness. In order to further our understanding of the ways in which components like self-efficacy, apprehension and gender affect DSP, each component needs to be isolated and studied in conjunction with DSP. For instance, self-efficacy's role can be substantiated in large part by students' performance in the courses that they ultimately choose. Passing grades would indicate, at least to a degree, that students are choosing wisely. In addition studies need to be conducted examining whether females or males are more successful in the courses they have chosen in order to determine if males and females are equally as adept at placing themselves. Additionally, ethnicity should be studied to examine if there are trends among particular groups of students to place themselves in one course as opposed to another. In order to ascertain the role that writing apprehension assumes in DSP, case studies should be conducted with students by employing the Daly and Miller Writing Apprehension Measure and comparing the results with students' placement decisions, thereby further examining the parallels in writing apprehension and that which students are willing to attempt in terms of writing. Although data that appears to support the DSP initiative is currently being accrued, as is evident in this volume, further longitudinal studies are necessary to determine the retention rates, attrition rates, and grades in contiguous writing courses of students who have been directed in self-placement. Finally, research and results need to be shared among English departments that utilize DSP so that trends and patterns may be more closely examined and understood.

REFERENCES

Bandura, Albert. *Social Foundations of Thought and Action: A Social Cognitive Theory.* Englewood Cliffs, NJ: Prentice Hall, 1986.

Bers, Trudy H. and Kerry E. Smith. "Assessing Assessment Programs: The Theory and Practice of Examining Reliability and Validity of a Writing Placement Test." *Community College Review* 18 (1990): 17-27.

Bruning, Roger H., Carolyn Colvin Murphy, and Duane F. Shell. "Self-Efficacy and Outcome Expectancy Mechanism in Reading and Writing Achievement." *Journal of Educational Psychology* 81 (1989): 91-100.

Daly, John A. "Writing Apprehension and Writing Competency." *Educational Research* 72 (1978): 10-14.
Daly, John A., Lester Faigley, and Stephen P Witte. "The Role of Writing Apprehension in Writing Performance and Competence. *The Journal of Educational Research* 75 (1981): 16-21.
Daly, John A. and Michael D. Miller. "The Empirical Development of an Instrument to Measure Writing Apprehension." *Research in the Teaching of English* 9 (1975a): 242-49.
——. "Further Studies on Writing Apprehension: SAT Scores, Success Expectations, Willingness to Take Advanced Courses and Sex Differences." *Research in Teaching English* 9 (1975b): 250-56.
Daly, John A. and Deborah A. Wilson. "Writing Apprehension, Self-Esteem, and Personality." *Research in the Teaching of English* 17 (1983): 327-341.
Fox, Paul W., Mary A. Lundeberg, and Judith Puncochar. "Highly Confident but Wrong: Gender Differences and Similarities in Confidence Judgments." *Journal of Educational Psychology* 86 (1994): 114-21.
Jessel, David and Anne Moir. *Brain Sex: The Real Difference Between Men and Women.* New York: Bantam Doubleday Publishing Group, Inc., 1991.
Johnson, Margaret J. and Frank Pajares. "Confidence and Competence in Writing: The Role of Self Efficacy, Outcome Expectancy, and Apprehension." *Research in the Teaching of English* 28 (1994): 313-31.
Knudson, Ruth E. "Development of a Writing Attitude Survey for Grades 9 to 12: Effects of Gender Grade and Ethnicity." *Psychological Reports* 73 (1993): 587-94.
McCarthy, Patricia, Scott Meier, and Regina Rinderer. "Self-Efficacy and Writing: A Different View of Self-Evaluation." *College Composition and Communication* 36 (1985): 465-71.
McLeod, Susan. "Some Thoughts About Feelings: The Affective Domain and the Writing Process." *College Composition and Communication* 38 (1987): 426-35.
Roberts, Tomi-Ann. "Gender and the Influence of Evaluations on Self-Assessments in Achievement Settings." *Psychological Bulletin* 109 (1991): 297-308.
Schunk, Dale H. "Self-Efficacy and Academic Motivation." *Educational Psychologist* 26 (1991): 207-31.
Stitt, Beverly A. *Building Gender Fairness in Schools.* Carbondale: Southern Illinois University Press, 1988.
Wellesley College Center for Research on Women. *How Schools Shortchange Girls: The AAUW Report.* New York: Marlowe and Company, 1992.
White, Edward M. "Placement Question." 11 May 1998. Online Posting. WPA-L.
Wood, Robert and Edwin Locke. "The Relation of Self-Efficacy and Grade Goals to Academic Performance." *Educational and Psychological Measurement* 47 (1988): 1013-24.

II

PRACTICES

5

DIRECTED SELF-PLACEMENT AT BELMONT UNIVERSITY

Sharing Power, Forming Relationships, Fostering Reflection

Robbie Pinter
Ellen Sims
Belmont University

WHY CHANGE TO DIRECTED SELF-PLACEMENT?

Until the spring of 1998, the writing faculty at Belmont first encountered new students during the English Placement Test, a 90-minute essay exam designed, proctored, and holistically scored by the writing faculty. Only recently did we consider our well-honed placement test to be at odds with our pedagogy. Although we think of ourselves an accessible, student-centered faculty, our entering students probably perceived us initially as judges who closely monitored the placement exam, collected the resulting essays precisely according to schedule, and usually held fast to the placement decisions if students challenged their English placement scores. Although our classrooms emphasize the writing process, our previous placement instrument allowed for no authentic revision. Although our course objectives include improving critical reading skills, our former placement test did not ask students to respond to a reading selection. Although our classrooms encourage participatory, empowered learning and dialogic exchange, our placement instrument suggested that students should acquiesce to the experts' judgments and that faculty control students' education. And even though our required first-year writing courses[1] challenge students to become self-aware and self-reflective writers, our former placement process devalued personal insights students could bring to the placement decision. Thus, our means of placing students into our classes contradicted our means of educating and relating to students that once they found their way into those classes. Belmont faculty explored and eventually adopted DSP in January 1998 primarily to align our placement process with our writing program's philosophy, pedagogy, and practices. We also saw DSP as a way to present ourselves to students in a consistent manner—as their teachers, coaches, co-learners, and interested readers of and respondents to their writing instead of as autocratic arbiters of acceptable writing.

Other problems with our former placement test motivated the change. For example, our Admissions and Student Services Offices had for several years expressed concern about "scaring off" potential students with the onerous battery of placement tests our department and others on campus administered to new students during their summer orientation sessions. Repeatedly, different campus constituencies asked the English Department to consider using SAT/ACT or some other standardized test score or a portfolio analysis to place students in their first English course. Our concerns about the validity of the former and the expense of the latter placement methods prevented us from adopting either approach. But we felt our test no longer reflected the philosophy of our writing program nor met campus needs for a student-friendly process.

Additionally, we were troubled by our occasional inconsistencies in upholding the placement scoring because we lacked absolute faith in what seemed a viable but still imperfect system. For instance, if students appealed their placement, the director of the writing program would hear their concerns and either offer to retest the students or encourage but never require the students to register for the basic writing course in which they had been placed. Sometimes, although rarely, adamant students registered for English 101 even though they had been placed into English 90, a developmental writing course. Therefore, the faculty placement decisions were not truly binding, as two or three persistent students each year came to realize.

As Belmont considered problems with our English placement test and alternative means of placement, we heard about Royer and Gilles' method of DSP, first from a WPA listserv and then at Gilles' CCCC presen-

---

[1] Until recently, Belmont's first-year students were required to take English 101 and 102, two 3-hour writing courses. Beginning in Fall of 2001, Belmont's general education curriculum requires English 110 a 4-hour writing course taken in the first or second semester, followed by English 210, a 1-hour writing lab attached to an "affiliate" course in another general education discipline and taken in the sophomore year.

tation in 1998. Grand Valley State University's (GVSU) DSP questionnaire attempted to assess what we had acknowledged for some time but did not know how to measure: Student success in first-year college writing courses was often related as much to confidence and experiences with writing as it was to intellectual gifts and demonstrable skills. We also appreciated how such a questionnaire, and DSP approach in general, could be adapted to fit our uses. In fact, our eventual DSP instrument is based on the GVSU model but with several modifications, including a reading and writing task and an additional questionnaire designed specifically for international students.

WHAT TO CHANGE?

English 103

As the writing faculty were wrestling with the problems in our placement process, we realized that our student population was changing; we were placing only a handful of students into English 90, our basic writing course. The university's admissions office had incrementally been raising its standards for 10 years, and by 1997 we were placing only about five students into English 90 each semester. Less than 10 years before, the department had been offering two sections of English 90 each fall, but by 1997, even with a slightly larger student body, we could hardly justify one section of English 90. Because very few of our students needed the basic writing course prior to taking English 101 (according to our former standards), our heroic efforts to identify a handful of students seemed out of proportion to the need. At this point we considered dispensing with an English placement altogether, eliminating English 90 entirely, and relying on regular student-initiated or faculty-prescribed visits to the Writing Center to assist those few students who were underprepared for English 101. In the past, these students would have been required to complete 4 hours of English 90 successfully before enrolling in English 101.

Our response to the changing student body was to discontinue English 90, but we were not ready to rely solely on the Writing Center to support the less prepared writers. We felt these students, and other students whose writing needs were not so acute, would benefit from a more structured, regularly scheduled form of assistance. To support the changing needs of our students, we stopped offering English 90 and began offering English 103, a 1-hour companion course to English 101 taken in the same semester with English 101. Because students enroll in English 103 concurrently with English 101, we assumed (and experience bears out) that they are much more willing to take the support course because it does not delay their taking the required English 101. English 103 is only a 1-hour course (rather than the 4-hour English 90 course), so the additional tuition dollars for the support course are not significant enough to deter students from registering for English 103. Because English 103 is a Writing Center-based, writing instructor-facilitated, small-group workshop course, it can provide students additional assistance with English 101 reading and writing assignments (rather than additional assignments) and regular communication between 101 and 103 instructors. Students in English 103 readily perceive how this course supports their progress in English 101 and are more genuinely engaged in the course than they were in its predecessor, English 90.

Through DSP, Belmont students now may elect to take English 101 their first semester as their only ENG course, or they may elect to take English 101 and its support course, English 103. Thus, English 103 became the lynchpin for our adoption of DSP, and DSP provided the impetus to reexamine and replace English 90 with a more serviceable course.

Orientation

The creation of English 103 allowed our program the luxury to use the time formerly allotted for the placement test to orient and educate incoming students about program standards and expectations. The placement *test* now became the placement *process*. Using DSP, we could give new students some sense of what to expect in college writing courses and some tips about succeeding in English 101. Additionally, students could get help from writing faculty regarding which section of English 101 to take. More than half of the writing program's first-year, first-semester writing courses are computer-enhanced, and the program also offers several service-learning sections of English 101. As our menu of English 101 options grew, we felt students might need more assistance in selecting the particular section of English 101 that was right for them, and DSP enabled us to provide exactly such guidance.

Just determining preparedness for English 101 was no longer the sole objective for our placement procedure. We could now assist students in selecting the specific version of English 101 that suited their interests and needs. Our DSP also functions in part as an orientation to the first-year writing courses by immediately asking students to begin making their own choices. For example, the proctors introduce the process and emphasize the students' roles in taking responsibility for their own education. We then explain English 103 as an extra hour of support directed through the Writing Center. Proctors explain that students who elect to take 103 are often good writers who may nevertheless feel insecure about their first semester of college, or may feel they lack the self-discipline needed to work consistently on papers through the semester, or may realize they have not had extensive, challenging writing experiences in the past.

The Placement Instrument

The placement instrument itself grew out of the Royer and Gilles DSP questionnaire. The GVSU questionnaire addressed key determiners of success in first-year writing courses: general academic preparedness as well as self-perceptions of student attitudes toward, success with, and habits of reading and writing. We modified the questionnaire to reflect our specific expectations of entering students (such as revising) and to assess the skills of our international students.

Although we were ready to relinquish the task of evaluating nearly 500 student essays each summer, we were not eager to give up the writing sample entirely during the placement process. We felt that students could better determine their need for English 103 if they received examples of college-level reading and writing assignments and heard about college faculty expectations for reading and writing skills. Thus, in addition to the questionnaire we included a reading and writing sample to demonstrate a typical reading and writing assignment, asked students to produce a brief writing sample in response to the reading, and then asked the students to self-evaluate what they produced. (*See the writing sample in appendix.*) We chose a passage from Mike Rose's *Lives on the Boundary* for our reading sample; it is not only a fairly challenging text, but it also articulates something of our educational philosophy.

The process of guiding the students through their own self-placement is critical. The proctor gives students 30 minutes to read this paragraph and respond to the writing prompt; he or she then asks students to read silently what they have composed thus far. A proctor next reads aloud a typical summary of the Rose excerpt to see if students understand the main idea. Students are told that the passage is considered a challenging one, but missing the main idea entirely could indicate that students should consider taking English 103 with English 101. We also ask students to assess the essay they produced using five main evaluative criteria, printed in the placement booklet. By elaborating on the criteria, we are giving students an early introduction to criteria we will use to evaluate their writing in the future. In addition, we are demonstrating a process of self-evaluation and reflection we will encourage in our writing courses. Admittedly, many students cannot at this stage recognize their own organizational problems or lack of supporting detail or mechanical errors. But when encouraged to reread and reflect, students may become aware of some of their own writing problems, even if they do not yet know how to correct them.

Faculty members next answer any remaining questions the group may have about the English 101 options and about English 103. Finally, the faculty proctor directs students who feel confident they already know which course to register for to circle their choice on the first page of the placement booklet, which they retain as a reminder of the course they will register for the following day. Academic advisors, with whom students will meet the following morning, check this sheet to confirm the student has been through the placement process and has remembered correctly his or her placement decision. This sheet also lists the placement director's office location and phone number, and students are encouraged to visit her that afternoon or call her the next morning if they have second thoughts or other questions about their placement. Most of the students leave the placement room at this time.

Students who need more time and assistance choosing their first-semester English course or courses are invited to stay for a few minutes longer to meet with the waiting writing faculty. These faculty members are available to answer students' questions or to read students' responses to the writing prompt. Usually 10% to 15% of a placement group will linger for an additional 10 to 15 minutes to confer one-on-one with the writing faculty present. Sometimes in this informal conversation with a listening faculty member, students will recognize more about their writing experiences and self-assessed skills. Sometimes students will ask for an "expert" opinion. If students ask us to read their writing samples and offer our opinions about their readiness for English 101, we do so, but we remind them that the choice is theirs. Again, we want to take the stance of an interested and informed counselor, not of a judge.

HOW TO CHANGE?

Although DSP seemed pedagogically sound, we feared it could be risky. Could we really trust our students to enter into DSP with the seriousness, honesty, and responsibility necessary for accurate placement? What if large numbers of students who were not prepared for English 101 enrolled in English 101? And how would the campus perceive this decision to let the students themselves decide which writing course they should take their first semester? We had spent years educating advisors, admissions personnel, and support staff concerning our placement methods and enlisting their help to make our system work. We had created a veritable cottage industry around regular training sessions for graders, creation of new prompts, administration of the testing and grading sessions themselves, reporting of scores to academic advisors, education of faculty advisors, record keeping of scores, and management of the appeals process initiated by students unhappy with scores and assertive enough to challenge the system. Dismantling or changing a system we had worked hard to maintain would not be easy. What if, after all our reforms, the new system produced more problems than it solved? Although we found the GVSU rationale for DSP compelling and our own version of DSP workable, we were initially stymied by several logistical and political concerns.

These concerns led us to establish several safety nets that would allow us to anticipate and minimize problems with our new placement system and to ensure a more successful transition from the traditional placement to DSP. For example, we piloted the placement instrument with two English 101 classes in Fall 1997, asking students who had been placed by taking the former placement test and were recently enrolled in their first-semester writing course to complete the DSP instrument as if they were at orientation and then to offer feedback about the instrument. Because these students went through both placement processes, they offered useful feedback from a student's perspective. They appreciated DSP for empowering them, but argued vigorously that no incoming student would ever self-select English 90. Perhaps they were dubious about peers being willing to self-select a basic writing course because, despite our best efforts, students attached to English 90 a stigma of failure. The students' vehement response to English 90 gave us one more reason to delete it. The following semester, a spring term when English 101 courses have significantly lower enrollments, we implemented DSP with all new students at Belmont. The timing allowed us to experiment with the process, again trying to minimize potential risks in the change.

Another safety net served to identify the students who needed the support course. A pre-existing admissions committee that includes a writing faculty member screens for the occasional student admitted with barely admissible verbal standardized test scores, a weak application essay, and/or marginal grades in high school English. The writing faculty member of the Admissions Committee can stipulate these students must take English 103 as a condition of their admission. These students are also usually prevented from taking more than 12 hours during their first semester, again as a stipulation for their conditional acceptance.

Finally, the program guards against underprepared students taking English 101 without the supplementary course by asking all first-year writing faculty to elicit a writing sample on the first day of class. Although we continue to authorize the students themselves to decide on their English placement (except for the few given conditional admission to Belmont), their English 101 teachers can and do advise students who produce a weak writing sample to register for English 103. We can even, at this point, allow an occasional student to enroll in English 103 after the drop/add period is over. Because ours is a small program, we have the flexibility to accommodate students' individual needs and situations.

In Fall 1998, we discussed the new placement procedure with our departmental colleagues. Our rationale for revising our placement procedures used Paolo Freire's philosophy that teachers should empower their students through their education. Freire, writing in Horton and Freire, describes himself as "going as far as [he] could in helping people develop the capacity to make decisions and to take responsibility, which is . . . the role of an educator" (125). We also talked with colleagues about student empowerment that Ira Shor advocates when indicting the English placement tests of the 1970's that had, along with other educational experiences, predisposed his students to expect the teacher to "do education to them" (2). Shor acknowledges that all facets of schooling can "socialize students into critical thought or into passive habits of following authorities, waiting to be told what to do and what things mean" (13). Members of our department agreed with Shor's call for a respectful, reciprocal relationship between learners and teachers. Opportunities for learners to reflect on their own educational experiences could begin, we believed, in our very first encounter with students during a DSP process. Although we recognized that providing new students with an opportunity to self-determine their English placement would not, in itself, empower learners, we came to believe that it could be a small step toward that process of empowered learning to be reinforced by student-centered classrooms. In fact, DSP can signal to students that the institution itself sanctions and even expects students to participate in and question critically their own educational experiences.

The remaining public relations task was to educate colleagues outside our department concerning DSP. "You let the students themselves decide?" some faculty asked in astonishment. Surprisingly, we did not hear that question frequently. Very few people find the change a problem, and most are excited about the concept. In the annual fall faculty workshop in 1998, we distributed a flyer to explain the shift to DSP, primarily to inform advisors that we would no longer report to them the scores for the English placement test.

HOW TO ASSESS THE CHANGE?

The writing faculty and other faculty and staff have overwhelmingly supported the change to DSP, but student response has been most telling.

Since 1998, at the request of the writing faculty, the questionnaire given to all students who complete the first-year orientation has included one general question about DSP. The evaluative instrument, based on a Likert scale, concludes with the following statement: "I found the English Department's DSP process helpful in making my decision about the first English course I should take at Belmont." The 169 students who voluntarily evaluated their 1999 orientation that included the placement process reported the following: 25 strongly agreed with the statement that DSP was helpful in deciding which English course they should take; 58 agreed; 26 disagreed; 9 strongly disagreed; and 51 did not respond at all to this particular statement. Of course, these students had not yet begun classes at Belmont, so presumably they could not accurately judge the appropriateness of their decision.

Anecdotally, students seem to support the faculty impression that students do take seriously their role in DSP, appreciate being brought into the process, and find the process helpful. In a questionnaire one teacher gave her students, 10 of the 12 responding agreed with the statement "The English placement process helped me understand what to expect in English 101," whereas two students disagreed. Eleven of the 12 students agreed with the statement "I had sufficient time to complete the English placement process," but one student disagreed. All 12 respondents agreed with the remaining statements:

- "The oral and written instructions for completing the placement were clear."
- "The purpose of the English placement process was made clear."
- "I appreciated the way the English placement process made me responsible for my own English placement."

A significant measure of the success of DSP is found, we believe, in student satisfaction with English 103. Students, in fact, often now recommend to peers this elective course. English 103, the companion course to English 101, is now often elected by capable but insecure writers. Of the nearly 300 first-semester students, 72 elected to take English 103 in Fall 1997. The sheer numbers attest to the success of the curricular and placement changes. Whereas English 90 used to enroll three to five students (admitted through increasingly more stringent admissions criteria) now students self-select English 103 in numbers as high as 77 per semester. The most unexpected byproduct of English 103 and DSP is that the English 103 groups became so popular we created English 103 sections for the second-semester first-year writing course and our sophomore literature courses. When we have the faculty to teach them, we now offer 103 groups for selected classes in other disciplines. Anecdotal evidence strongly supports these offerings because enrollments remain high, even though students still self-select for these companion courses.

Finally, the success of DSP at Belmont may also be seen in the influence of DSP on larger curricular reforms on our campus. For example, while our institution has been revising its general education curriculum, we have borrowed from DSP to begin creating a self-placement instrument for students to use in determining computer proficiency.

Our perceptions about the impact of DSP are that students who need English 103 are, for the most part, receiving 103; that students enrolled in English 103 are genuinely engaged in English 103 because they have self-selected the course; that far more students are self-selecting English 103 than faculty were placing in English; that DSP presents to students a more accurate preview of Belmont's writing courses and college-level reading and writing expectations; that students use DSP to make informed decisions about an increasingly complex menu of English 101 offerings; and that our relationships with our future students now begin in mutual respect toward mutual goals.

CONCLUSIONS ABOUT DSP AT BELMONT

Recently a sophomore, reflecting on his English 101 experience at Belmont, remarked that the course had been an orientation to college for him. As Belmont's writing faculty reflect on the new placement process, we feel that it serves as an "orientation to the orientation." As such, we can, in some ways, set the agenda for the kinds of reading, writing, and thinking expected at the university. Although we overwhelmingly support DSP, believing that it serves students better than our former placement test, our approval of is largely based on anecdotal evidence and impressions. We like how it feels to meet new students in a teaching and advising role rather than as judges who screen out the unworthy. In addition to these informal impressions, we have also gathered some data from questionnaires completed by faculty and students and institutional data comparing numbers of students who self-selected ENG 103 to numbers of students who were placed into ENG 90 through a placement test. This preliminary assessment suggests that DSP does offer an appropriate means of placing students in their first-semester writing course. As an orientation, Belmont's DSP presents the course options for ENG 101, introduces students to college-level reading and writing expectations, requires students to assume responsibility for a major decision in their education, engages students in intellectual habits of reflection and collaboration, and launches student–teacher relationships that are mutual rather than adversarial. As faculty involved in this process, we feel we can now be instructive rather than judgmental. We now answer for ourselves the question "Why change to DSP?" with the response "We really can improve the way we teach students to write."

APPENDIX: DIRECTED SELF-PLACEMENT BOOKLET DEPARTMENT OF LITERATURE AND LANGUAGE BELMONT UNIVERSITY

Most entering freshmen register for one of the English 101 sections; however, an additional hour of assistance with writing is available to you through the Writing Center. This self-placement process will let YOU determine if you would benefit from an extra hour per week of tutoring along with English 101. If you determine you would indeed benefit from an additional hour of assistance with your writing, you should register for English 103 as well as English 101. NOTE: Multilingual speakers should see page 8.

DESCRIPTIONS OF FIRST-SEMESTER ENGLISH COURSES

English 101: is a beginning-level course designed to strengthen students' critical thinking, reading, and writing skills. Students work individually and collaboratively with classmates to complete a series of related essay assignments. They also record responses to reading assignments and class activities. The class reviews the rules of English grammar and mechanics as necessary—but the emphasis in the work of the course is on the processes of critical thinking, reading, and writing. Thoughtful and enthusiastic participation in class discussions and group activities is essential and contributes toward the students' final grades for the course.

> *Some English 101 sections include a suffix to designate a particular approach to English 101. All of the ENG 101 sections, even those section numbers that precede a letter suffix, fulfill the ENG 101 requirement and achieve the same writing goals. For the purposes of this placement instrument, English 101 will refer to all options of English 101 including ENG 101C, 101SL, and 101SC that are explained below:*

English 101C: Some sections of the ENG 101 are designated as 101C. These classes are the same as English 101 except they are conducted in a computer classroom and papers are composed on computer. No previous computer skills are required but basic typing ability is a plus.

English 101SL: are sections of ENG 101 with a required community service component. Students who take these "service-learning" sections will commit to tutor at-risk children in a literacy enrichment program with other ENG 101 students for at least 8 hours during the semester. The Belmont students who tutor these children will become encouragers and friends for the children and interested readers of the children's writing. The Belmont student tutors will benefit by becoming aware of their own literacy histories, needs, and goals and by earning 1 hour of convocation credit (required for graduation) for every hour of tutoring. Eight hours of tutoring are required for the course but more tutoring hours are possible.

English 101SC: are computer-enhanced sections of ENG 101 that also include the "service-learning" approach. Therefore, these sections combine features of ENG 101C and ENG 101 SL. Students in these sections will meet in the computer classroom and will also spend 8 hours over the course of the semester tutoring and mentoring a child.

English 103: is a writing workshop that meets once a week for 50 minutes in the Writing Center. Students work in small groups, usually of three or four, to give and receive feedback that will strengthen their papers for English 101. Group members assist one another in a) interpreting reading assignments; b) interpreting writing assignments; c) developing first rough drafts; d) revising intermediate rough drafts; and e) editing final drafts. You will sign up for ENG 103 in addition to ENG 101.

English 100: is a writing course for international, multilingual students to strengthen thinking, reading, writing in English on computers. Meeting 3 hours a week, it introduces internationals to U.S. academic writing before they take English 101.

Now detach this first page from the placement booklet. After completing the placement process, you'll return to this page and circle the first semester ENG course/s you have determined you need for this semester. Before you leave the placement site, have one of the faculty proctors initial your choice on this page. (Your advisor may request to see this form before signing your fall schedule.) Also turn in the remainder of the placement booklet (pages 2-8) to a proctor. If you or your advisor has any questions about your English placement, please call the Dept. of Literature and Language.

Belmont's Directed Self-Placement Process

NAME _____ SOCIAL SECURITY # _____ TODAY'S DATE _____

STEP ONE:
READING AND WRITING SAMPLE

Read the following excerpt from the book *Lives on the Boundary* by educator and author Mike Rose. Then write a response to this excerpt according to the brief writing assignment or prompt which follows. You will be given 30 minutes to complete this college-level reading and writing assignment:

■■■

READ   A friend of mine recently suggested that education is one culture embracing another. It's interesting to think of the very different ways that metaphor plays out. Education can be a desperate, smothering embrace, an embrace that denies the needs of the other. But education can also be an encouraging, communal embrace—at its best an invitation, an opening. Several years ago, I was sitting in on a workshop conducted by the Brazilian educator Paulo Freire. It was the first hour or so and Freire, in his sophisticated, accented English, was establishing the theoretical base of his literacy pedagogy—heady stuff, a blend of Marxism, phenomenology, and European existentialism. I was two seats away from Freire; in front of me and next to him was a younger man, who, puzzled, finally interrupted the speaker to ask a question. Freire acknowledged the question and, as he began answering, he turned and quickly touched the man's forearm. Not patronizing, not mushy, a look and a tap as if to say: "You and me right now, let's go through this together." Embrace. . . . . No-nonsense and cerebral, but a relationship in which the terms of endearment [could be] the image in a poem, a play's dialogue, the winding narrative journey of a novel.

More often than we admit, a failed education is social more than intellectual in origin. And the challenge that has always faced American education, that it has sometimes denied and sometimes doggedly pursued, is how to create both the social and cognitive means to enable a diverse citizenry to develop their ability. It is an astounding challenge; the complex and wrenching struggle to actualize the potential not only of the privileged but, too, of those who have lived here for a long time generating a culture outside the mainstream and those who . . . immigrated with cultural traditions of their own. This painful but generative mix of language and story can result in clash and dislocation in our communities, but it also gives rise to new speech, new stories, and once we appreciate the richness of it, new invitations to literacy.
****

WRITE   In the above passage from *Lives on the Boundary*, Mike Rose describes education as a "communal embrace" and argues that "a failed education is social more than intellectual in origin." In your own words entirely, summarize your understanding of Rose's main idea. Then respond to his concept of education being a "communal embrace" that is as much social as it is intellectual—agreeing with it, disagreeing with it, or modifying it somewhat. Support your position with details that may come from personal examples. On the lined pages that follow, develop as much of a response as is possible in this 30-minute time limit.

Use these pages to complete a written response to the excerpt from *Lives on the Boundary:*

Your Name_____

REFLECTING ON STEP ONE:
SELF-EVALUATION OF YOUR READING AND WRITING

Review your just-completed writing in response to the excerpt from Mike Rose's book. How challenging was the reading selection and how challenging was the following writing assignment for you? Based on your perception of how well you understood the above college-level reading and how well you responded in writing, do you feel prepared for college-level reading and writing assignments? To help you assess your readiness, consider the following criteria the ENG 101 instructors use in evaluating writing.

Does your response:

- reflect that you understood the reading assignment well?
- summarize the passage's main idea accurately?
- advance a clear thesis?
- present arguments in a well-organized way?
- support that thesis with sufficient detail?
- use mature, varied sentence structure and clear, concise language?
- use standard punctuation, spelling, and language?

If you feel fairly confident of the quality of your written response to the above assignment, you should at this point consider yourself a good candidate to register for English 101 only. If not, you may need to consider registering for English 103 along with English 101. Reflect honestly on your experience with this college-level reading and writing assignment. At this point, do you believe you would benefit from taking English 103 in addition to English 101?

REMEMBER, if the Admissions Committee has stipulated that you must take ENG 103 as a condition of your admission, you must register for both ENG 103 and ENG 101.

A TIME FOR QUESTIONS

STEP TWO:
QUESTIONNAIRE OF READING/WRITING EXPERIENCES

This final section consists of ranking your response to several statements about your writing experiences and abilities. Use the following statements to guide you in determining your readiness for ENG 101. Place an X along the continuum to suggest which statement best reflects your background and experiences. Remember that the farther to the right or left you place your X, the more you are indicating strong agreement with the statement on the right or the left. If you don't know how to answer a response, leave it blank.

Example
If you felt your high school was slightly below average in its academic reputation, you might mark the first continuum as follows:

•<--•-----X--------------------------------------->•
I attended a high school with a strong academic reputation.   I attended a high school not noted for its rigorous academic program.

* *

•<--•--->•
I attended a high school with a strong academic reputation.   I attended a high school not noted for its rigorous academic program.

•<--•--->•
My high school teachers often gave me helpful written and/or oral responses (not just correction marks and grades) to my writing.   My high school teachers usually offered very few comments about my essays.

•<--•--->•
I am accustomed to writing several drafts before submitting a final draft; I see revising as an important part of the writing process.   I usually write just one or two drafts for a writing assignment. The only revision work I do is to edit for spelling errors and other careless mistakes. I'm not really aware of other ways to revise.

•<--•--->•
I often generate ideas for an essay (through invention or prewriting strategies like clustering, listing, outlining, freewriting, etc.) before I begin drafting the essay.   When I begin a new writing assignment, I usually start writing immediately about the first idea that comes to mind. Often I feel I don't even know where to begin.

•<--•--->•
I am aware of some patterns in my own writing: tendencies I have to produce certain kinds of errors, my personal writing habits, and recurring analytical, organizational, and stylistic strengths and weaknesses.   I'm not really sure what are my writing strengths and weaknesses. Besides, I have the impression that good writing just happens and there's not much I can do to become a better writer.

•<--•--->•
I like to play with language: changing and rearranging words or sentences I've written, experimenting with different ways to express an idea, adding new words to my reading and writing vocabulary.   I'm either unaware of multiple ways of expressing an idea or unwilling to experiment with different ways of wording an idea. Whatever phrase or sentence I record first is often the only way I know to express an idea.

•<--•--->•
Although I may find it difficult to do, I have a fairly clear understanding of how to organize a written argument around a controlling thesis with distinct, well-organized points supported in detail.   I'm not certain what is meant by a controlling thesis idea or how to support that thesis with significant details. I'm also often uncertain how and where to divide my papers into paragraphs.

•<--•--->•
I read newspapers and magazines regularly. In the past year I have read books for my own enjoyment.   Generally, I don't read when I don't have to.

•<--•--->•
In high school, I wrote several essays per year   In high school, I didn't produce much formal writing.

•<--•--->•
My high school GPA placed me in the top third of my class.   My high school GPA was less than the top third of my class.

•<--•--->•
I have used computers for drafting and revising essays.   I've rarely used computers for writing and revising essays.

•<--•--->•
My ACT English score was above 23, or my SAT verbal score was above 540.   My ACT English score was below 23, or my SAT verbal score was below 540.

•<--•--->•
I consider myself a very good reader and writer.   I don't think of myself as a strong reader or writer.

(This questionnaire was based in part on the Placement Guide published by the English Department at Grand Valley State University.)

REFLECTING ON STEP TWO:
SELF-EVALUATION OF QUESTIONNAIRE

Now review your responses to the previous questionnaire. If several of your responses fell to the right of the center along the spectrum, you should at least consider registering for ENG 103 in addition to ENG 101. **NOTE: If you have a suspected or diagnosed learning disability that affects your reading and writing, you should also consider registering for ENG 103.**

At this point, non-international students should be able to select ENGLISH 101 or ENGLISH 101 plus 103. If you are not certain, please feel free to ask the advice of the writing instructors administering the self-placement. For more information about the varieties of ENG 101 sections, see a proctor.

A TIME FOR QUESTIONS

Do you believe you need to register for ENG 103? If so, please sign your name after the following statement of your intention to register for ENG 101 and 103:

I believe I should register for ENG 101 only _____ *(your name)*

I believe I should register for ENG 103 as well as ENG 101 _____ *(your name)*

FOR INTERNATIONAL AND MULTILINGUAL STUDENTS ONLY

Multilingual speakers who have taken the TOEFL or who are not fluent in English should consult with the International Student Advisor here after completing the questionnaire below. Together the student and advisor will determine if the student should register for English 100, a 6-hour per week writing course for multilingual students who need more preparation in writing <u>before</u> taking English 101.

•<--•-->•

| I attended a high school where English was the primary language. | I attended a high school where English was not the primary language. |

•<--•-->•

| I have been studying English for more than 5 (five) years. | I have been studying English for less than 5 (five) years. |

•<--•-->•

| I am able to "think" in English. | I think in another language before translating my ideas into written or spoken English |

•<--•-->•

| I learned to speak English before I was 12 years old. | I learned to speak English some time after I turned 12. |

•<--•-->•

| I believe I do not need a writing course that is especially designed for international students. | I believe I would benefit from a writing course that is especially designed for international students |

REFLECTING ON THE MULTILINGUAL QUESTIONNAIRE

At this point, if most of your responses to the multilingual questionnaire fell to the left of the continuum, you may wish to consult with the International Student Advisor now to discuss your decision. If most of your responses to the multilingual questionnaire fell to the right of the continuum, you should register for ENG 100.

According to the above section of the questionnaire, do you believe you should register for ENG 100?

I believe I should register for ENG 100

_____ *(your name)*

I believe I should take the English Placement Test to determine if I might be eligible to take English 101 _____ *(your name)*

---

[i] Until recently, Belmont's first-year students were required to take English 101 and 102, two 3-hour writing courses. Beginning in the fall of 2001, Belmont's general education curriculum requires ENG 110, a four-hour writing course taken in the first or second semester, followed by ENG 210, a 1-hour writing lab attached to an "affiliate" course in another general education discipline and taken the sophomore year.

REFERENCES

Gilles, Roger. "Directed Self-Placement: A New Approach." Conference on College Composition and Communication, 1998.

Horton, Myles and Paulo Freire. *We Make the Road by Walking: Conversation on Education and Social Change.* Chicago: U Chicago P, 1992.

Shor, Ira. *Empowering Education: Critical Teaching for Social Change.* Chicago: U Chicago P, 1992.

Rose, Mike. *Lives on the Boundary: The Struggles and Achievements of America's Underprepared.* New York: Free Press, 1989.

6

INTRODUCING DIRECTED SELF-PLACEMENT TO KUTZTOWN UNIVERSITY

Janice Chernekoff
Kutztown University

The English Department, administration, and faculty senate of Kutztown University (KU) agreed to pilot directed self-placement (DSP) during the Summer 1999 orientation for new students. The primary focus of the following discussion is the initial trial implementation of DSP and the issues that arose in the process. As I write, I imagine an audience of compositionists interested in implementing DSP. Alternately, this chapter may also interest readers who are curious about the effects of DSP on a college composition program. Now 3 years into our experiment with DSP, I believe that KU will continue with it because it suits our needs in a number of ways. Philosophically, DSP dovetails nicely with the emphasis on student responsibility and decision making in our orientation program. Practically, it creates only a minimal staffing, financial, and time burden for the university as well as the orientation program organizers. The English Department and administration have carefully observed the results of DSP over the last three years. I am happy to provide information on what we have learned and how it has affected our composition program. For example, Table 6.1 lists first-year composition (English 001) grades for the last four fall semesters, the final two following summers in which we employed DSP.

Table 6.1. Grade Distribution in English 001
(Fall 1997–Fall 2000)

Fall 1997: Before DSP				
A	B	C	D	F
15.2	41.8	25.6	5.6	7.1
Fall 1998: Before DSP				
A	B	C	D	F
18.9	42.2	24.2	3.9	7.2
Fall 1999: With DSP				
A	B	C	D	F
17.0	37.2	23.9	7.1	10.3
Fall 2000: With DSP				
A	B	C	D	F
20.9	42.3	22.3	3.7	6.5

Although DSP certainly has its skeptics, it is an interesting and theoretically important response to a whole range of placement problems. Ironically, if one were to summarize the effects that DSP has had on KU's composition program, one might be tempted to say that it has had very little effect at all. By that I mean that grades have not fallen (it appears that the opposite is happening—see Table 6.1), composition-teaching faculty (with two or three notable exceptions) are not complaining about dramatic changes in their English 001 classes, and some students are still enrolling in Developmental English (DVE). So the composition program has not collapsed, and other predicted dire effects that I discuss later have not come to pass. However, it would not really be accurate to say that nothing has changed. DSP has created the need for our department to talk about its goals and pedagogies related to composition because DSP is most successful when one is able to accurately explain to students what they will experience in their writing classes. Obviously, the department must be more or less in agreement on its composition program goals and the methods for achieving them if one is to give students accurate descriptions of the available classes during DSP. In other words, DSP has been the catalyst that has made it necessary for us to re-examine what we all do in composition, what we all should be doing, and why and how.

METHODS

This chapter includes material from interviews with several of my colleagues: the former coordinator of composition, members of the department's Composition Committee, the chair of the department, the department secretary, the acting dean of Liberal Arts and Sciences (usually the assistant to the dean), the director of Connections (KU's orientation program), and the faculty coordinator for new student scheduling. I have relied heavily on the memories and opinions of my interviewees in the sections where I describe KU and where I write about its placement history. In these two parts of the chapter, my purpose is to contextualize the situation in which the decision to pilot DSP was made and also to offer a way for readers to compare their situation to ours. When we began discussing DSP in the Composition Committee and with the dean's office, some of the first questions were about Grand Valley State University's (GSVU) program and students; it therefore seemed valuable to provide such information about KU.

In order to broaden my understanding of the effects of DSP, I also distributed an end-of-semester survey to all students who participated in DSP, and another to faculty who taught English 001 or DVE during the first fall semester following DSP. Using this information, I explain and evaluate the initial effects of DSP for everyone involved. Wherever possible, I include the thoughts and reactions of others so as not to rely exclusively on my own perceptions. Finally, I have added recent information about changes effected by DSP in the last two sections of the chapter.

DESCRIPTION OF KU

KU is one of the 14 campuses that compose the Pennsylvania State System of Higher Education. Kutztown has approximately 8,000 students, three quarters of whom are undergraduates. Originally a teachers' college, KU is now an "open access" school that admits roughly 1,500 students per year, mostly from local high schools, although a small percentage of our population comes from Philadelphia to the south and New Jersey to the east. Given the relatively high number of public, semi-private[1] and private universities, as well as community colleges, in the state of Pennsylvania, students are presented with a wealth of choices when they set out to select a university. As a result, competition for students is fierce, and according to local lore, KU does not typically draw many students from the top 15% of the graduating high school class. Additionally, KU's incoming class each year includes up to 40% first-generation college students. It is often said that our students are not confident in their academic skills; sometimes they seem unsure as to whether they even belong in college. Many of our students also work full-

---

[1] Penn State, for example is one such school. Essentially private, this university still receives substantial support from the governor's budget.

or part-time jobs while attending college. Perhaps these factors account for the unimpressive retention rate and the delayed graduation rate—two problems that are currently receiving considerable attention. In summary, KU primarily serves the local working class and middle-class families. The most popular majors include elementary and special education, business, Telecommunications, fine arts and professional writing. Not many of our students continue on to graduate school.

THE HISTORY OF ENGLISH PLACEMENT AT KU

In their 1998 *College Composition and Communication* article, Royer and Gilles describe a method of placement used at GVSU prior to DSP that was not unlike the one employed by KU. On both campuses, test scores—ACT and SAT, respectively—were used for the initial screening of incoming students. Although the exact scores used to demarcate the various populations at KU varied slightly from one year to the next, generally speaking, students who scored below 440 on the SAT-Verbal test were automatically placed in DVE. Those students with scores of 520 and above were placed into English 001. Students whose scores fell into the middle range were given the opportunity to write an essay during orientation to demonstrate that they did not need DVE.

During the first day of the 2-day orientation cycle, according to Angela Scanzello, former coordinator of Composition, students who elected to take the written test were given 50 minutes in which to write an essay on an assigned topic. These essays were then scored, apparently with great difficulty due to the lack of a stable, "normed" pool of readers. Time constraints and scheduling problems also created friction between the coordinator of Composition and the orientation staff who needed the results to create student schedules. Both students and parents viewed this process, repeated eight times in the month of June, as arbitrary, subjective, and punitive. The dean of Liberal Arts and Sciences, the English Department chair and the coordinator of Composition all received complaints as a result (Scanzello; Nott). Not surprisingly, students placed in DVE, by whatever means, often began the class with "attitude." I taught two such DVE courses in my first semester at KU, witnessing first hand the sullen resentment and frustration of many of these students. Some openly expressed their feelings, whereas others conveyed their thoughts just as eloquently through their reluctance to be drawn into discussions or activities. Such attitudes made it necessary for me to expend an inordinate amount of time and energy in justifying the value of the course to them. I've learned from colleagues that my experience was not unusual. Almost everyone—from students to administrators to professors—was unhappy with this system.

Although Scanzello believes that the old system may have worked if properly understood and supported by the department and administration, she explained that a number of factors worked against its success and reliability. The fact that she sometimes had to write grants just to obtain funds to pay the readers seems to support her point. To make matters worse, the readers were temporary faculty who had other summer commitments and were not available for all of the orientation sessions in June, making the validity of the placement recommendations questionable. Additionally, others involved in orientation who believed their needs more pressing, occasionally interrupted the time allotted for the essay test. Scanzello recounted an instance, for example, in which a school official came in and interrupted her testing procedure to speak to the group because he had been busy at the time when he had been scheduled to speak. As her frustration grew, she also became increasingly certain that her testing results were unreliable. When I asked her why she initially supported the idea of DSP, she replied that she could no longer support the old system. To be clear, her initial support for DSP was based more on her lack of belief in the old system than on a strong belief in the proposed system. After seeing the results of the first trial run with DSP, she said that she continues to support this system on a conditional basis because she believes that we need to standardize our composition courses to some degree to ensure that students actually get the classes that I describe during DSP sessions.

A similar lack of confidence in the old placement system was expressed by others in the English Department. Arnold Newman, a former chair of the department, claimed that the number of sections of DVE that the department offered in the fall semester had doubled in recent years. And having taught DVE consistently through the years, he maintained that the DVE placement had been inappropriate for a significant number of his students. Another colleague, Sam Keiser, contends that students simply did not take the essay test seriously during orientation because there is too much going on during those two days. Elaine Reed, current chair of the English Department, believes that the essay tests may not have yielded valid results because students do not always choose to show what they know, even in placement tests. Finally, there is also the underlying question that most of us asked about this type of writing test: How much can one show about one's writing skills in 50 minutes?

As I prepared to assume the responsibilities of coordinator of Composition, I was assigned the task of exploring and recommending other possibilities for English placement. Being familiar with the body of composition theory that has argued against the validity of using SAT Verbal scores to place students in writing courses, I did not want to continue this practice. However, I knew it would be difficult to find a system that I considered ethical and efficient *and* that required little in terms of time, money, and staff. With these prerequisites in mind, and with extensive support from my chair and Carl Brunner, dean of Liberal Arts and Sciences, I started to dialogue with composition program directors from other universities in Pennsylvania. It was during a conversation with Joseph Harris, then at the University of Pittsburgh, that I first heard about the concept of DSP. When I described KU's predicament to him, he suggested that I read the article by Royer and Gilles.

WHY DSP WAS INITIALLY APPEALING

I read the *CCC* article and was immediately intrigued by the idea of DSP. It seemed a nice philosophical fit for me, and it promised to eliminate the impossible situation that my predecessor had found herself in. I would not have trusted timed essays even under more favorable conditions than she had experienced. Having been a reader of Subject A[2] exams for the University of California, San Diego, as well as a reader for the Educational Testing Service, I had learned that it is impossible, even with regular "norming" sessions, to grade essays (especially illegibly written ones) objectively and fairly. DSP would not put me in this position. In fact, it would give students the message that we believe they are capable of making an appropriate decision. Generally speaking, I would rather err in the direction of trusting students too much because this act of trust usually yields more favorable consequences in the long run. I also believe that students live up (or down) to our expectations of them. If students are challenged, they are likely to achieve beyond their own expectations of themselves. From the beginning, I was aware that skeptics would be suspicious of students' motives in judging their own abilities, but are the motives of faculty or administrators less suspect? If professors and administrators subscribe to the commonly expressed notion that students do not learn anything in high school, doesn't this affect English placement? How do the political pressures surrounding budget cuts and staffing problems affect placement methods and decisions? In other words, placement is not a "pure" activity, no matter who makes the decision about which English class the student will take during his or her first college semester. Why not give students more of a say in the matter?

---

[2]Subject A is a basic writing course that does not grant students credit toward graduation. There is an exit exam that students must pass before they are allowed to enroll in first-year writing courses.

Royer and Gilles claim that DSP gives students an "authentic educative experience" by upsetting "prevailing student/teacher relations" (54). I liked this aspect of DSP because it would convey to students the message—before they had even begun their academic careers at KU—that they should be active participants in their education. Being an advocate of critical pedagogy, it seemed to me that Royer's and Gilles' DSP would at least implicitly support Paulo Freire's idea that students "cannot enter the struggle [or the classroom] as objects in order *later* to become human beings" (50). In other words, if educators hope that students will become mature decision makers and active citizens, shouldn't we give them practice in the skills they will need to assume these roles? And if we don't begin these lessons as soon as they arrive on campus, then when? The work of other important critical pedagogues and compositionists also seemed to me to theoretically support DSP. Linda Brodkey, bell hooks, and Bronwyn Davies, for example, argue that teachers need to encourage the development of students' voices and critical thinking abilities, partially by giving up the notion of being the expert who is always right, and just as importantly, by listening to and dialoging with students. DSP promised to create a situation in which students would be making responsible choices based on conversations with school representatives. The faculty and/or administrators explaining the composition program might legitimately claim to be experts in their program, but they would not need to make the less legitimate claim to expertise in individual students' abilities.

In their article, Royer and Gilles argue that when students select their composition class, they have something invested in making their decision work for them. Students placing themselves into DVE might be assumed to desire the extra time and attention in order to feel comfortable and confident with their writing abilities, whereas those selecting the first-year composition course might be assumed to believe they can and will pass the course. Either way, the DSP decision that students make is educational and usually a confidence builder for them. Even those who do not succeed the first time will have learned that their decisions have consequences—and that they have only themselves and their original placement choice to look back to (Royer and Gilles). In our first year with DSP, we discovered that this view is shared by students and their families, too, because the acting dean of my college, Walter Nott, received no complaints from parents or students regarding English placement during the subsequent fall semester. We did learn, however, that we needed to make it clearer to students who selected DVE that they could not change their minds mid-semester, disappear from the course, and then expect to be able to enroll in English 001 the following semester. The only way to erase the "U" (Unsatisfactory) that these actions would earn one would be to repeat the course.

Many of us worried about the potential problems for those students who might overestimate their skills in DSP. Some argued—and continue to argue—that so-called basic writers are the least capable of making a good decision, the most vulnerable in terms of dropping out, and the most likely to overestimate their abilities. Whether DSP was a suitable method of placement for this part of our community was, and still is, being debated. From the perspective of promoting active learning and participatory education, however, it was, and is, hard to justify eliminating this learning opportunity for those who have the most to gain if they succeed in it. When is it the right time to hand over responsibility to the so-called basic writers, and how will they be transformed into clear-thinking, capable individuals? Don't we need to start the training in critical thinking and decision making with students at the beginning of their college careers—*no matter where that beginning is for an individual student?*

However, it was clear from the beginning of our discussions about DSP that strong resistance to it would arise with the suggestion that students admitted conditionally to the university should participate in it. Presently, the conditionally admitted students include those entering through the Developmental Studies Summer Program as well as those admitted through the ULTRA[3] Program. Most of the students in these programs were and are placed in traditional ways. In the second year that we used DSP, however, ULTRA students whose SAT-Verbal scores were 450 and above were allowed to participate in DSP. Politically, the stakes are high with these special groups; if students are not retained or do not succeed, the programs and their funding come into question. It is understandably harder for the university to give up control of the placement of students in these groups.

Within my department, people may have had various initial reactions to DSP and its underlying philosophy, but it was clear to me that my colleagues wanted to "do the right thing" by our students, even at a time when we faced drastic financial constraints. Temporary faculty contracts are being steadily reduced in number, so the teaching of composition has become an increasing burden to the tenured and tenure-track faculty who are primarily trained in and committed to literature or professional writing. Because virtually everyone in the department is now teaching composition, we have a difficult time offering enough courses for the majors. DSP was appealing, therefore, in that it seemed to hold out the promise of a reduction

---

[3]ULTRA is a funded program for students with projected grade point averages of less than 2.0 and/or combined SAT scores below 880. In their first semester at KU, these students take both DVE and English Composition, Developmental Math and the required math course, and University Studies—a course in critical thinking, reading, and writing.

in the number of sections of DVE that would need to be offered. It seemed to provide the best solution to our placement woes in financial terms, *and* it seemed to have a sound theoretical basis.

WHY FACULTY AND ADMINISTRATORS (CONDITIONALLY) APPROVED DSP

The general dissatisfaction with the old system allowed many people to feel that, at the very least, DSP could fare no worse than the old system. Even with "Kutztown students," often characterized as less capable than most of making good educational decisions, it was felt that DSP would probably result in more satisfying placements for them. Many of my English Department colleagues hoped that the new system would change the tenor of DVE classes as well. As some of them said when I inquired about changes in DVE, it is so much easier to work with students who come to class willingly. Moreover, English 001 professors would suddenly be in the position of being able to say to a student: "Look, you made the decision to take this class. That's fine, but here's what you need to do if you hope to pass it." Professors would be in a stronger position with regard to recommending tutoring, the writing of extra drafts, and office visits. Students would perhaps be more inclined to listen to such advice if they wanted to prove that they had made the right decision in signing up for a class that was a bit above their skill level.

Arguments about an anticipated change in the attitude of students, particularly those in DVE, were persuasive. Several colleagues remarked on the idea that happier students make for better classes—and many had experienced the same sullen resentment in DVE students as I had. Moreover, just the *idea* that students were being trusted to make a smart choice entailing responsibility for themselves changes the atmosphere *in* all composition classrooms to some extent. As Jim Nechas remarked, DSP conveys to students the message that they should "take back some control" over their writing. According to him, it further tells them "that they are an important part of the process, and that they do have some control over what they write and how they get to the point of writing well."

In my interview with Nott, he also focused on the importance of students having more control over how their writing skills are evaluated by the university. According to him, students are too often the passive recipients of other peoples' evaluations about their writing. He feels that students are generally encouraged to not trust their own perceptions about their writing and this results in feelings of powerlessness regarding writing, how it is evaluated, and what it means to be a good writer. Like my English Department colleagues, Nott also viewed DSP as a step in the right direction toward a more comprehensive review of writing, or literacy, on the campus of KU.

Several of my colleagues who have been supporters of the composition program over the years also explained that DSP seemed to provide "an incremental step" in the right direction with regard to making more sweeping changes (Keiser; Nechas). Historically, divisiveness between literature and professional writing faculty made it hard to implement program changes, including changes in composition. Although fences have been mended, people are also reluctant to raise issues that might divide the department again. However, as it was explained to me, implementing DSP required little from anyone, provided necessary changes, and allowed people to hold onto the feelings of collegiality that had flourished recently (Keiser; Nechas).

These issues—students' responsibility toward themselves and the building of what Erica Reynolds calls self-efficacy (chapter 4, this volume)—were themes that came up repeatedly in discussions with colleagues and administrators. The director of the Connections Program, Andrea Kirshman, reiterated these themes in my interview with her. She is making a concerted effort with her programming to stress the development of critical thinking skills and responsible decision making, goals that are in line with the mission statement of the university (*KU Undergraduate Bulletin* 7). From her perspective, DSP is philosophically compatible with Connections and has the added advantage of being a relatively painless method for handling a historically problematic task. In my interview with her, she added that her student facilitators had also expressed their support of this system. Because they assist with DSP, distributing and collecting materials, and also helping to answer students' questions, they become very familiar with the process. There is a pleasing resonance, too, in working with a group of students all of whom have obviously been academically and socially successful at KU, and in having them help us convey the message to their peers that the decision they make during the DSP session is a significant one.

INITIAL DOUBTS AND QUESTIONS

Despite their general acceptance of DSP, my colleagues understandably had some questions and doubts when I explained the process to them. How could they be sure that they would not have to "dummy down" their English 001 classes because they would be filled with students who should have taken DVE? Would anyone take DVE? Was this a sneaky way of eliminating the jobs of the "temporary" faculty who had been there for a number of years? (Was the administration behind this move?) Who else was using this method of placement? How closely did GVSU compare with KU with regard to size, type of student, and SAT score average?

These questions were also asked by many on the KU campus. The faculty coordinator for new student scheduling, John Schellenberg, stated during my interview with him that he had been one of DSP's "greatest skeptics," based on 20 years of experience talking to disgruntled students and their parents about DVE placement. He had been certain that *no one* would select DVE. He had also been worried that the failure rate for first-year composition would dramatically increase and rob new students of seats in composition classes the following year. Others, I believe, were certain that the English Department was going from bad to worse with regard to its placement methods. It was actually harder to sell DSP, even as a pilot project, to the Faculty Senate than to the English Department. Thanks to the solid support of provost and vice president for Academic Affairs, Dr. Linda Goldberg, however, who argued that this was just part of a plan to review the entire composition program, we were able to persuade the Senate to approve a trial run.

The administration, although supportive, had many similar concerns. Nott also worried whether anyone would enroll in DVE, whether students would take the placement system seriously, and whether the pass rate for composition would plummet as a result of the new system. Additionally, he was and is particularly concerned about the conditionally admitted students, most of whom do not participate in DSP. The ULTRA and Developmental Studies groups are already under scrutiny because some believe that they do not belong at KU. Although the acting dean philosophically agrees that these students should participate in DSP, he also believes it would be much more difficult to sell this idea given the general feeling that these students are seriously underprepared and unaware of what is needed to succeed in college. Concerns about academic standards being lowered (yet again, some might say) would likely resurface if ULTRA and Developmental Studies students were all permitted to participate in DSP.

WHAT WE ACTUALLY DID—AND HOW WE DID IT

After reading Royer and Gilles' article and corresponding with them about their new placement system, I met with the Composition Committee to discuss DSP and the procedure that had been implemented by GVSU. In particular, we reviewed their survey, a crucial aspect of the process, and decided to try DSP but to add several items to the survey that we would use. Elaine Reed argued that we should take advantage of this new placement method to try to increase interest in the Honors Program, something that the administration was also promoting. The committee reasoned that the additional survey questions that we eventually agreed upon would permit us to include Honors English as a choice for students. Students selecting Honors English would still have to meet the Honors Program requirements, but those who could truthfully answer "Yes" to virtually all 13 questions (shown in Table 6.2) would be likely candidates, we believed.

Overall, the 13 items in our instrument solicit information about students' recent reading and writing experiences as well as about their facility with Standard English grammar and academic conventions. The SAT-Verbal score item is intended to indicate that it should be considered as a factor but one that is no more or less important than, say, the habit of regular reading or the experience of having written regularly for the previous 2 or 3 years. We also thought that the longer list would allow students to put together a more detailed review of their language knowledge that would help them make an appropriate decision as to which class they should take.

Students received the DSP brochure, explaining the system and previewing the survey, in the mail several weeks before the 1999 Summer Orientation. We hoped that they would study the information about the course options, think about the survey, and prepare to make a realistic course choice at orientation. The English Department received only a few

Table 6.2. Survey of Reading and Writing Experiences

Y/N	I read magazines and newspapers regularly.
Y/N	I read books regularly.
Y/N	I read publications about hobbies and interests.
Y/N	I consider myself a good reader and writer.
Y/N	I have learned writing as a process that includes at least some of these steps: brainstorming, drafting, evaluation, revision, and editing.
Y/N	I am at ease composing and revising essays on a computer.
Y/N	I write letters and e-mail messages regularly.
Y/N	English was one of my strong subjects in high school.
Y/N	My writing demonstrates my competency in English grammar and punctuation.
Y/N	In high school English, I wrote several essays, for at least 2 or 3 years.
Y/N	I stay current with political and social issues.
Y/N	My SAT Verbal score is 500 or above.
Y/N	I have experience in doing library research to write a paper.

calls about DSP prior to the orientation sessions, so its introduction apparently did not alarm or confuse too many people. At the orientation sessions, it was obvious that some students had carefully read and studied this information, whereas others had not even looked at it. Therefore, as part of my talk with students, I reviewed the survey and what I meant by such phrases as "I read books *regularly*." I wanted to be clear about our expectations of students while at the same time encouraging capable students to select the more challenging courses.

The physical conditions for the placement sessions that first year were functional but not ideal. Between 120 and 180 students attended each session, and we gathered in a hot lecture hall immediately after lunch. Smaller groups would be easier to work with, but that was not an option for reasons having to do with space, staffing, and other logistical issues. Given these constraints, the assistance of the Connections student staff was vital. They assumed responsibility for a number of key tasks during the DSP sessions: ensuring that students arrived on time, distributing and collecting materials, assisting in answering students' questions, and setting a tone of seriousness for the 45-minute sessions. Unfortunately, conditions have not improved very much over the 3 years, but the presentation of information in the allotted time has been streamlined, and my working relationship with the Connections staff and student facilitators has been fine-tuned. The student facilitators are now an important and integral part of DSP for us.

After the very first orientation session, however, we felt certain that students were not getting enough information about the courses, were not taking the process seriously, or, as many had feared, were acting "practically" in deciding not to take a course that did not earn them credits toward graduation. For whatever reasons, only 6% selected DVE during the initial orientation session. We[4] panicked and then made a decision to change our process slightly. Thereafter, we began each session with an additional survey asking students to write detailed responses to questions about their specific reading and writing experiences over the previous 2 or 3 years (Table 6.3). We asked students to return these inventory cards to us but allowed them to remain anonymous. This strategy proved successful in getting students to more carefully reflect on their actual reading and writing histories.

In the second session, roughly 25% of the participants selected DVE, and likewise in the third session. After the introduction of the preliminary questionnaire, students also asked more questions than before. In other words, this tool functioned as we hoped it would: students slowed down and thought about the writing they had done rather than only about the class they

---

[4] I say "we" because Nott and I worked very closely together last summer. I appreciate the support, assistance, and the advice he has given me on this matter.

Table 6.3. Directed Self-Placement Inventory

How many books have you read in the last year?

What is the name of the last book you read?

How many times have you read the newspaper in the past week?

How many magazines have you read in the past week? What are the names of the magazines that you read?

How many papers did you write in your last year of high school?

What kind of papers did you write in the last 2 years?

What range does your SAT Verbal score fall in?

Above 520___ 450–520___ Below 450___

How would your last English teacher describe your skills in reading and writing?

How would you describe your skills in reading and writing?

Please note that the information requested on this card has two major functions:

1: To assist you in making an honest appraisal of your reading and writing skills prior to selecting a composition course.

2: To help the English Department understand how to place students in order to ensure success in college writing.

---

wanted to take. Over the eight June orientation sessions in 1999, we averaged just over 12% placement in DVE. This result represented a reduction of more than 50% in DVE sections—higher than expected. The English chair and the dean's office transformed classes slated to be DVE into English 001 with minimal disruption. Although we felt cautiously successful with our experiment, I am sure I was not alone in feeling some trepidation about how the semester would go, especially in first-year composition classes.

THE RESULTS OF OUR FIRST SUMMER WITH DSP

Probably the strongest evidence of success was that none of my colleagues noted any drastic differences in their English 001 classes in the Fall 1999 semester. At the same time, everyone teaching DVE noted improvements in student attitude and performance. Although DSP is still considered a pilot project at KU, the results are encouraging, so much so that the deep skepticism of some has somewhat abated and the support of others is more enthusiastic than before. Kirshman is so pleased with the "fit" between DSP and her orientation program, that she has said, "Leave it alone. Don't change anything." Even my colleagues, who are understandably more cautious, have been indirectly encouraging with comments like this one: "No matter what, let's not go back to the old system." DSP may not yet be institutionalized at KU, but it gained guarded approval after its initial run from the administration, the department, and those involved with the orientation program. This acceptance is no doubt partially due to the fact that the pass rate for composition in the Fall 1999 semester was 90%, down just 3% from the previous two fall semesters (see Table 6.1).

In fact, the slight increase in the failure rate was reversed in Fall 2000. Students in the Fall 2000 semester actually seem to have done better overall than students in either the Fall 1998 or Fall 1997 semesters when we still employed the old method of placement. With regard to DVE, the failure rate was reduced by roughly 4% in 1999 although it increased by 0.5% in 2000. At this point, I might cautiously suggest that DSP has had no negative effects on the outcome of English 001 or DVE. Schellenberg, assured that the same number of first-year composition seats as usual would be available to incoming students, remarked that the survey does seem to be encouraging students to take stock of their writing skills. This view is spreading, or at least there is a level of acceptance of DSP that did not exist during the first year. Now, 3 years into KU's experiment with DSP, when I speak with the faculty advisors who counsel new students and help them create their first-semester schedules, our conversations center on helping particular students make the best choices rather than about the system we're using to serve the students.

Additional evidence of general satisfaction with DSP was provided by the surveys that I distributed to students as well as in questionnaires completed by all faculty teaching composition in the Fall 1999 semester. Faculty teaching DVE reported that both attitude and performance of students taking this course were markedly improved over previous semesters. And although the faculty remarks about composition were not overwhelmingly positive, neither were they negative. In general, the opinion seemed to be that if no improvement had occurred in their first-year composition classes, there had not been any negative changes, and it was just too early to really decide how DSP was working. English department members were also reluctant to make quick judgments about DSP for several other reasons. For most of the Fall 1999 semester, a possible faculty strike loomed over everyone. Twice, in fact, I went home expecting to be walking a picket line the next morning. To make matters worse, these two "11th-hour" stand-offs happened several weeks apart. The result was a semester of confusion, demoralization, and a lack of focus—for everyone. Many English Department faculty felt that this issue must be factored into any evaluation of grades from English 001 and DVE classes for the Fall 1999 semester. Added to this was the perception that the admission standards for KU had eased considerably so that the preparedness of the incoming student body was questionable. In other words, there seemed to be enough variables to make most on campus willing to continue the experiment and see what would happen. As Table 6.1 indicates, grades for ENG 001 classes did rise substantially in Fall 2000, following the second summer during which we used DSP to place students. With the exception of two or three professors who believe that we should return to the former system of placement, there seems to be a general agreement that we have made a positive change. However, it might be wise to say that we need to employ DSP for several years, keeping careful records about a whole host of variables, before we can really say what effect it has had on our program.

Students surveyed in 1999 indicated that the new process worked well for them; 95% believed that they made the appropriate course selection for themselves. Of the 5% who indicated that they felt they had made an inappropriate choice, most thought that they should have selected the more difficult course, that is, first-year composition rather than basic English. Additionally, students generally believed that the brochure was accurate and helpful, and that the presentation given to them during their orientation session was informative. Further evidence of student satisfaction exists in the fact that neither the dean nor the department chair received complaints about placement during the summer or at the beginning of the semester. In a climate where "customer satisfaction" becomes increasingly important, this last fact has been noted appreciatively by everyone with any administrative responsibilities for English placement.

This is not to say that there have been no questions or problems at all. As previously mentioned, we have had some difficulties with a handful of students who selected DVE during placement but changed their minds about the class once the semester was underway. Many of these students seemed to think that if they were free to choose DVE, they were also free to choose to stop taking it. However, if a student simply stops attending, he or she will earn a grade of Unsatisfactory for the class, which counts as a grade of F until the class is retaken. To try to prevent this problem I have added a statement to the description of DVE in the brochure explaining that enrolling in this class obligates one to pass it before proceeding to first-year composition. Now, I also ask instructors to remind students of this stipulation during the first week of classes. Additionally, I can offer students relief from the class if they drop it or withdraw from it officially. Students who tell me that they dropped the class because they decided it was too easy or was simply repeating material that they were familiar with, are not students that I feel compelled to take a tough stand with. If the student assumes the responsibility of dropping the class and coming to see me, I will not make the student repeat DVE. I think that the content of DVE classes at KU varies enough that I need to respect students' opinions about it.

Lack of standardization is somewhat of a problem with DVE in particular because students do not receive credit toward graduation in this course. When I explain DVE during orientation, I have felt myself to be on somewhat shaky ground because of the differences between DVE classes. Some professors focus heavily on grammar, punctuation and sentence-level work, whereas others treat their courses as an introduction to critical thinking, reading, and writing. Many use traditional basic writing textbooks, but a few do not. To make it possible to provide students with an accurate description of DVE, the Composition Committee has begun to review the official curriculum for this course. In fact, at a 1-day seminar on composition in which the entire department participated during the 2000-2001 school year, we spent a considerable amount of time discussing the goals of DVE.

THE FUTURE OF DSP AT KU

Although DSP is still a pilot project at KU, it is likely to gain institutional approval. The significant positive results so far have included shifting responsibility for the placement decision to students and a major change in attitude in DVE classes; meanwhile there have been virtually no negative outcomes. Added to this is the fact that the percentage of students passing first-year composition with acceptable grades has remained more or less the same, and student and parent complaints about placement have ceased. As explained earlier, we must decide whether or not to permit the conditionally admitted students to participate in DSP, an issue currently under discussion at KU. One possible course of action is to *gradually* lower the SAT Verbal score required to participate in DSP; as more at-risk students demonstrate their ability to make this decision successfully, we would move closer to integrating almost everyone into this placement process.

In general, however, fewer students seem to be selecting DVE. In 1999, 12% chose DVE, whereas in 2000 the figure was 10.33%, and in 2001 only 8.45%. I am not yet sure whether this is a matter for concern. My ambivalence about DVE in its present forms leads me to feel less concerned about the low DVE placement rate. If we were able to revise the DVE curriculum into a more challenging course, and one that would earn students credit toward graduation, it would be a course that I would feel stronger about recommending. At present, when "marginal" students approach me (and many do at the end of each orientation session) during DSP and ask which course I think they take, I do my best to think of what is best for the students rather than about our statistics. I question students about their motivation level and their willingness to work hard, revise repeatedly, visit the writing center regularly, and spend more time on assignments than some of their peers might. If they think they're up to the challenge, I tell them that they may want to enroll in English 001; if they think they need the extra time and easier paced course, I tell them to consider DVE. At this point, while DVE is under consideration and review, I would say that the results of the 2001 DSP placement are cause for question and study rather than concern. We need to see how students do this semester. Just as importantly, we need to conclude our review of DVE.

The summer of 2001 is also notable, however, for the increase in interest in Honors English. Although DVE placement decreased by about 2%, and the percentage of students requesting English 001 remained the same, interest in the Honors class increased by 2%. The interest in the Honors course was so significant, in fact, that we added an additional section of the course for the Fall 2001 semester. Before DSP, we generally offered one section of Honors English each fall. In 2001, however, we offered two, and in 2002 three were offered. This is unquestionably good news. It means that we have more first-year students willing to challenge themselves and asking us to challenge them in their course work. Presumably, many of these students will join the Honors Program and boost its numbers, something that did in fact happen in 2001. Because it has been a stated goal of the administration to expand the Honors Program, this result will certainly be pleasing to that portion of the academic community.

Another issue that needed to be resolved was the matter of staffing and payment for administering DSP. From an administrative viewpoint, DSP appears deceptively simple. One English faculty member—with some student assistance—can assist 100 to 200 students in selecting their composition classes in less than 1 hour. However, there is a substantial amount of work to be done before and after the actual orientation sessions and for the faculty member involved, DSP consumes the entire month of June at KU. Overall, I estimate that DSP tasks consume at least 70 hours in the summer. To illustrate some of the more "invisible" work that must be done to ensure effective results, on the mornings following the afternoon DSP sessions, I attend meetings with the counselors who do student scheduling. For the entire month of June, then, I have scheduled obligations Mondays through Thursdays. I also write letters to students who express interest in Honors English but who are found ineligible and respond to phone calls resulting from these letters. I consult with my chair, the dean's office, the new student coordinator, and the orientation program about any problems or questions that arise. Although I did not include a discussion of payment in the original DSP proposal and consequently was not paid for the first 2 years, we now seem to have the matter resolved. For the last 2 years I have been paid the equivalent of one summer course. Clearly, this is an issue that should have been addressed before we began to implement DSP. With this experience behind me, I would certainly recommend that any school considering DSP discuss payment up front and be careful to compile a realistic estimate of the time needed for the work.

Another matter, fortunately one that we did address in our second year with DSP, the 2000-2001 academic year, has to do with the need for a Writing Center with well-trained staff to provide the support that some students need to succeed. Because some students select the course that will really challenge them, it is necessary to provide them with the means to be successful if they apply themselves fully to the task. One of my colleagues addressed this issue in my interview with him. Acknowledging the fact that the University Writing Center (UWC) staff engaged in more rigorous training last year, he observed that the stronger tutors really allowed his weaker students to achieve the goals they had set themselves (Keiser). According to him, students who utilized the UWC had their decision to enroll in first-year composition instead of basic English reinforced for them once they realized they would succeed if they regularly worked with tutors. In other words, an essential piece of the puzzle in making DSP work is to ensure that the writing center staff is able to adequately serve the students. Because KU anticipates receiving more underprepared students in the future, we will need to ensure that the UWC services continue to expand and improve.

DSP may also be responsible for revitalizing the awareness of a need for a campus-wide conversation about writing and its place in our academic community. It is generally acknowledged that KU presently lacks a coherent vision on this issue. Some colleagues in other departments tell me that they make their students write papers and/or do written exams; however, I also hear from students who report being able to complete their degrees without writing other than for their first year composition classes. Perhaps some of the initial resistance to DSP had to do with an unrealistic expectation of what students could achieve in one semester of writing. In other words, while I would not expect students to be polished writers after English 001, others might. Although I think of English 001 as the introduction to a student's study of writing, others might see it as the conclusion. With the introduction of this new placement method, and the reality that most of our students are now taking only one composition course, DSP is creating the opportunity for us to discuss important writing questions. What does it take to make students into writers? How can we better facilitate this process? Why should we be doing this? How does DSP affect what we do and when we do it?

For students at KU, perhaps the most significant benefit of DSP so far is that they have some control over the evaluation of their writing and are, therefore, a little less at the mercy of what they perceive to be the subjective and whimsical opinions of composition instructors. In other words, DSP provides students with a means to intercede in the external evaluation of and control over their writing. The typical conversation I have with students at orientation sessions now illustrates this. Instead of telling them that they are good, bad, or so-so writers, I ask them about their writing experiences, review their surveys with them, and work around to the point of making them tell me which class is best for them. Allowing students to regain some control and demonstrate some responsibility on this issue could presumably have ripple effects in other areas. Students might wish to assume a more active role in their selections of courses, or other departments and faculty might begin to believe that students should be more involved in important educational choices and decisions. If DSP has helped KU to begin a conversation about students as responsible people and decision makers, could it have a positive effect on other significant policies and procedures?

DSP reiterates the goals of liberatory education, goals that are now widely accepted as being appropriate and effective for college students in whom we hope to instill the capacity for critical thought and socially responsible action. DSP reminds us of these goals and provides us with a way to move toward them. DSP forces faculty to let go of some of their control and to simultaneously realize that it is safe to do so (Nechas). I believe that I am correct when I say that for those of us who initially supported directed self-placement at Kutztown, there is a sense of satisfaction in having taken what appeared to be a big risk, albeit a risk in an ethical and pedagogically sound direction, and in seeing that so far it is working out just fine.

REFERENCES

Brodkey, Linda. "On the Subjects of Class and Gender in 'The Literacy Letters.'" *College English* 51.2 (1989): 125-41.

Davies, Bronwyn. *Poststructuralist Theory and Classroom Practice*. Geelong, Vic.: Deakin UP, 1994.

Freire, Paolo. *Pedagogy of the Oppressed*. Trans. Myra Bergman Ramos. Rev. 20th Anniv. ed. New York: Continuum, 1994.

hooks, bell. *Teaching to Transgress: Education as the Practice of Freedom*. New York: Routledge, 1994.

Keiser, Samuel. Personal Interview. 19 April 2000.

Kirshman, Andrea. Personal Interview. Fall 1999.

Kutztown University Undergraduate Bulletin 1998-2000. Kutztown, PA: Kutztown University, 1998.
Nechas, James. Personal Interview. 17 April 2000.
Newman, Arnold. Personal Interview. 3 May 2000.
Nott, Walter. Personal Interview. 6 March 2000.
Reed, Elaine. Personal Interview. 26 April 2000.
Royer, Daniel J. and Roger Gilles. "Directed Self-Placement: An Attitude of Orientation." *College Composition and Communication* 50.1 (1998): 54-70.
Scanzello, Angela. Personal Interview. 28 April 2000.
Schellenberg, John. Personal Interview. 10 May 2000.

7

THE CASE OF A SMALL LIBERAL ARTS UNIVERSITY
Directed Self-Placement at DePauw

Cynthia E. Cornell
Robert D. Newton
DePauw University

The history of the DePauw Writing Program, like the history of any writing program that has been in place long enough to have a history, is one of accommodation and experimentation: accommodation to political pressures, to the mood of the culture, to economies of time and money, and to competing agenda, principles, and pedagogies. Our directed self-placement (DSP) procedure is the most recent in our history of accommodation. We adopted DSP in 1995, reluctantly and under pressure from competing agenda, and we have been monitoring it ever since, expecting that the data produced would show that our at-risk students were disadvantaged in some measurable way by choosing to avoid our beginning writing course. But the more data we collect, the clearer it becomes that *mandatory* placement of such students in our first course is not justified. For that reason, DSP has become for us not an accommodation but a matter of principle.

For 4 years, we have followed the academic success and persistence at DePauw of our at-risk first-year students, some of whom chose to take our first course, College Writing I (English 120, originally called "Basic Writing") and others of whom chose to move directly into College

Writing II (English 130, originally called "Expository Writing"). We have been able to compare our data for these students with the results of earlier studies of a similar group of students who had all been mainstreamed into the second course. We quickly discovered that our findings do not support the kinds of claims we had been making for the College Writing I course when, earlier, we had required it of at-risk students or when, more recently, we have recommended it to them. Because our data do not show that taking the basic writing course enhances their chances of success in College Writing II or other college courses, we are reluctant to require it as a "remediation" for a writing deficit. And because we cannot show that at-risk students who take basic writing are more likely to persist to graduation from the university than at-risk students who avoid the first course, we are reluctant to present it to students as a key to successful adjustment to the culture of the university. Our data do show that the at-risk students who choose to take basic writing but eventually drop out of the university persist slightly longer than the at-risk students who avoid College Writing I and later drop out of the university, but the data cannot show whether that persistence is a result of taking the College Writing I course or a function of the same personality characteristics that might have led a student to elect the course in the first place. What we can say is that students are virtually universally satisfied with their right to choose the level at which they will begin our writing program, and that the students who elect the first course value it for itself—for the experience that the course provides— more than they value it as a prerequisite to their success in the writing program.

Although the center of this chapter is the data from our 4-year study of DSP, we begin with a description of the context of our study: who we are as an institution, how our writing program is structured, what procedures we follow to place students and help them place themselves. Then we present data from a mainstreaming experiment in 1993 and 1994 in order to explain why we chose to try DSP in the first place. The second half of the chapter presents the data from which we try to answer the following questions: Is there a profile of the kind of student who elects College Writing I that is different from the profile of the kind of student who chooses to go directly to College Writing II? Is there evidence that students are disadvantaged academically by not taking the basic writing course? Is there evidence that students' rate of graduation from or persistence at the university is compromised by their choices? And finally, how do the at-risk students themselves evaluate their choices and their freedom to choose? Our study focuses on the lower levels of our writing requirement, but we have some incomplete but suggestive data on DSP at the upper level, which we include in our discussion of why we began to experiment with DSP. (See Preliminary Study 3 and Preliminary Study 4 sections.)

INSTITUTIONAL BACKGROUND: WHO ARE WE?

DePauw University is a small liberal arts university in central Indiana that offers bachelor's degrees in the liberal arts, education, and music performance. Its enrollment is almost exclusively traditional: young men and women, mostly middle class, who enter college immediately after graduating from high school and live on campus. All first-year students live in dormitories, but by their sophomore year, nearly 75% join a fraternity or sorority and move into an associated house. During the years of our study, "Greek" rush for first-year students took place midway through the first semester. The university is described as "more selective" than some colleges and universities in terms of admissions, but nevertheless, in each year of our study, we had a group of 100 to 120 students (between 15% and 18% of the entering class) who appeared, according to conventional predictors, to be at risk for completing college successfully. The standardized test scores of the middle 50% of our new class rose slightly over the period of our study: SAT-Verbal scores for the middle 50% of the class entering in 1994-1995 ranged from 490 to 600 and for the class entering in 1998-1999 from 540 to 640; SAT-Math scores ranged from 540 to 670 in 1994-1995 and 550 to 660 in 1998-99. ACT-Composite scores ranged from 23 to 28 for the class entering in 1994-1995 and from 25 to 29 for the class of 1998-1999. Eighty percent of the entering classes during our study period were from the top 25% of their high school graduating class; 97% were from the top half. We have considered our at-risk group to be students with Verbal SATs of 530 or below, and these scores dipped as low as 320 in the newly recentered system, with a median score of 480 and the largest number clustering between 420 and 520. In the absence of SAT scores, we use ACTs to classify students as at-risk. In this case, the ACT-English cut off is 22, with scores dipping as low as 11, and the largest number clustering between 15 and 22.

Majority students comprised roughly 82% to 85% of our entering class during our study period. Multicultural enrollment ranged from 15% to 18%, with African-American students representing between 6% and 8% of the entering classes, Hispanics between 3% and 5%, Asian Americans roughly 2%, and multiethnic roughly 2%. DePauw is currently a site for the Posse Foundation's experiment in sending multicultural students to college from New York City, and a "posse" of these students are included in the last 2 years of our study. Fourteen foreign countries are represented in the remaining 2% to 4%. Although DePauw is regarded as a national rather than a regional liberal arts college, most students come from the Midwest. The percentage from Indiana increased from 44% to 50% as part of a statewide effort funded by the Lilly Endowment and headquartered at DePauw to encourage Indiana students whose parents have not attended college to continue their education. English is the first language of at least 98% of incoming students.

First-year students enroll for between three-and-one-half and four courses each semester, each course meeting 4 hours a week. They are taught almost exclusively by faculty with the terminal degree. Because DePauw has no graduate programs, we have no graduate instructors, teaching assistants, or graders. The student–faculty ratio during the period of our study has been a little less than 12:1.

THE DEPAUW WRITING PROGRAM: WHAT IS IT?

The Original Course Definitions

The Writing Competence Program was established by faculty vote in 1979 as part of a revision of the graduation requirements. It was designed to implement one of three competencies: writing, speaking, and quantitative reasoning. For about a decade before this time, a course in expository writing had been simply an elective, but in 1979 a three-tier writing requirement was mandated. It was the time of the "Why Johnny Can't Write" hysteria, and some of our weakest students had difficulty writing coherent sentences about academic matters. Additionally, introductory courses had ballooned in size, and students were sometimes not asked to write a paper until they got into their smaller upper division courses. Following the current thinking of the time, a writing task force designed three new courses: a developmental one (English 120: Basic Writing, later called College Writing I), a foundational one (English 130: Expository Writing, later called College Writing II), and a lower division writing-across-the curriculum course (called W) to be attempted before the end of the student's sophomore year. The first two courses were conceived as skill-building classes, working from sentences, to paragraphs, to personal experience narrations, description, classification, definition, and comparison/contrast, to academic summary, analysis, argument and library research. Emphasis was on invention, prewriting, and overcoming writing anxiety. English 120: Basic Writing focused in particular on overcoming writing anxiety and developing fluency in sentences, paragraphs, and short essays in the conventional modes, most of which took personal experience or observation as their subject; it was a pass/fail course, but it counted as a full credit toward graduation. English 130: Expository Writing concentrated on more academic, text-based writing, but tended still to be organized according to modes of discourse. A final grade of C- was required in English 130 in order for a student to continue to the W level.

The W course was at first conceived as a writing-intensive course housed in departments across the curriculum and designed to extend the students' writing experience and instruction beyond the English Department, with a focus on writing for a general educated audience. But, for many faculty and administrators, its role was to provide a forum outside the English 120 and 130 courses more objectively to "certify" students as competent in writing.

The Original Placement Procedures

Ed White visited our campus in August 1979, and helped us establish our first placement procedure, training us in the holistic reading of placement essays. The scores on placement essays, SAT-Verbal, and a mechanics and usage test were combined to form an English Placement Index (EPIX) by which students were ranked for placement. The bottom 30 students were assigned to English 120: Basic Writing, the next 75% to English 130: Expository Writing, either fall or spring semester, and the top 20% were placed directly at the W course level. Those students assigned to English 120 took it in the fall of their first year, followed by English 130 in their second semester. Students had the opportunity to appeal their placement by presenting appropriate evidence of writing competence or by the writing of a second placement essay. Additionally, a second impromptu was administered in all sections of English 120 and 130 on the second day of class as a corrective for possible errors in placement.

Changes in Course Definitions

As the years passed, so did the definitions of the courses and the nature of the placement procedure. Wishing to decrease the remedial connotations of the Basic Writing course and bring the courses, in students' minds, more clearly into the regular curriculum, we changed the names of Basic and Expository Writing to College Writing I and II. We decreased the emphasis on personal experience writing in the College Writing I course, moved directly into short essays, stressed revision of drafts, and increased the intellectual challenge of the course so that the combination of College Writing I and II felt more like a "stretch" version of the second course. Both courses were designed to help students perform effectively and with greater confidence in a culture of books and writing, to engage them in the "intellectual conversation and inquiry that we associate with a liberal arts education" (Soliday 95), but the smaller class size, ungraded format, and greater emphasis on processes of thinking and writing were intended to make College Writing I a safer space for at-risk students in their first semester of college than College Writing II. Both courses became text-based, centered on a visit of a major writer or acting troupe, and consequently, both began to look more like first-year seminars than skills courses.

Our W courses also changed from "certification" courses to writing-intensive courses that integrated both informal and formal kinds of writing with the exploration and mastery of course materials. The professors of those courses began to take more seriously their role as writing instructors, stressing the writing process and writing in the discipline as well as writing for a general audience.

Changes in Placement

Changes in our placement procedure came slowly. By the mid-1980s, we had dropped the mechanics and usage test as too expensive to administer, both in time and money, and as not useful in terms of the information it provided us about students' writing abilities or intellectual development. We continued to administer the writing placement essay exam on the first Sunday of student orientation, to grade it in a marathon session with all W course and College Writing faculty, and to create an EPIX score by a weighted combination of the writing sample score and the SAT-Verbal or, in its absence, the ACT-English.

WHY WE BEGAN TO EXPERIMENT WITH DSP

The Crisis: The End of Writing Placement as We Had Practiced It

Major changes in our placement procedure did not come until 1993 when DePauw, like other small liberal arts colleges across the country, was suffering enrollment declines that called for budget cuts and quick solutions to student attrition, especially among our first-semester students. Our dean, historically a strong supporter of the writing program, announced in May of that year that he wanted to suspend the placement essay writing and simplify the placement procedure. He argued that the writing of placement essays was one thing too many in a hectic and threatening orientation week for new students; his new goal was to make orientation week as comfortable and supportive for students as possible. He produced figures from our program that demonstrated that the use of an SAT-Verbal or ACT-English score alone for placing students would produce results closely comparable to the results of the EPIX. He also reminded us of the university's need to cut costs, and he felt that, on balance and at this time, the benefits of our placement procedure did not justify its considerable cost.

The Writing Program Placement and Monitoring Committee wrestled with the implications of the dean's announcement. Our first concern was the impact of using SAT-Verbal and ACT-English scores, particularly for the placement of minority students with cultural differences and students with learning and performance style differences that compromised their success on standardized tests. Earlier studies of our program had confirmed that minority students at DePauw were distributed at the lower end of these scales in greater proportion to their numbers than majority students even though they were distributed in equal proportion to the majority students on the writing sample scores. For several years, we had looked individually at the writing sample and entrance essays of minority students in order to identify disparities between the writing sample and the SAT-Verbal and to distribute minority students more equitably across the three levels of the writing program. We had an opportunity to do the same thing for students with reported learning disabilities, which were only now, because of federal legislation, beginning to become visible to the university. We worried that if we abandoned the writing sample, we would have no pre-registration method to correct for the cultural or learning style biases associated with standardized tests.

Portfolios were out of the question. Not only was it too late to ask incoming students to assemble them; the dean told us that there simply was no money to pay for training in portfolio assessment and for a reading session, nor would there be in the near future of economic uncertainty. After all, if reading impromptus was expensive, reading portfolios would be, according to White, about five times as expensive.

Strong arguments were made instead, by both the dean and members of the English Department, that we should simply drop College Writing I from the curriculum and mainstream all students, except for the top 20%, into College Writing II. If we did this, we would no longer need a complicated and expensive placement procedure. Proponents of this proposal questioned the benefits of tracking our apparently weakest students into the developmental class, reminding us that these students were often demoralized by this placement (see Adams 22), and wondering whether, as a result, they might perform *down* to the level of their placement. They argued that in their experience our weakest students were equally likely to *rise* to the level of higher expectations.

Others, especially the staff who regularly taught College Writing I, argued passionately that the withdrawal of College Writing I from the curriculum was irresponsible, depriving our least well-prepared or least confident students of highly effective developmental support. They testified to the success of students in their classes and to their own feeling that the teaching they did in this course consistently had a more discernible positive impact on their students than they perceived it as having in other courses. The retention of the course was also defended, almost universally, by the senior English Department members, who had contributed to the original design of the program, and by faculty teaching W courses, who feared that students would come to them less prepared in writing if the basic course were dropped.

The Compromise: Mainstreaming and DSP for a Few

We ended this debate with a series of compromises. For 2 years, 1993-1994 and 1994-1995, we would suspend the offering of the developmental course, English 120: College Writing I, on an experimental basis, thus simplifying the placement procedure. The students with the weakest SAT-Verbal or ACT-English scores, most of whom would have been placed in College Writing I, would be mainstreamed into the fall English 130: College Writing II sections. In exchange, the dean allowed us to reduce these sections in size from 18 to 16 so that instructors would have slightly more time for tutorial work. We would work out the appropriate placement procedure at the end of this 2-year experiment, based on data we would collect about it. He also agreed that if, after 2 years, we were still committed to offering College Writing I, we could do so, providing that we would systematically begin collecting data about the students taking the course—data that would give us a firmer basis on which to decide its ultimate fate in our curriculum.

For these 2 years, then, we agreed to use verbal aptitude scores and class rank to place the top 20 percent at the W course level and to divide the remaining 80% so that the lowest 40% took College Writing II in their first semester and the next 40% took it in their second semester. In principle, we believed that College Writing II was a course that all students should be required to take, as a core first-year experience introducing them to college-level thinking and writing. But, again, the practicalities of staffing had, from the beginning of the writing program, led to the compromise of exempting the "best" students from it. As part of our compromise, we set up a new procedure through which students scheduled to take College Writing II second semester (our 40th to 80th percentile) could appeal their placement. We scheduled a placement essay exam in late October, immediately after students had received their midterm grades for their first semester at the university, and we invited, but did not require, all students assigned to College Writing II in the second semester to take it. This would give us, and the students, more, and more relevant, information for their placement than we'd ever had: a writing sample, a midterm reading on their success in college level courses, papers that they had written for these courses, and advice and recommendations from their teachers and adviser.

Out of a group of 200 students, 57 wrote the placement essay, most of them from the 610 to 650 (recentered) SAT-Verbal range. The essays were graded easily by a small group of faculty, at no cost to the university. As a result of this placement procedure, we allowed 28 students to move directly to the W level if they chose to do so.

FOLLOW-UP STUDIES ON MAINSTREAMING AND PLACEMENT

Did Mainstreaming Hurt Students and How Do We Know?

As the 2 years of our mainstreaming experiment drew to a close, we needed to (a) decide whether to return to our earlier system, (b) withdraw College Writing I from the curriculum permanently, or (c) come up with a new arrangement. In working toward this decision we asked ourselves the following question: Were the students who earlier would have been placed in College Writing I but who had instead been mainstreamed into College Writing II damaged by our experiment in any measurable way? This led to our second question: Do we have measurements by which to place the most needy students into our basic course and our most capable students into W courses?

Preliminary Study 1. Our first study focused on the students entering in 1993. All students except the top 20% were placed in College Writing II. The lowest 40% were placed in the first semester sections of that course. Using the scores from a writing sample taken in the first week of the course and graded by the course instructor, we calculated EPIX scores like those that might have been used to place students under our original mandatory placement procedure. On the basis of these scores, we identified one group of 24 students whose EPIX scores would have placed them in College Writing I and another group of 29 just above those 24, who would have been placed into College Writing II for their first course. We used the mean grades in College Writing II as the tentative measure of the success of these groups.

We found that the mean grade for the cohort of 24 was 2.64, whereas the mean for the cohort of 29 was 2.83. Both of the means are located in our B- range, and the differences between the two are not statistically significant. It looked as if the success of the cohort of 24 was not damaged by skipping the College Writing I course.

Preliminary Study 2. We realized, of course, that group justice does not translate into justice to all individuals in the group. In both cohorts—the one that would have been placed in College Writing I and the one immediately above it, which would have been placed in College Writing II—there were individuals whose performance in the second course was significantly less than the mean. This led to the first part of our second question: Do we have indicators for incoming students that would have helped us accurately to put such students in a preliminary or basic course like our College Writing I?

In 1994, we again placed *all* entering students ranked in the lower 40% of their class in SAT-Verbal into the first semester sections of College Writing II. Then, at the end of the semester, we asked the faculty teaching those sections to identify any students who they felt had needed a preliminary course in order more easily to meet the exit standards of College Writing II. They identified 20 such students. Creating an EPIX score for all first-year students on the basis of a writing sample written on the first Friday of the semester and SAT-Verbal or ACT-English scores, we generated a descending order EPIX list. Then we located the "needy" students on this list. We found that they were not clustered together, as one might expect or hope; rather they were spread out among a group of 332 students with the lowest EPIX scores, more than 50% of the entering class. Then we tried several other ranking devices. Using SAT-Verbal or ACT-English ranking, we found the 20 students distributed among a group made up of the lowest 246 students. Using high school class rank, we found them in a group of 555 out of a class of 641; using the writing sample score, we found the "needy" students in a group of 405.

Looking at the data in another way, we became even more skeptical of the ability of our original placement procedure, or anything like it, to identity students like those that the faculty had reported to need a course preparatory to College Writing II. How many of the 20 needy students identified by the faculty would have been among the 30 students that our EPIX placement system would have identified? The answer is only 5. If we had used the SAT-Verbal, only 6, and if we had used high school class rank, only 3. We included portfolio placement in our skepticism. Even if we could persuade our administration to finance, and our overworked faculty to participate in, portfolio placement, is it likely that students who had achieved success in high school, ranking them in the top 10%, would present us with portfolios that identified them as needing remediation? Yet such students had been identified by faculty as needing College Writing I.

Preliminary Study 3. Our third and fourth preliminary studies focused on the placement of students at the W level of the program, exempting them from both College Writing courses. We considered this placement issue less critical than placement choices for our apparently weaker students. At that time, we were placing students with SAT-Verbal scores of 660 on the recentered scale directly into W. The cut-off point depended on how many students we could accommodate in College Writing II, a compromise that we could live with because we allowed those above the cut-off to elect College Writing II if they chose to, and because we had designed that course as a core first-year course, not a remedial one. But we were still curious about how students in the upper quintile of the class who had not taken College Writing II as opposed to those who had taken the course fared in their W course. Did College Writing make a difference in the level of success that students experienced in their W course? Did SAT-Verbal scores predict level of achievement in the W course?

For purposes of comparison, we divided students immediately on either side of the 660 cut-off into three groups, which we called *high*, *middle*, and *low*, relative to one another. The high group was composed of 28 students with scores from 670 to 690. The middle group consisted of a 31 students from either side of the cut—17 students with scores of 660 or 670 and 14 with scores of 630 or 640 who had taken the fall writing sample and, on its basis, were allowed to bypass College Writing II. The low group consisted of students immediately below the cut-off point, with SATV scores from 630 to 650, who either had not appealed their placement or had failed in their appeal. We compared the three groups in terms of their W course grade, and found the following:

1. For the high versus the middle group, there was virtually no difference in the mean grade for the W courses: 3.34 versus 3.33, respectively.
2. For the high versus the low group, again there was no statistically significant difference in the mean grade: 3.34 versus 3.18, respectively.
3. For the middle versus the low group, there was no statistically significant difference: 3.33 versus 3.18, respectively. *For this group of students*, from the 630 to 690 range of the SAT-Verbal, taking or not taking College Writing II did not make a significant difference to their success in the final course of the writing program, the W course.

Preliminary Study 4 Our second study of placement at the upper level of the writing program focused on 30 students just below the cut-off point (SAT-Verbal 660) between placement in College Writing II and placement in the W course. We divided these students, who had scores from 630 to 650, into two sets: those who took College Writing II (16 students, labeled Group A) and those who were allowed to enter the writing program at the W level because of their performance on the fall mid semester writing sample (14 students, labeled Group B). Here we did find a statistically significant difference in the mean grade of the two groups in their W course. Group A—those who had taken College Writing II first—had a mean grade of 2.93 in their W course; Group B—those from the same SAT-Verbal percentiles as Group A who appealed their placement successfully and went directly into the W course—had a mean grade of 3.55, a mean that was higher than our "high" group in Study 2. We noted with considerable interest that, without having taken College Writing II, these students with verbal SATs from 630 to 650 had outperformed, in the W course, their peers who had taken College Writing II and equaled the performance of an automatically exempted group with SAT-Verbal scores 40 to 60 points higher.

What can we conclude from this? This procedure invited students to think about their placement and gave them an institutional space to do it—a formal testing occasion in which they could write an essay for us. They could choose to do this or not to do it. It took a level of self-confidence even to take the placement exam in the first place, and it would appear that some of the students who did so had an accurate perception of their capabilities, as well as the confidence or motivation to choose a higher level at which to enter the writing program and to excel in that choice. On the other hand, what can we say about the students who chose to appeal their placement, failed in their appeal, and performed less well in the W course? Did they have less self-knowledge and an overconfidence in their abilities? Or did they perform down to the level of faculty judgments of them? Or, to look at it in a different way, because all students from this study group of higher ranking students were successful in their W course, did their placement assignment matter in any practical way?

OUR EXPERIMENT WITH DSP

The data that we had collected from our preliminary studies of the relation between writing placement and success in writing courses left us unable to show which at-risk students might be disadvantaged by not taking College Writing I and which higher scoring students might be disadvantaged by not taking College Writing II. In fact, it showed that lower ranking students could succeed in College Writing II without taking the preparatory College Writing I. And it showed that upper middle ranking students could succeed in the W course without taking College Writing II. Our preliminary findings called into question our entire placement procedure assigning students to particular levels of the writing program.

As we reassessed our placement procedure in 1995, we focused on the at-risk students. Because we were uncomfortable defining who our at-risk students are, in the first place, and then requiring that these students, however we defined them, take College Writing I, we set in motion an experimental program of DSP. Unknown to us, similar experiments were taking place elsewhere.

In late spring 1995, 1996, and 1997, we sent letters to our at-risk students, a group that we now defined more broadly than we had when we simply placed the 25 to 30 students at the bottom of our EPIX list into College Writing I. Each spring, the letter went to more than 100 students with SAT-Verbal scores of 530 or below, or ACT-English scores of 22 or below. The letter explained our writing program and the nature and purposes of the courses in it. In the earliest version of the letter, we emphasized our *recommendation* that they consider taking College Writing I, but we changed that language in 1996 to emphasize students' *choice*. In all versions of the letter, we offered the students the opportunity to talk with faculty in the writing program, by phone, at any time during the summer, or, once they had arrived on campus, to write an impromptu essay for diagnosis by writing faculty at a time set aside in orientation week.

In spring 1998, we attended the session on DSP that Roger Gilles and Dan Royer presented at the CCCC meeting in Chicago, and, as a result, modified our mailing to the students somewhat. Our letter now offers additional guidance on making the choice by suggesting that the students seek advice from their high school English teachers and that they fill out a questionnaire about themselves as readers and writers. The questionnaire is modeled on the one Gilles and Royer presented in their CCCC session. The students return a request form for their writing course along with their summer registration forms. From these returns we are able to plan how many sections of the course we will offer. A sample of our letter and attached questionnaire follow:

Dear New DePauw Student,

This summer we are asking you to choose one of two courses—English 120 or English 130—as your first writing course at DePauw.

The Writing Program at DePauw consists of three courses: (1) English 120 (College Writing I), an elective course taken during the first semester; (2) English 130 (College Writing II), a required course taken during the first or second semester; and (3) a W course, a required writing-intensive course in a discipline, normally taken during the sophomore year. The elective course, English 120, emphasizes shorter units of writing than English 130, is graded pass/fail, and enrolls only fifteen students per section to allow for more instructor feedback and closer attention to the process of writing academic papers. (There is an additional writing course, English 100, offered for those students for whom English is a second language.) Whichever course you choose, you will be placed in that course for the fall semester in addition to the other two courses you have requested.

Most DePauw students enter the Writing Program by taking English 130 (either their first or second semester) and then proceed to a writing-intensive course. However, the faculty in the writing program recommends that some students take an additional course, English 120, so that they will have a full year of writing instruction and practice. We realize that a student's SAT-Verbal or ACT-English score is only one indication of verbal skill, but our experience in past years predicts that most students with SAT-Verbal scores below 540 or ACT-English scores below 22 will profit from the two-semester sequence.

You are not required to take English 120; it is your choice. You may begin your writing curriculum at DePauw with English 130, College Writing II, if you think that is more appropriate for you. In making your choice, you should consult the questionnaire on the following page and discuss your writing skills with your high school teachers or others who know you. (We can also answer questions this summer.)

We are asking you to state your preference on the attached sheet and return it to us by June 30. If you are still uncertain about your choice, you may do a timed writing sample on the Sunday before registration and consult with one of us or your adviser before you register for your courses. The optional testing session for the writing sample is scheduled for Sunday, August 24, at 8:30 a.m. in the Julian Science and Math Center, Room 120.

Welcome to DePauw and our best wishes for a productive and exciting four years.

Sincerely,

Chair, Department of English   *Coordinator of Writing Placement*

Which Course Should I Take?

Yes No

☐ ☐	I read newspapers and magazines regularly.
☐ ☐	I read books for my own enjoyment.
☐ ☐	I wrote several essays per year on my reading or research in high school.
☐ ☐	I've used computers to write and revise essays.
☐ ☐	My GPA was in the top one third of my senior class.
☐ ☐	My ACT-English score was above 21, or my SAT-Verbal was above 530.
☐ ☐	I consider myself a good reader and writer.
☐ ☐	I am comfortable with the rules of grammar and punctuation.

Generally speaking, you are well prepared for English 130 if you have done quite a bit of analytical reading and writing in high school. If this has not been the case, English 120 will give you an opportunity to develop your analytical and critical reading and writing skills, and will help build your confidence before enrolling in English 130.

If you answered "Yes" to many of the statements above, you are probably ready for English 130. If you don't think you are ready, you should enroll in English 120.

Still Unsure?
Call the director of Writing Placement or the chair of the English Department. Their names and phone numbers appear on your cover letter.

Name: _____
    Last   First   Middle

Please enroll me in:
___English 120: College Writing I
___English 130: College Writing II
___August writing sample for further placement information

Return this form and your summer registration form by June 30 in the enclosed envelope.

When the new students arrive on campus in August, academic advisors explain, again, the two routes that they can choose to begin the writing program; at this point there may be some adjustment in students' initial choices. The opportunity to make further adjustments is available during the first week of classes, when students write a diagnostic essay in all sections of College Writing I and II, allowing their writing professors to advise them further on their choices.

WHO CHOOSES WHAT?

Profiles of College Writing I and College Writing II Electors in the At-Risk Group

We have readiness, achievement, and persistence data on the 435 at-risk students who were free to choose either College Writing I or College Writing II, the first semester of their first year from 1995 to 1998. From their readiness scores (SAT-Verbal, SAT-Math, ACT-Composite, ACT-English, ACT-Math, and high school centile (HSCN) and from a breakdown of these students in terms of gender, race, and college generation, we can draw a rough profile of the kinds of students who chose College Writing I and College Writing II. On our tables and in the remainder of this chapter, we call the first group W1s and the second W2s.

Students in our at-risk study group sorted themselves into the W1 and W2 cohorts in ways that led to some significantly different readiness means for students in each course. As shown in Table 7.1, the readiness means of the W1s were lower than those of the W2s in all indicators, and statistically significantly so in all but the ACT-Math. It would seem, on first glance, that the students sorted themselves higher and lower in correlation with their readiness scores.

Table 7.1. Readiness Means for At-Risk Groups

Skill or Readiness Scores	W1s Mean	N	W2s Mean	N	Significance
ACT-Composite	20.7	104	21.4	122	.015
ACT-English	19.4	103	20.4	123	.004
ACT-Math	21.3	90	22.0	116	.184
HSCN	74.5	188	79.1	199	.003
SAT-Verbal	473	183	494	199	.000
SAT-Math	508	183	528	199	.004

Even though these means are significantly different, it is important to emphasize that there is a full range of scores for the individuals of both cohorts. For the W1s, the SAT-Verbals ranged from 320 to 550; for the W2s, from 330 to 580. SAT-Math scores for the W1s ranged from 340 to 710; for the W2s, from 330 to 690. ACT-Composite scores for the W1s ranged from 13 to 26; for the W2s, from 16 to 27. ACT-English scores for W1s ranged from 11 to 26; for W2s, from 14 to 28. The HSCN for the W1s ranged from 20 to 99; for the W2s, from 34 to 99.

From this analysis, we see that even though the at-risk students, when presented with a self-placement choice, sort themselves into cohorts with significantly different readiness "potentials" as exhibited in the mean scores, nevertheless each cohort contains a similarly wide range of scores for each readiness variable. The mean readiness scores for each cohort may be significantly different in a statistical sense, but it is clear that we cannot predict from individual readiness scores what course individual students will choose. We hypothesize that the self-placement choices reflect additional factors, such as "self-efficacy" ("people's judgments of their capabilities to organize and execute courses of action required to attain designated types of performances" [Bandura 391]), writing apprehension, or some other as yet unidentified factor.

How do gender, race, and college generation affect the choices the at-risk group of students will make? Of the 435 at-risk students, 48% (209) placed themselves into W1 and 52% (225) into W2. In general, female students and those of European descent were more likely to choose College Writing II than College Writing I. Male students were equally likely to choose either. First-generation college students were more likely and African-American students were much more likely to choose College Writing I (Table 7.2).

Within these social groups that make up the whole at-risk group, we see the same kind of self-sorting in terms of mean readiness scores as seen

Table 7.2. Placement Choices by Gender, Race, and College Generation

Social Group	n	% College Writing I	% College Writing II
Female	228	46.1	53.9
Male	207	50.2	49.8
African-American	74	58.1	41.9
European-American	306	46.4	53.6
First-Generation College	159	52.2	47.8
Second-Generation College	276	45.7	54.3

in the group as a whole. For each group, the readiness scores of the W1 cohort are lower than those of the W2, in most cases statistically significantly so. The only social group for whom we do not have sufficient data to establish statistical significance is the African-American group. Again, however, we must note that the readiness scores of all these social groups in W1 and W2 range widely for individuals in the group, and that it would be impossible to predict which individual would choose College Writing II rather than College Writing I on the basis of these scores. As seen in the next section of the chapter, it would be unjust to place individuals at one level or another, based an any score or combination of scores.

Does the greater likelihood that one social group rather than the other will choose College Writing I correlate with differences in the readiness scores of the two social groups? In the case of African American and European-American students, most definitely. Table 7.3 reveals that, in terms of group means, the correlation is significant in SAT-Verbal, SAT-Math, ACT-Math, and ACT-Composite, with the readiness scores of African Americans in the whole at-risk group being significantly lower than those of European Americans. In the case of first- and second-generation college students, the correlation is limited to only one readiness mean: As a group, first-generation college students have a statistically significant lower SAT-Verbal than the second-generation students (476 to 488). The situation is more mixed in terms of gender. Although male students are more likely to choose College Writing I than their female peers, the males score higher than the females in math readiness scores, lower in ACT-English and HSCN, but show no significant differences in SAT-Verbal or ACT-Composite scores. Again, such inconsistencies point to the importance of other factors than readiness scores in our students' choices.

ACHIEVEMENT DATA

Are Students Disadvantaged Academically by Their Choices?

We would abandon our DSP program if we could show that students who chose to avoid College Writing I were disadvantaged in a practical way by their choice. But the achievement data that we have collected do not show that. For our study, we compared the W1 and W2 at-risk groups in terms of means for five measures of academic achievement (See Table 7.4.): first semester GPA (GPA1), second semester GPA (GPA2), cumulative GPA (CGPA) for however many semesters they have been at the university (one to eight), grade in College Writing II (W2G), and grade in the W course

Table 7.3. Readiness Scores by Race and Gender

Skills or Readiness Scores	African American Mean	N	European American Mean	N	Significance	Female Mean	N	Male Mean	N	Significance
ACT-Composite	20.0	40	21.4	164	.000	20.9	125	21.4	101	.152
ACT-English	19.3	38	20.0	167	.138	20.3	125	19.5	101	.018
ACT-Math	19.4	34	22.2	153	.000	21.1	113	22.4	93	.010
HSCN	76.6	59	76.2	279	.790	78.4	205	75.1	182	.032
SAT-Verbal	470	63	490	269	.003	482	198	486	184	.244
SAT-Math	463	63	531	269	.000	502	198	536	184	.000

Table 7.4. Achievement by At-Risk Groups

Achievement Scores	W1s Mean	N	W2s Mean	N	Significance
GPA1	2.36	208	2.53	222	.006
GPA2	2.53	200	2.67	206	.013
CGPA	2.53	207	2.67	220	.002
W2G	2.54	197	2.73	220	.004
WG	2.70	145	2.86	169	.012

(WG). On all five measures, we found a statistically significant difference in achievement means, with the W2s scoring higher than the W1s. Additionally, fewer W2s failed the College Writing II course than W1s, and fewer missed the cut-off of C-. Of the 226 at-risk students in the W2 cohort, 4 failed the required College Writing II course, and 2 more received less than the C- required at the time for entry into the W course. Of the 209 students in the W1 cohort, 5 failed the College Writing II course, and 6 more failed to make the C- requirement. Although the differences are very slight, *statistically the at-risk group who avoided the "preparatory" course achieved at a higher level than those who chose it. So we cannot say that the at-risk students—as a group or as individuals—were disadvantaged by being allowed to choose to enter the Writing Program at the second level—* at least not in terms of preparation for success in the required College Writing II, the required W, or subsequent academic work.

On the other hand, can we conclude, from our evidence, that the W1 students were disadvantaged by their choice to take College Writing I? Would they have performed at a higher level if there had been no College Writing I to choose—if we had said, as Peter Elbow suggests in chapter 1, "We know you are smart, we know you can make it, and we will never give up on you" (25)? We have no way of knowing this. We assume, and they tell us, that they gained advantages from taking the first course that we have not measured, or that we cannot measure. Our profile of the W1s in comparison with the W2s, which we previously presented, suggests that the W1s are less ready than the W2s for the rigors of college. It should not be surprising that their academic performance lags slightly behind that of those who selected themselves into College Writing II and that they never quite catch up. On the other hand, like Adams and Elbow, we worry that the W1s may have paid a cost in self-confidence, diminished already by their identification as at-risk and, possibly, by stigmatization for their enrollment in the preparatory course, even if voluntary. This concern, however, has less to do with self-placement than with the question of whether we should have a "basic writing" course in our curriculum in the first place.

IS THERE A CORRELATION BETWEEN SOCIAL GROUP AND ACHIEVEMENT?

Our next step in terms of looking at achievement was to try to isolate factors other than those measured by standardized tests and high school rank that might account for the slight differences in performance means between W1s and W2s in subsequent course work. We broke down our data in terms of the possible impact of four social factors on the mean achievement grades for both cohorts of the tracked at-risk group. We looked at year of students' entry into the writing program, college generation, race, and gender. Year of students' entry made no difference in terms of the mean scores in readiness and achievement for either group. For the W2s, only gender showed any significant difference in any mean score: the W2G for W2 females was significantly higher than that of the males (2.84 vs. 2.61, with a significance of .012). This is particularly interesting because on all readiness scores for this pair of subgroups of the W2s, males are statistically either equal to or higher than females, with the exception of ACT-English, where the score for females is 20.8 and the score for males 19.9, with a statistical significance at the .038 level. In all other achievement scores, males' and females' performance was statistically similar, African Americans and European Americans similar, and first-generation college and second-generation college students similar.

On the other hand, for the W1s—those who elected College Writing I in the fall—differences in college generation, race, and gender make a significant difference in some of the performance means.

Let's consider the first- and second-generation college groups in the W1 cohort. Although the readiness means for the first-generation group are below the second-generation group in all measures except HSCN, the differences are not statistically significant on any of the measures. But on their achievement measures, two of the means are significantly lower—their GPA2 and their CGPA (Table 7.5). And the difference between their mean grades in their W course (WG) approaches statistical significance (Table 7.5).

Table 7.6 shows that there are statistically significant differences between the means for African-American and European-American students in the W1 group in two achievement measures: CGPA (2.39 vs. 2.57) and

Table 7.5. Achievement by College Generation

Achievement Scores	W1 First Generation Mean	N	W1 Second Generation Mean	N	Significance
GPA1	2.26	82	2.42	126	.108
GPA2	2.43	78	2.60	122	.045
CGPA	2.39	82	2.63	125	.004
W2G.	2.52	78	2.56	119	.720
WG	2.60	52	2.76	93	.078

W2G (2.33 vs. 2.61). On the other three achievement measures, there is no significant statistical difference between the two groups, even though African-American students have significantly lower readiness scores on four of the six measures (Table 7.7).

But it is the gender difference in performance of the W1 cohort that is the most striking. The mean grades on four of the five achievement measures for females are significantly higher than those for males, with the measures for the differences in GPA2, CGPA, and W2G being significant at the .000 level (Table 7.6). A look at Table 7.7 shows that this is true despite the fact that there is no significant difference in four of their six readiness means, including ACT-English, and that, in the other two—SAT-Verbal and SAT-Math—male scores are significantly higher than those of females.

Furthermore, when we compare W1 females with W2 females, we see that even though the readiness scores of the W1 females are significantly lower than those of the W2 females—SAT-Verbal 466 versus 496, SAT-Math 491 versus 511, and ACT-English 19.6 versus 20.8—there is no statistically significant difference in their performance. *If the W1 cohort had been only females, their achievement scores would have suggested that choosing W1 does help the less ready make up the gap between them and the slightly more ready cohort.*

Some factor or factors other than "readiness" as measured by standardized tests depress some performance scores of W1 first-generation college students and W1 males in comparison with second-generation students and females. The picture in regard to African Americans is not so clear, perhaps because the numbers in our study group are limited. It does look, however, as if something in the African-Americans students, as with females, causes them to perform at a higher level than their "readiness" scores might indicate.

Table 7.6. W1 Achievement by Race and Gender

Achievement Scores	W1 African American Mean / N	W1 European American Mean / N	Significance	W1 Female Mean / N	W1 Male Mean / N	Significance
GPA1	2.29 / 43	2.38 / 141	.339	2.50 / 104	2.21 / 104	.002
GPA2	2.52 / 41	2.54 / 136	.836	2.71 / 103	234 / 97	.000
CGPA	2.39 / 43	2.57 / 140	.037	2.70 / 104	2.36 / 103	.000
W2G	2.33 / 40	2.61 / 134	.026	2.72 / 100	2.36 / 97	.000
WG	2.78 / 33	2.67 / 97	.333	2.76 / 78	2.64 / 67	.209

Table 7.7. W1 Readiness by Race and Gender

Skills or Readiness Scores	W1 African American Mean / N	W1 European American Mean / N	Significance	W1 Female Mean / N	W1 Male Mean / N	Significance
ACT-Composite	19.5 / 19	21.1 / 77	.006	20.6 / 53	20.9 / 51	.584
ACT-English	18.7 / 16	19.4 / 78	.254	19.6 / 52	19.1 / 51	.308
ACT-Math	17.7 / 15	22.0 / 69	.000	20.8 / 44	21.9 / 46	.129
HSCN	76.0 / 36	72.9 / 132	.344	76.3 / 96	72.5 / 92	.132
SAT-Verbal	461 / 39	480 / 121	.012	466 / 94	480 / 89	.023
SAT-Math	456 / 39	527 / 121	.000	491 / 94	524 / 89	.002

Is there a practical use to which we can put this information? Certainly not in terms of a placement procedure that assigns students to one or another level of the first-year writing course at DePauw. Does it tell us that any of these social groups were "damaged" by their freedom to choose their level? The students who identify themselves as basic writers fall below the academic mark set by those that mainstream themselves most likely for dispositional and cultural reasons—traits of motivation, self-esteem, acculturation, and maturity. Those dispositions may become intensified or complicated by the choice—or the imposition—of a basic writing identity. But we do not know that nor can we know how those dispositions might have performed if there had been no preparatory course like College Writing I for them to enroll in.

IS STUDENT PERSISTENCE AT THE UNIVERSITY COMPROMISED BY DSP?

In his 1995 article on the importance of placement and basic studies, White makes the case for basic writing by claiming that at-risk students who enroll in basic writing courses are helped to persist in their college study more than similar students who do not enroll or are not required to enroll. He cites two important studies, one in New Jersey and the other in California, that support his claim. To evaluate his claim with respect to *our* at-risk students, we prepared the following analysis of persistence.

We have students in our survey group who are at different stages of their college careers as well as students who have completed those careers. Also, we have students who have dropped out of their college study, at least from DePauw. We constructed an index of persistence (PINDEX) as follows. For students who had completed college or were still in process, we assigned the PINDEX number of 1. For students who withdrew from DePauw (56 W1s and 36 W2s), we calculated a PINDEX number representing the ratio of their length of study by the usual length of a student's study. For examples, for a student who completed two semesters of study before withdrawing, we divided 2 by 8 for a PINDEX of 0.25; for a student who completed five semesters of study before withdrawing, we divided 5 by 8 for a PINDEX of 0.625. In this way we avoided the problem of fluctuating indices as not-yet-finished but still-persisting students moved toward the end of their college careers.

Considering the whole survey group of at-risk students, those who chose College Writing II (the W2 cohort) persisted longer than those who chose College Writing I (the W1 cohort). The difference appears small, but given the numbers of students involved, the difference is statistically significant. From this we conclude that W2s as a group were not harmed by placing themselves into College Writing II. When we consider the data from the perspective of social group, we find that there is no statistically significant difference in the rate at which W2 and W1 African Americans, females, first-generation college students, or second-generation college students persist. But W1 males and W1 European Americans, as groups, persist for a significantly shorter time than their W2 peers. The situation for W1 males and W1 European Americans raises the question again of whether they were harmed by their choice of College Writing I. Nevertheless, the decreased persistence of males of the W1 cohort is consistent with their lower performance and is more likely a function of dispositions—motivation, concentration, and maturity—than a result of their choice. It is apparent to us that their dispositions influence their choice, their performance within that choice, and their persistence.

When we examine *only* those who *withdrew* from DePauw before completing their college careers here, we find that *those who chose College Writing II persisted for a shorter period of time than students who placed themselves into College Writing I* (Table 7.8). This is the reverse of the trend for the study group as a whole. For all social groups, there is a consistent pattern of longer persistence on the part of W1s than W2s, although the difference is statistically significant only for female, first-generation, and second-generation students. *In the case of withdrawals*, it is a credible hypothesis that enrollment in the College Writing I course selectively and for a time affected some social groups electing it, perhaps by easing their entrance into a program of study that they were ultimately destined to leave. In any case,

Table. 7.8. Persistence of At-Risk Groups by Race, Gender, and College Generation

PINDEX Table	W1s	W2s	Significance
Survey Group	.818	.876	.046
African-American	.826	.903	.238
European-American	.820	.902	.014
Female	.844	.869	.520
Male	.792	.885	.033
First-Generation College	.776	.862	.097
Second-Generation College	.846	.883	.280
Withdrawing Students	.321	.222	.002
African-American	.375	.250	.256
European-American	.311	.238	.053
Female	.370	.232	.003
Male	.279	.208	.086
First-Generation College	.284	.192	.032
Second-Generation College	.354	.239	.010

we are not prepared at this time to call this effect a benefit. Even if we were to do so, however, certainly the very small impact on persistence that enrollment in College Writing I might have had does not justify a program of institutionally mandated placement in that course.

WHAT DO THE AT-RISK STUDENTS THINK?

In the first 3 of our study years we asked students in the W1 and W2 at-risk groups to fill out a questionnaire on their attitudes toward the courses they had placed themselves in and on the elective nature of College Writing I. Our survey was designed to contribute to our debate about whether or not to continue to offer College Writing I, but it nevertheless has implications for a discussion of DSP. (Obviously, there is no need for DSP at the initial stage of the writing program if there are no longer two levels at which the student can begin.) From the W1 cohort we have 190 responses for Questions 1 and 6 and 128 for the remaining questions. From the W2 cohort we have only 56 responses.

Of the 56 responses from the at-risk students who placed themselves into College Writing II (the W2s), 88% were unqualifiedly happy with their choice, 89% felt that they were well-prepared for the course, and 75% felt College Writing I would not have helped them more than College Writing II did to adjust to college (Table 7.9). Clearly, the overwhelming majority of the W2 cohort felt that they were benefited by their opportunity to choose College Writing II. At the same time, the majority expressed satisfaction with the fact that College Writing II was required and College Writing I elective.

The responses from the at-risk students who placed themselves into College Writing I (the W1s) were positive in regard to their choice, although not as overwhelmingly so as those of the W2s (Table 7.10). Of these students, 58% were happy with their choice. When asked if College Writing I helped prepare them for College Writing II, 64% agreed. When asked if it prepared them for other college courses, 55% agreed. Almost 70% thought that taking College Writing I was not a waste of their time, and 61% felt that it helped them adjust to academic expectations of college. Just over 72% thought that College Writing I should continue to be elective and only 2.3% thought it should not be offered in the curriculum at all.

When we broke the responses of the W1 cohort down into social groups, we found very few statistically significant differences in each groups' mean evaluation of their choice and their chosen course. Only on two survey questions did our results reach statistical significance. Males and females differed significantly in the strength of their agreement that College

Table 7.9. Satisfaction of W2 Students with their Choice

Survey Answers of At-Risk W2 Students	Agree or Strongly Agree	Unsure	Disagree or Strongly Disagree
1. If choosing again, I would take W1 instead of W2.	3 5.4%	4 7.1%	49 87.5%
2. I was adequately prepared for W2.	50 89.3%	4 7.1%	2 3.6%
3. W2 prepared me for other college courses.	42 76.4%	9 16.4%	4 7.3%
4. W2 was a waste of time.	4 7.1%	6 10.7%	46 82.1%
5. W1 (more than W2) would have helped me to adjust to college.	4 7.1%	10 17.9%	42 75.0%
6. W1 should be required rather than elective.	5 8.9%	14 25.0%	37 66.1%

Table 7.10. Satisfaction of W1 Students with Their Choice

Survey Answers of At-Risk W1 Students	Agree or Strongly Agree	Unsure	Disagree or Strongly Disagree
1. If choosing again, I would still take W1 instead of W2.	110 57.9%	23 12.1%	57 30.0%
2. W1 helped prepare for W2.	82 64.1%	19 14.8%	27 21.1%
3. W1 helped prepare for other college courses.	70 54.7%	35 27.3%	23 18.0%
4. W1 was a waste of time.	19 14.8%	20 15.6%	89 69.5%
5. W1 helped prepare for academic expectations of college.	78 60.9%	22 17.2%	28 21.9%
6. W1 should be elective if offered.	137 72.1%	31 16.3%	22 11.6%
7. W1 should not be taught.	3 2.3%	13 10.2%	112 87.5%

Writing I helped their academic achievement. Whereas 56% of females agreed to that statement, 68% of males agreed. First- and second-generation students differed significantly in the strength of their agreement that College Writing I prepared them for College Writing II (68% vs. 62%) and that taking College Writing I was not a waste of their time (81% vs. 63%). In general, male and first-generation students were more positive about their choices than female and second-generation students, but all four social groups were positive. Although African-American students were less likely than European Americans to say that they had made the right choice, they nevertheless tended to be more positive than the European Americans about the value of College Writing I as an academic experience (preparation for other college courses, help in academic achievement, not a waste of their time).

Open-ended student comments on those surveys helped explain the reservations that some students had about their choice. In general, the students who said they would not elect to take College Writing I, if they had the gift of hindsight, had been unclear about the nature of the course or motivated in the first place more by fear and uncertainty than by a clear sense of their own academic needs. Their most obvious misunderstanding was about the elective nature of the course. When asked why they chose College Writing I, negative respondents would say things like "It was forced upon me by my adviser," or "I didn't [choose it]; the university told me I had to," or "I did not know I had a choice," or "I was worried that the English Department was right—I wouldn't be able to handle English 130 [College Writing II]." On the other hand, many of the positive respondents used language of choice and self-knowledge in their responses or alluded to the additional guidance they had gotten by doing a writing sample during orientation week. For example, "I chose to take it because I felt it would give me a headstart and have me better prepared upon entering English 130 [College Writing II]"; or "I chose to take English 120 [College Writing I] because I knew that I was not completely comfortable with my writing ability. I looked at English 120 as a way to write for a college professor without having to be judged with grades. I thought it was a way I could ease into writing at college." As a result of our first set of surveys, we revised the letter sent to students to emphasize the elective and pass/fail nature of College Writing I, and we asked all first-year advisors to emphasize these things when they talked with their advisees.

The Future of DSP at DePauw

The students in our at risk group are very positive about their freedom to choose their entry point into our Writing Program. They endorse the elective nature of College Writing I and the required nature of College Writing II. The faculty who teach both courses find the classroom climate to be a far more cooperative one than existed under our earlier placement system, when we told students where they "belonged." We have found that College Writing I has not died as a result of DSP: One out of every two students who are invited to consider it, elect it. This proven pattern makes it fairly easy to plan for the number of sections of the two courses that we will offer in the first semester. We also find that DSP has not compromised the rate at which students meet the minimum requirement in College Writing II (now a C-) for entry into W courses, nor can we say that, despite some interesting performance differences between social groups, especially males and females, it has compromised their level of achievement in either their writing courses or their other course work at the university.

All our data tell us that we cannot, in good conscience, require or advise our students to enroll in our first writing course on the basis of an assumption, or implicit promise, that they need it in order to perform well in subsequent writing or other courses at DePauw. This may be a function of our particular students, who, if motivated, can virtually always rise to the level of the demands we make of them in our second writing course and in our W courses. We may still have some students with low standardized test scores, but we are convinced that they all come to us these days better prepared in, and less fearful of, writing than they did in the 1970s and 1980s. In our small classes and with the help of our Writing Center, they can quite quickly develop writing strategies to which they have not previously been exposed. It may be that they could always have done this, and that, earlier, we underestimated their ability to rise to the level of our expectations. In any case, it took a financial crisis in the institution to drive us to look carefully at the students we had *labeled at-risk* and at our requirement that they take both semesters of College Writing.

Our monitoring of our experiments, first, in mainstreaming students, and next, in DSP has convinced the DePauw students, faculty, and administration that DSP is not only theoretically preferable to any other placement system, but is also the most practical. We have shown that writing samples, SAT or ACT scores, and high school class rank cannot accurately identity or predict those individuals who might fail to make the minimum grade in College Writing II or the grades those individuals might earn in other college courses. We have shown that students who appear, by standard indicators, to be underprepared or at-risk and yet choose to accelerate their progress in the writing program frequently perform at a higher level than those who proceed with caution. Finally, we have shown that *at DePauw*, the choice of taking one or two semesters of first-year writing is *not* a critical one, and does not warrant complicated, expensive, *and* stigmatizing placement procedures. So, as long as we have two first-year writing courses at DePauw, conceived not as a developmental sequence but as a stretch, we are committed to DSP. It works because it both respects and supports our students.

Our commitment to DSP does not mean, however, that we have developed the best system. As a result of our study, we would suggest some modest changes in our procedure. First, we should reconsider our practice of "targeting" a group of at-risk students to receive our invitation to consider taking College Writing I. Although targeting the 100 students scoring lowest on standardized tests is a practical way to limit numbers of sections of College Writing I, there surely are individuals above our cut-off points who would appreciate the choice and might prefer to begin with College Writing I.

Second, we would modify the letter sent to incoming students to remove the implication that standardized test scores are the most prominent factor to be considered in their choice. In DSP, what is most important, in our view, is the student's writing experience, writing confidence, and above all writing motivation. Our revised letter should, therefore, urge the students to place these factors foremost in making their choice, perhaps advising them to talk about these things, while looking at their high school writing portfolio, with their parents or high school teacher. This, by the way, is the only place where we see portfolio assessment as appropriate in our placement procedure. We believe that faculty-mandated placement by portfolio might well fail to reveal those factors of motivation and social adjustment that are most likely to put our students at risk, and, more important, we are convinced that portfolio placement is, ultimately, another unnecessary and damaging way of taking agency away from the student.

REFERENCES

Adams, Peter Dow. "Basic Writing Reconsidered." *Journal of Basic Writing* 12.1 (1993): 22-36.

Bandura, A. *Social Foundations of Thought and Action: A Social Cognitive Theory.* Englewood Cliffs: Prentice Hall, 1986.

Soliday, Mary. "From the Margins to the Mainstream: Reconceiving Remediation." *CCC* 47.1 (1996): 85-100.

White, Edward M. "The Importance of Placement and Basic Studies: Helping Students Succeed Under the New Elitism." *Journal of Basic Writing* 14.2 (1995): 75-84.

8

DIRECTED SELF-PLACEMENT AT A LARGE RESEARCH UNIVERSITY

A Writing Center Perspective

Phyllis Frus
*Hawaii Pacific University**

In 1999, the University of Michigan (UM) adopted a program of directed self-placement (DSP) modeled on that at Grand Valley State University (GVSU). Our experience may be of interest to large public research universities as well as to selective public or private institutions not only because we have found DSP an efficient way to assess large numbers of students (more than 5,000 enter the UM every fall), but because our results show that it is appropriate for students who meet high admission standards to choose their first college writing course. We make this claim despite the long-standing belief that assessing the writing of incoming students and assigning them to one of three tracks toward fulfilling the introductory composition requirement has been the mainstay of the writing program since 1978, when the College of Literature, Science, & the Arts (LS&A) faculty established the English Composition Board (ECB), predecessor of the Sweetland Writing Center.[1]

---

*Author was formerly at the University of Michigan.

[1] The College of LS&A is the largest of university's undergraduate colleges with an enrollment of 15,550. For an account of establishing the writing requirements and the ECB, see Stock. See Hamp-Lyons and McKenna for an explanation of the importance of assessment to the writing program.

179

Faculty also directed the college's writing center—first the ECB and now Sweetland—to support writing through faculty development, and so faculty are an important constituency in considering the success of an assessment plan. Instructors want students who are ready to write at the college level, and DSP, at the UM at least, may result in courses composed of students with a wider range of abilities than under faculty placement. This disparity between best and least prepared writers may have increased under DSP as well because there are no longer exemptions made for timed essays or outstanding portfolios.[2] Even though one of the elements that attracted the university to this model is that it shifts responsibility from instructor-evaluators to student writers, we do not want students who are not ready to take on that responsibility, and who show it by taking a course for which they are not prepared, to slip through the cracks. A primary goal, therefore, is to identify such students in order to get them the one-to-one support they need. We prefer, therefore, that they identify themselves (with the help of advisers and parents) by enrolling in Writing Practicum, the course that prepares them for academic writing, rather than bypassing it in favor of introductory composition. Like other writing centers, we have found it easier to give less well-prepared students the help they need in a tutorial course than to get them to come to the writing center to work with instructor-tutors or peer tutors regularly. In the interest of getting those who should benefit from it into Practicum, we have tinkered with the particulars of self-assessment since we adopted it in 1999.

This chapter reports on those changes and the results we have obtained in the first 3 years of the program. Additionally, we hope that the experience of the Sweetland Writing Center illuminates the relationship between writing centers and student self-placement more generally. One caveat remains to be stated about the somewhat unusual way the writing program is organized at the UM. Because of the decentralized structure within the college as well as the university, the Sweetland Writing Center, which is charged with assessing entering writers and certifying students who have completed the first-year writing requirement, has little influence on the two courses the majority of students take to meet the requirement. This separation of responsibilities persists despite the fact that, since 1997, the Writing Center has been located administratively within the Department of English, and our English Department colleagues oversee the courses taken

---

[2]Hamp-Lyons and McKenna say that direct assessment of students was designed to place "students along a continuum of writing instruction work so that in any class the instructor would encounter a narrower range of writing needs than in the former composition courses taken by everyone" (257). My colleague George Cooper has argued that assessment, which assigned weak students to remedial writing, was handed to the writing center in order to save "the real" faculty.

by approximately 3,500 students a year, English 124: Writing and Literature and English 125: College Writing. Because of the division of powers, although we in Sweetland are responsible for assessing students and certifying transfer courses as equivalent to the university's in order to exempt some students who have met the requirement elsewhere, we lack any way of influencing curriculum or instituting exit criteria for these courses. These are factors that would seem to affect the success of a DSP program.

FROM PORTFOLIOS TO STUDENT SELF-PLACEMENT

The change to DSP in 1999 coincided with several other changes to the writing programs at the UM. The ECB, the autonomous unit that for 20 years assessed the writing of incoming students and taught the developmental writing course for those deemed not ready for college writing, was transformed into the Gayle Morris Sweetland Writing Center and placed within the Department of English.[3] As part of the reorganization, administrators of the College of LS&A, which provides the Writing Center's operating budget, urged the unit to find a more streamlined method of evaluating incoming students' writing than its noted portfolio assessment.

Although portfolio placement demonstrated clear pedagogical benefits, such as providing some continuity between high school and college writing and encouraging writing in departments other than English in high schools, as a placement practice it proved to be more complex than its results warranted. In the last years of requiring portfolios of all entering students, Sweetland instructors read nearly 5,000 portfolios over the summer and throughout fall term while placing fewer than 10% of students into Writing Practicum, and exempting from the introductory composition requirement approximately the same percentage.[4]

Portfolio assessment had been used for all entering students only since 1994, and yet in 5 years it had become a national model of a program that evaluated students on the basis of writing done in high school to pre-

---

[3]The Sweetland Writing Center also continues the ECB's programs offering students one-to-one conferences with lecturers (Writing Workshop) and peer-writing tutors, and it bears primary responsibility for the Upper Level Writing Requirement, which students meet through the Advanced Writing in the Disciplines Program. (For a description of this program, see Hamp-Lyons and McKenna.)

[4]Most of the remaining students not in the Honors Program or the Residential College (approximately 3,500) ended up in one of the two English Department writing courses, with a few taking History 195, The Writing of History, or a first-year seminar that meets the introductory composition requirement. Students in the Honors Program take Great Books or Western Civilization and those in the Residential College take a first-year semi-

pare for college rather than by judging a writing sample produced specifically for assessment purposes. Its proponents argued that this entrance requirement not only communicated expectations of the kind of writing that is required at the university but also conveyed something about the philosophy underlying composition courses, for students were asked to show evidence of revision (such as an earlier draft with comments) and to include a reflective essay. Advocates of portfolio assessment also claimed that these criteria for placing students influenced the kinds of writing high school teachers assigned. For example, they believed students were being asked to write fewer book reports and more analytical essays. Similarly, they reasoned, helping students prepare a portfolio would be better use of high school instructors than teaching the timed in-class essay that prepares students for writing an impromptu essay for placement.

As outlined by Dan Royer and Roger Gilles in their essay, "Directed Self-Placement: An Attitude of Orientation," student self-assessment seemed to offer us some of the pedagogical and other benefits of portfolio placement, such as the ability to communicate the kinds of writing we expected students to have done in high school. Sweetland administrators and faculty also looked forward to fewer appeals of placement decisions, a less-resistant population of students in the developmental writing course, and an entering class with morale improved by having been given the privilege of as well as the responsibility for making an important choice.

Our results for the first 2 years resemble those at GVSU and other schools making the switch. Our placement in Practicum dropped from 6% to 8% in the last years of portfolio placement to less than 3%. Although this represents more than a 50% drop in placement, total enrollment did not fall off so steeply, because we had students left over from portfolio placement enrolled in the first year, and in both first and second years of DSP the College of Engineering continued portfolio placement on its own. This meant that 50 engineering students were placed into Practicum in 1999-2000, whereas 89 were assigned to take it in 2000-2001. Despite the mix of placed students and "volunteers" in Practicum, overall, instructors in the preparatory course reported more students interested in learning because a significant number had chosen to work intensively on their writing for a term before tackling first-year composition.

We realized that we had been placing into Writing Practicum students who would have done well enough in a first-year writing course. This should not have surprised us, because our results are very consistent with

---

nar. The College of Engineering has no first-year writing course; students not being placed (or, beginning 2001, placing themselves) into Practicum go directly into Introduction to Engineering, which has a writing component but is not a writing course.

our selective admissions policy.[5] The fact is that our students are the best Michigan high schools have to offer. For example, 96% of the entering class in 2000 graduated with a high school GPA of 3.0 or higher; and the average SAT composite score ranged from 1180 to 1380, while the ACT composite average score ranged from 25 to 30. This indicates that a first-year writing course is probably appropriate for 96 percent of entering students, nearly the percentage that chooses it each year.

Concerned that some overconfident students might be at risk of doing poorly in first-year writing, we asked course instructors to collect substantive writing samples the first 2 weeks of class in order to identify and counsel students who seemed underprepared, and we offered to discuss the best ways to help them should they remain in the course.[6] Then, at the end of the term, we asked these instructors to identify students who had struggled and who, in their view, might have been better off with a developmental writing course before taking their course. They named 47 students in the fall and 38 in the winter. In the second year of DSP, they identified even more, 55 in the fall and 35 in winter term. Because we were also getting reports from instructors of first-year courses that there were more students who seemed underprepared in their courses, and we knew from our records that these students were coming neither to the evening peer tutoring center nor to the daytime instructor-staffed Writing Workshop, we made some changes in our materials for the third year of DSP.[7]

We were satisfied with the numbers of students enrolling in Practicum, but we wanted to get the right 3% of entering students—those who would benefit from the extra practice before embarking on the required course. Although a primary rule of DSP is to inform students of the possible

---

[5]In 1999, for example, the first class to undertake DSP, of the 21,000 students who applied for admission, 13,000 were accepted, for a selectivity rate of 62%. In 2000 the rate was 55%.

[6]These essays are in some sense "diagnostic," although they are not the basis of a different placement for the student writer; rather they help the instructor identify how many and which students may have difficulty in the class. Those demonstrating poor preparation can then be asked whether the writing represents their best effort or if it was a last-minute effort. In the latter case, their instructor or Sweetland Writing Center faculty members advise the students about their prospects, and if they decide to remain in the course, they are referred to the writing center for regular work.

[7]We looked up the results of 130 students who had been placed in Practicum in the last years of portfolio placement and who took the first-year writing course (English 124/125) in Fall 1999; their average grade was a B. Compare this to the average grade in 1999-2000 of the students who selected first-year writing without taking Practicum first, although their composition instructors identified them as struggling and even at risk; their average was a C+. This suggests that Practicum helps some students perform better in first-year writing.

consequences of choosing inappropriately and then let them make the choice, we are unable to demonstrate that those apparent overreachers will suffer significant consequences. Few of the 47 students identified by their instructors as underprepared for introductory composition in Fall 1999 term suffered serious penalties: No one failed English 124 or 125 (although 5 withdrew) and the average grade was C+ (2.3). Of 38 singled out in Winter 2000 term, no one failed, 2 withdrew, and the average grade was squarely between C+ and B- (2.5).[8] Because our questionnaire about students' reading and writing background the first year was too idealistic—that is, it presumed a very well-prepared and confident writer—it triggered many "No" answers, and so students for the most part ignored the suggestion that if they answered two or more of the questions in the negative, Practicum would be a good course for them. Therefore, in the second year, we shortened the survey and made it more realistic—that is, more appropriate to the actual level of our students. (See the appendix for both questionnaires.) In our advising and orientation materials we also tried to communicate more clearly the expectations we have of writers in the two courses. In 2000-2001 we had significantly fewer students placing themselves into Writing Practicum, although again the numbers did not drop precipitously because the College of Engineering continued portfolio placement into Practicum.

Then, when we had reports of even more students in over their heads in first-year writing courses in 2000-2001, we made two significant alterations in the way we inform students in Summer 2001, for our third year of DSP. First, the orientation leaders who tell students about the choice facing them say quite matter of factly that students who take Practicum before first-year writing do better in the latter course and may well do better in all their writing in college: "If your answers to the survey indicate that Practicum is the better course for you, you should take it first term—it will serve you well in the long run," is a typical statement. The second change is that students' responses to the survey trigger a writing course recommendation. Although in each of the first 2 years of DSP answers to the surveys were reported to the students and their advisers before students registered for courses, with a general recommendation that "if you answered no to two or more of the questions, Practicum is a good course for you," in the third year, placement reports for every student from the office of evaluations and

---

[8]As Elbow says, in the usual "time-serving" required course it is difficult to fail students who attend regularly and do the work, no matter how casually, but when the possible range of grades has shrunk from a four-point spread to 2 1/2 (A to C-), it's obvious that teachers are finding it hard to be demanding. Elbow suggests considering a more radical revision of the course, such as instituting competence-based exit criteria. In his view, students could leave the course as soon as they have demonstrated competence, which gives them an incentive to learn an effective writing-and-revising process (97).

examinations included a suggested writing placement, along with students' individual survey results.

This was not a deliberate addition; because results of the writing survey were reported online to advisors of all units and schools along with results of students' placement tests for math and foreign languages, programmers said that it would be more consistent to include a placement recommendation for writing. Sweetland agreed, and this recommendation seems to have triggered more self-placement in Writing Practicum from all colleges and units across the university except Engineering in Summer 2001 (very few engineering students enrolled in Practicum in the first year they were allowed to avoid it). The questions are unchanged from 2000, and we assume students are answering honestly, based on the two questions to which we already know the answers. That is, 15% to 17% percent of students do not have scores above the minimum ones suggested for first-year writing and 15% of admitted students do not rank in the top 20% of their high school class, and we are getting the correct percentage of negative response to each. Because 15% of entering students who fill out the survey answer "No" to two or more questions, that percentage of students gets the recommendation to take Practicum.

We can only conclude at this point that the suggested placement, following hard on the informal advice of peer-orientation leaders that if you need Practicum it is in your interest to take it, has made a difference in the course choice of many students. As we entered the final month of orientation and registration in 2001, we were on track to enroll in Practicum close to 6% of the 3,700 entering students in the colleges and units without their own first-year required class. Practicum enrollment fell slightly in 2002, to 5 1/2%

COROLLARY RESULTS OF DIRECTED SELF-PLACEMENT

We believe that the form of placement we adopt is not a significant factor in meeting our objectives as a Writing Center. In this we follow the experience of the ECB administrators and faculty who, soon after instituting portfolio placement, became less concerned with placement and more interested in ways of using portfolio assessment. Because DSP asks for similar background preparation of entering students, albeit in abbreviated form (a checklist and a brochure, rather than instructions for compiling a writing portfolio), it is possible for Sweetland to keep many of the advantages of portfolio placement, such as communicating our expectations about desirable experience that would prepare students well for college writing.

Brief though it is, the survey we administer communicates our expectations of good high school preparation. Although we do not compare students to one another or against a standard set of criteria, we ask students to measure their own writing experience and acquired abilities and consider whether those experiences and skills have prepared them well for college writing. Obviously, a large factor in this readiness is the quality of the students' high school. Building on what we learned from portfolio assessment, we would like to play a modest role in improving the teaching of writing in Michigan high schools so that students enter the university better prepared. Even before portfolio placement began, high school outreach was an important element of the ECB's program beginning in the late 1970s (see Stock 88-89). As it happened, the university's discontinuing of portfolio placement did not have a significant impact on Michigan high schools because by 1998, under the Michigan Educational Assessment Program, they were mandated to require both elements emphasized by our portfolio requirement: students' independent assessment of their writing and writing in every discipline. Beginning in 1999, Sweetland held two annual day-long institutes for high school instructors teaching writing across the curriculum. Sweetland faculty also lend their expertise to high schools directly, as in an ongoing collaboration between a Detroit high school and two Sweetland faculty members who are helping to coordinate an oral history-based theater project. Its goals include energizing schools' curricular objectives at various levels and encouraging collaboration between schools and local communities.

In assessing DSP at the UM going into its fourth year, we are satisfied that we are sending students a clear message about our values, expressing a belief in the importance of students taking a role in their own education, and communicating at least something about the elements of writing. We think that students on their own can comprehend that academic writing is different from high school, and, without the stigma of a placement into a tutorial class, can tell that they may not be as well prepared as some of their peers for analytical reading and writing.

From DSP, we have learned that students can be adequate judges of their own writing ability—or that, if they are wrong, it does not hurt them very much. When the great majority of them bypass the developmental writing course, enroll directly in introductory composition, and come out with an average grade of B+, they prove the irrelevance of a faculty placement system to their success, if not their improvement. If, as faculty continue to insist, many undergraduates cannot write clearly, sustain a complex argument, and support it convincingly, it is not where they are placed that is the important factor. We should find ways to help improve their writing regardless of whether they take one course or two to meet the introductory requirement. Other areas to focus on are those in which we have experience and expertise: foundational writing courses, faculty development work, and writing center tutorial programs (in our case Writing Workshop and peer tutoring). The Sweetland Writing Center needs to devise creative solutions to the problem all too common in an elite research university as well as in less-selective undergraduate institutions—the presence of too many students who do not communicate effectively in academic writing.

Our continuing problems are both different from and similar to those experienced by other institutions. We would like to find ways to overcome the split between Sweetland Writing Center and First- and Second-Year Studies because that limits the effect DSP can have on pedagogy in introductory composition. Grading continues to be a problem, as it is nationally. Some plans we are implementing or considering are to increase Writing Workshop hours, offer more workshops for first-year students on particular writing topics that instructors can put on the syllabus (which is a potential way to affect curriculum), and devise ways to get at-risk students to come to Writing Workshop, such as by interviewing those who came when urged to do so by the instructor. We would also like to link some Writing Workshop instructor-tutors with particular first-year writing course instructors (it seems appropriate to begin with Graduate Student Instructors teaching for the first time, if we can secure the cooperation of the English Department administration). In a pilot program in fall 2000 we placed experienced peer-writing tutors in a first-year writing course in order to increase the use of peer-writing tutors by students in introductory writing classes. We learned that tutors' participation in classroom writing projects and group work spurred student writers to seek frequent feedback to drafts of their essays and at various stages of their individual and group projects.

It seems reasonable to conclude with this summary of what the Sweetland Writing Center is doing to support writing and writing instruction in the college and, because so many students from other schools and programs take courses in LS&A, across the UM. The Writing Center faculty will continue examining the relationship between innovative writing center pedagogy and the teaching of writing in first-year writing courses. DSP worked for UM primarily because it taught those of us in the Sweetland Writing Center where to look to find ways to improve writing across the university.

REFERENCES

Cooper, George. "Adventures of Assessment: Questioning Writing Assessment and Its Relation to Responsible Writing Pedagogy." Conference on College Composition and Communication, Minneapolis, 13 April 2000.
Elbow, Peter. "Writing Assessment in the 21st Century: A Utopian View." *Composition in the Twenty-First Century: Crisis and Change.* Eds. Lynn Z.

Bloom, Donald A. Daiker, and Edward M. White. Carbondale: Southern Illinois UP, 1997.

Hamp-Lyons, Liz, and Eleanor McKenna. "The University of Michigan." *Programs That Work: Models and Methods for Writing across the Curriculum.* Eds. Toby Fulwiler and Art Young. Portsmouth, NH: Boynton/Cook Publishers, 1990.

Royer, Daniel, and Roger Gilles. "Directed Self-Placement: An Attitude of Orientation." *CCC* 50.1 (1998): 54-70.

Stock, Patricia L. "A Comprehensive Literacy Program: The English Composition Board." *Fforum.* 4.2 (1983): 192-200.

APPENDIX
UNIVERSITY OF MICHIGAN
SURVEY ON STUDENT WRITING 1999-2000—GAYLE MORRIS SWEETLAND WRITING CENTER

	Definitely yes	Probably yes	Probably no	Definitely no
Reading experiences During the PAST TWELVE MONTHS,				
... did you read at lease three novels of more than 200 pages (such as a novel by Toni Morrison or Alice Walker, Ernest Gaines, or Tom Wolfe)?	o	o	o	o
... did you at least twice a week read one or two well-written periodicals (such as *Wired*, the *New Yorker*, *Rolling Stones*, or *Sports Illustrated*)?	o	o	o	o
... did you at least twice a week read a substantial and well-written newspaper (such as the *New York Times*, *Washington Post*, *LA Times*, or *Wall Street Journal*)?	o	o	o	o
... did you read a volume of short stories or poetry every month?	o	o	o	o
... did you read at least three book-length nonfiction works (histories, biographies, or autobiographies)?	o	o	o	o

	Definitely yes	Probably yes	Probably no	Definitely no
Writing experiences				
Did you write at least three substantial essays (i.e., 3 to 5 pages each) during the past year?	o	o	o	o
In your senior year or last year, did you write a research paper at least 10 pages long that required some library research?	o	o	o	o

APPENDIX (cont.)
UNIVERSITY OF MICHIGAN
SURVEY ON STUDENT WRITING 1999-2000—GAYLE MORRIS SWEETLAND WRITING CENTER

Did you write regularly for high school courses other than English?	○	○	○	○
Computer experiences	Definitely yes	Probably yes	Probably no	Definitely no
Are you comfortable with at least one word-processing program, including using spell-check before finishing a paper?	○	○	○	○
Experiencing in revising essays	Definitely yes	Probably yes	Probably no	Definitely no
Did you revise at least half of the papers that you wrote during the past two years, where "revise" refers to substantially re-thinking the ideas of the paper?	○	○	○	○
Level of correctness	Definitely yes	Probably yes	Probably no	Definitely no
Over the past year, did your writing (including papers for school, letters to friends, e-mail messages) almost always show a high standard of correctness, and did you make very few errors (no more than one per piece of writing) that interfered with clear communication?	○	○	○	○
Your standardized test scores	Definitely yes	Probably yes	Probably no	Definitely no
If you took the ACT, was your ACT-English score above 25? Or if you took the SAT, was your SAT-Verbal score above 570?	Yes ○	No ○		

UNIVERSITY OF MICHIGAN
SURVEY ON STUDENT WRITING 2001-2002
GAYLE MORRIS SWEETLAND WRITING CENTER

Yes	No	
O	O	I read newspapers and periodicals regularly.
O	O	During the past year I've read at least four books—fiction, biography, history—outside of class.
O	O	In class I wrote several 3-5-page essays per year.
O	O	Some of my essays were written for classes other than English.
O	O	I graduated in the top 20% of my high school class.
O	O	I am comfortable using a computer to draft and to revise and polish them.
O	O	I have learned the correct forms of standard written English and make few mistakes in sentence construction, punctuation, and usage.
O	O	My ACT-English score was 26 or above, AND/OR my SAT-Verbal score was 580 or above.

For Non-Native Speakers

Answer the questions below if English is NOT your native language. Think about the questions and then describe yourself honestly.

Yes	No	
O	O	I have used computers in writing.
O	O	I wrote two or more essays/papers in English in the last year.
O	O	I read regularly in English.
O	O	I have had regular experience drafting and revising essays.
O	O	I can revise my papers without the help of a native speaker of English.
O	O	I have written and essay/paper in English in response to something I have read.

9

DIRECTED SELF-PLACEMENT IN A COMMUNITY COLLEGE CONTEXT

Patrick Tompkins
John Tyler Community College

Placement testing, like all acts of writing, always occurs in a context, and I think this is an important point that those of us who criticize most current placement practices fail to sufficiently acknowledge. When we speak of proper or correct placement, we must remember to define our terms and ask "Proper for whom?" and "Correct in what sense?" Like most situations where a number of interests are involved, no answer to these questions can wholly satisfy or treat with equal justice all parties. This is the reality of being human, and the reality educators must grapple with as they attempt to construct effective writing programs. Instead of arguing, then, that directed self-placement (DSP) is or is not a more effective placement method—for my research will not adequately support either conclusion—I want to situate a pilot study of DSP at John Tyler Community College (JTCC) affected within the interdependencies among the writing program, the college, the Virginia Community College System (VCCS), the public, and, of course, students and faculty.

Most schools rely on national, standardized tests to make decisions about admission and placement. And to a large degree, these tests are effective. Despite well-documented pitfalls—most especially regarding test bias against some minority groups—the SAT, for example, remains a fairly trustworthy predictor of college success. The Educational Testing Service can share plenty of data to prove the point, but if you have ever taught at an institution where the students score above 1100 on the SAT and taught at a school where students score well below 1100, you don't need any statistical corroboration to know that, at least in terms of making broad distinctions within large populations, the SAT provides schools with the very information about their applicants' chances for success that they want.

This point is especially important, because it speaks to the management issue that colleges and their administrators necessarily face. When several thousand students enter a college each year, how can educators most efficiently and effectively determine which courses are appropriate for students?

The main argument with standardized writing tests, such as the Test of Standard Written English, ETS' Computerized Placement Test (CPT), or ACT's COMPASS, is that they purport to measure writing without having students write. Such a methodology seems to beg common sense and to be inherently unfair. As a reaction to this, researchers like Edward White established protocols for designing and evaluating effective essay exams. The great body of literature about essay tests, and particularly about holistic scoring, attests to the widespread acceptance of this method. Obviously, an essay test addresses the major weakness of the standardized test because students write and trained scorers evaluate their writing performance. In the best of circumstances, an essay test may actually approach or nominally exceed the validity and reliability of standardized measures, but only in the best of circumstances, for the essay writing test is fraught with weaknesses.

Other educators have argued for the use of portfolios for admission and placement, and many schools have adopted this method. The argument here is that at least the evaluator makes a decision based on a student's actual writing, and therefore the placement decisions are more informed. But again, I would argue that evaluation is always context-specific, and we have to question the relevance of a high school portfolio (usually) to the college curriculum. Or if we concede that the portfolio does speak to the skills and abilities a student will need in college writing, we have to assume that the evaluator is part of a writing program with clearly stated course objectives, evaluation criteria, and scoring methodology. Liz Hamp-Lyons and William Condon have critiqued the assumptions and practice of portfolio assessment, and interestingly, they find, as I argue here, that the major benefit of a method may not be our ability to prove it is more trustworthy than some more trustworthy method, but how its design and implementation can affect a writing program.

We also have to acknowledge that the holistically scored essay and portfolio evaluation methods are time and resource intensive. Pearl Saunders' survey of higher education institutions found that most writing programs rely on standardized tests (including nonwriting skills tests such as SAT and ACT) for placement, in violation of the stated positions of professional organizations such as the National Council of Teachers of English (NCTE) and College Composition and Communication (CCC). The reason is quite simple: Standardized tests are cheaper and no one has been able to conclusively demonstrate that there is a more effective method. If you are an administrator and you are faced with a choice between a cheap, easy to apply, and fairly effective method for placing students against another measure that is costly and cannot be shown to be much more effective, which one would you choose? Remember, we all have our constituencies and our priorities, including which battles are worth fighting. If a school has a pool of faculty especially dedicated to a comprehensive effective placement methodology that includes essay or portfolio evaluation or if an institution has the resources to hire scorers and do the other things necessary to make such placement programs effective, then they live in happy days indeed. But many of the rest of us are faced with very real, very pressing constraints on our time and resources, and we find ourselves as servants, not only to the theories of our discipline, but to students, administrators, state governments, and the public who demand documentable accountability, both in terms of predictive validity and, as importantly, in terms of cost and efficiency.

In the next section, I discuss inaccurate placement in some detail, but for now I note that educators have been frustrated with the inability of either standardized tests or essay or portfolio evaluation to significantly reduce the problem of inaccurate placement. The development of DSP, and its attraction to writing educators, is borne out of the confluence of emerging pedagogical theory and a wall of inaccurate placement that previous methodologies have failed to breach.

PLACEMENT IN THE CONTEXT OF THE VCCS

Virginia belongs to the Southern Regional Education Board (SREB) whose studies provide a broad picture of placement policies in 15 southeastern states. A 1989 survey of 826 higher education institutions found that these schools used 125 combinations of 75 different tests (38 tests just for writing). In 1992, the SREB concluded in its Recommendation 2: "Institutions and states should make a concerted effort to establish a coordinated definition of college-level study that applies to all institutions in a state or institutional system. . . . The practice of using different tests and different cutoff scores on the same tests to place students in remedial or regular college courses can raise serious questions about how college-level is defined at the state or system level."

The VCCS illustrates the SREB findings in microcosm. In a 1997 study prepared by Dr. Bartholomay for VCCS Chancellor Dr. Oliver, the 23 Virginia community colleges applied nearly a dozen different tests to placement. ACT's COMPASS was the most popular, but the cut-off score between developmental and college-level writing courses ranged from a low of 50 to a high of 80. As a consequence of these arbitrary policies, in one case at least, a student was required to take 18 credits of developmental instruction at one VCCS college, whereas just down the road another VCCS school did not require the student to take any developmental courses. Dr. Bartholomay's report recommended the adoption of system-wide placement policies and procedures. In 1998, Chancellor Oliver put the issue out to the Advisory Committee of Deans and Provosts, which subsequently recommended the adoption of COMPASS as a system-wide placement instrument (ASSETT, the paper version of COMPASS, was recommended for institutions without computerized testing facilities).

Chancellor Oliver appointed the Developmental Education Implementation Task Force, with representatives from colleges, disciplines, and faculty/staff personnel from across the state, to put the Advisory Committee's recommendations into action. The Task Force was directed to accomplish the following:

1. Develop common system-wide guidelines for interpreting the results of the standardized test
2. Develop system-wide measurable objectives and exit criteria for developmental reading, writing, and mathematics.
3. Make recommendations concerning performance indicators and assessment methods that can be implemented system-wide for the purpose of monitoring the success of these new procedures.

The chancellor also sought to balance the need for consistency throughout the VCCS with the need for individual schools to tailor their placement policies to local contexts; he urged the Task Force not to lose sight of flexibility and local autonomy as they formulated new VCCS policies.

The current situation in the VCCS, then, is that we have all adopted the same standardized test and the same cut-off scores to evaluate students' skills in math, reading, and writing. But the Task Force tried to attend to the chancellor's desire for flexibility so that individual schools can design policies that best meet the needs of their specific student populations. First, using data gathered from participating VCCS institutions and crunched by ACT, the Task Force established cut score ranges for each subject area (see appendix). Rather than holding all schools to a single score, colleges have the latitude to set their cut scores anywhere within these several point ranges. Additionally, like almost any measure, COMPASS does very well identifying the strongest writers, and not too poorly identifying the weakest writers (except for problems with students who do not take the test seriously or whose performance is impaired by computer phobia, a learning disability, or some other influence), but the trouble for all of us is successfully placing the large middle group of writers. For this reason, the Task Force identified a "decision zone," a gray area of these students of middle abilities for whom it is very difficult to predict which course they will find best suits their needs. VCCS institutions are encouraged to establish individual policies for handling students in this "decision zone."

The Task Force also strongly encouraged schools to use multiple measures for determining placement. In writing courses, the Task Force suggests at a minimum that students be retested on the first day of class with a writing sample that is meant to confirm or question test placement. Other measures might include portfolios, high school GPA (a notoriously unreliable method), or interviews with students. Some schools have eliminated the decision zone altogether and have set their cut scores absolutely somewhere within its or the cut score range's boundaries. Other colleges, such as JTCC, are using methods like DSP to facilitate the placement of students in this range into writing courses. In the chancellor's letter to college presidents that formalized the Task Force's policies, he allowed that some schools might feel they have better methods of placement than COMPASS. Therefore, the chancellor permitted schools to study these methods until the end of the Spring 2001 term, and if they still wanted to use their method instead of COMPASS to provide evidence of research demonstrating its efficacy. This is how JTCC came to experiment with DSP.

Those college systems that have chosen to move toward regularization of writing assessment and placement have not done so maliciously or even without an understanding of the complexities of these issues, but instead with the intention of ending some of the abuses and mitigating some of the chaos of the diverse placement procedures in their systems. It is an effort to more effectively respond to growing demands for higher education and changes in the world economy and communication media that require greater integration and accountability. The desire then—argue against it if you can—is that schools should produce qualified graduates, that schools should be able to clearly demonstrate this to be so, and that schools should adhere to the same learning standards as other schools in the system. In this way, students, their families who support them, higher education administrative bodies, state legislatures, taxpayers, and potential employers can all be confident in the abilities of graduates.

DSP IN THE CONTEXT OF JTCC

At this point, I should insert myself more clearly into this text in order to provide some personal context for our discussion. I conducted two studies at JTCC (one that compared three placement tests and one on DSP), I coordinate developmental English at the Midlothian Campus of JTCC, I serve on the college's Developmental Education Committee, and I was appointed as a member of the chancellor's VCCS Developmental Education Implementation Task Force, which set current policies for testing, placement, education, and assessment.

After fielding complaints from faculty and students about JTCC's placement test (CPT at the time), after reading widely in evaluation research and theory, and after becoming acutely sensitive to the fact that some tests poorly reflect the abilities of certain populations—some minorities, some students with disabilities, and students with computer or test anxieties—I wanted to know which of the most common tests—CPT, COMPASS, holistically scored essay—best served the needs of JTCC students and faculty. My research indicated little correlation among the three instruments, and there was a large degree of "inaccurate placement."

For my purposes here, I define *inaccurate placement* as the number of students who passed a higher course than a test would have placed them into plus those students who were not successful in the course into which they had been placed. Viewed this way, the three tests would have inaccurately placed between 34% and 59% of students. These percentages suggest that although the tests are fairly good at placement overall, huge numbers of our students seem poorly served by these instruments. I must note, however, that ETS or ACT would strongly disagree with my definition of inaccurate placement. They would argue fairly that I should not include students who were placed into a course but did not achieve success, for according to the testing agencies these students were properly placed but, owing to factors outside the scope of the test, they failed to perform to their level of ability. We are all well aware that no test as yet can take account of ancillary issues such as a student's learning style or pressures at home (as DSP does), but the effect of this weakness in our methodologies is that some students who a test predicts will succeed end up withdrawing or failing whereas some others who the test tried to bar from a course will be able to pass.

A study of 1,500 students conducted by William Ziegler at J. Sargeant Reynolds Community College, another VCCS school, also failed to find strong correlations between test scores and course success or strong correlations between COMPASS and a locally designed and scored essay. Importantly, however, neither study demonstrated that standardized tests are better than random placement, neither study could show that a faculty administered essay test is more effective (even though the JTCC study used course placement as described by Brian Huot rather than a numbered scale for rating the essays), and neither study suggests a more effective placement instrument or methodology.

And so, as a member of the VCCS Developmental Education Implementation Task Force, I could not oppose the adoption of COMPASS in favor of another test, nor could I oppose a standardized test in favor of another method. I had not been certain as to whether my study would reveal one test to be any more or less accurate than any other test, but I did have a strong belief that as a system we needed to better coordinate our testing and placement policies in the interest of fairness to students throughout the system as well as for more effective accountability among the colleges. In choosing which battles to fight, I opted to urge the Task Force to recognize the imperfection of standardized testing, to recommend the use of multiple and alternative measures, and to address the notorious unfairness of standardized tests with regard to certain populations. Interestingly, this last battle is the one I lost most completely, for despite the then high-profile suits surrounding standardized tests and minority students and despite the recent focus on accommodating the needs of students with learning disabilities, members of the Task Force had little patience for what they saw as small and politically tired side issues.

Because my own studies and my review of other literature indicated so many weaknesses with standardized writing assessment, I appreciated Chancellor Oliver's invitation to colleges to conduct research on other placement methods during the study phase of COMPASS' implementation. I had read Royer and Gilles' article about DSP in *CCC*, where I was most attracted by their intangible claim that DSP "feels right." There is something seemingly so fair and so common sensical in asking students to make their own informed choices. I was persuaded then by Royer and Gilles' faith in student's self-efficacy, or as the term has been defined by Albert Bandura, "people's judgments of their capabilities to organize and execute courses of action required to attain designated types of performances" (cited in Reynolds, this volume), because self-efficacy is a cornerstone of JTCC's developmental writing program.

In the Summer of 1999, JTCC decided to experiment with DSP on a limited scale. Located outside of Richmond and serving suburban, urban, and rural counties, JTCC operates two campuses and a satellite location that collectively enroll about 2,500 full-time equivalent students with a head count around 5,300. The students range in age from 18 to 80, with a large clustering in the 20-40 range. Nearly 60% are classified as nontraditional students, two thirds are female, three quarters attend parttime, one third enroll in developmental writing, and students regularly complain about testing practices and placement decisions (we receive many more complaints about math than writing placement). Also, because JTCC is a community college, our students do not apply, take tests, or arrive at the same time. About 25 years ago, the college found the old system of having students write essays and the few faculty who were available and willing during the summer months rate them too cumbersome, and as a result switched to standardized testing, which can be administered cheaply, on a flexible schedule, and whose results are immediately available so that our very busy students can be advised and registered in one brief visit to the campus.

I intended to use about 150 students for the DSP study, which would reflect a sizeable portion of incoming students on the Midlothian Campus, but in the end only 65 students (24% of test-takers) participated. This small study, then, cannot demonstrate the efficacy, or lack thereof, of DSP, but the study revised Royer and Gilles' methodology in interesting ways and positively affected our writing program.

I decided to give all students the standardized writing placement test so that I could compare students' ultimate placement decision with how the test would have placed them. Although Royer and Gilles encouraged students to review their ACT scores, we must remember that the ACT does not purport to be a writing test, unlike COMPASS, so in that sense students' test scores at JTCC may be more helpful in assisting with placement decisions. After they took their test, I made a brief presentation, during which time I informed them of the study's purpose, reminded them of their rights and responsibilities as participants, provided them with an overview of the information provided in the placement package, and asked them to sign a consent form (they could choose traditional placement instead of DSP, if they wanted).

I also expanded the information provided to students in the Royer and Gilles study to assist JTCC students with their decision. The placement folder included a letter which explained the study and the materials in the folder, a consent form, a course placement chart that matched test scores to writing courses, descriptions for three writing courses (two levels of developmental and college-level), a self-inventory very much like the one devised by Royer and Gilles, and sample syllabi and writing assignments for each course. Students were then invited to make their own decisions, although the folder contained information on nearly every page about how to contact a counselor or faculty member for assistance.

As Royer and Gilles found at Grand Valley State University (GVSU), enrollment in developmental courses by DSP participants declined markedly. More significantly, I think, no student enrolled in a course below that which the test would have placed them into. Because of students' perceptions of the costs to them in time, money, and even self-esteem of developmental courses, I do not expect we'll ever have many students who would enroll in a lower course than the college would otherwise recommend. The success rate of students who enrolled in college-level writing courses despite their low test scores was impressive, with 63% earning a grade of A or B, compared with 49% of all college-level writing students.

But 27% of these DSP participants withdrew from the college-level writing class, a much higher rate than the 16% of all students who withdrew from this course. Perhaps, then, some students are very good at self-efficacy and can better judge which course is best for them; on the other hand, a misunderstanding of one's abilities leads to waste for students who want to bypass developmental instruction but nevertheless would benefit significantly from it. It is not only the student who suffers, for their tuition and fees account for barely one third of the cost of their education, and the costs of re-enrolling these students in the proper course or losing them to dropping out are quite high.

At the end of the semester, about half the DSP participants responded to a survey. When comparing the GVSU and JTCC studies, the most notable difference is that 35% of the JTCC survey respondents cited factors for their decision other than those mentioned in the GVSU study, including counselor advice, parental coercion, their belief that their hard work would lead to success, and the requirements of their programs of study. I think we can say with a fair degree of assurance that students at different institutions, particularly the local community college compared to a residential university, will make choices for different reasons, and that as a whole students, regardless of the location or kind of school they enroll in, will bring a multiplicity of issues—some internal, some external, and many issues quite specific to their individual situations—to bear upon their decision.

There can be little question that students found the DSP process informative and helpful. Most very highly rated the materials in the placement folder, especially the course descriptions and the placement test score/course enrollment chart. Of those students who wrote comments at the end of the survey, one third thanked JTCC for letting them make their own decision. Other than the one student who indicated he was "very dissatisfied" with his decision (he had enrolled in a marketing course), the only complaint expressed was by one student who said that the sample syllabus and writing assignment did not correlate well with her experience in the college-level writing course.

As I have maintained throughout this argument, the study of DSP at JTCC is not conclusive enough to encourage the college to make radical alterations in placement policies. For one thing, I believe that the study suffered in part from the Hawthorne effect, that is, that the behavior of the participants was affected by the special treatment of participating in the pilot program. I can assure you that when I stood before those students who were taking placement tests, they responded very well to me in large measure because for perhaps the first time in their academic lives, and certainly the first time during their placement test experience at JTCC, someone took a few moments to explain the procedures and the rationale for them, to inform them about what they might expect from JTCC writing courses, and most importantly, to allow them the rare opportunity to make their own choices about their academic future. I believe, based upon my reading of Royer and Gilles' account of the talk provided to GVSU students, that the GVSU study must also be read with the Hawthorne effect in mind. I'd be curious to see how GVSU findings change (or do not) after the faculty's enthusiasm for this new program is no longer so apparent to students, and, perhaps, after faculty become less thorough in trying to assure the successful implementation of DSP.

But the JTCC pilot DSP program yielded valuable benefits when examined in context. Not only were students affected by the special treatment of the program, but administrators, staff, and faculty were as well. We were genuinely surprised by some findings, which lead us to questions such as "Why did 37% of participants choose not to enroll in any writing course?" Some didn't enroll in college at all. We knew these populations existed, but we did not expect that they might be as large as the study suggests, and it yet remains for us to investigate the reasons why these people choose not to enroll and the degree to which we can better assist them.

At JTCC, the DSP pilot program must be understood within the context of the Division of Student Services. As test administrators and counselors, Student Services is placed at a dangerous crossroads of administrators, faculty, students, and often students' parents. When a student is placed into a developmental course based on test scores, it falls to the counselor to explain this fact clearly and empathetically and to assist the student in the construction of their schedule. But the student sometimes complains the scores are wrong, or that they don't care if the developmental course would be better for them, they want a course that counts for college credit and that is required for certificate or degree requirements. After placement and registration, counselors have to explain themselves to those instructors who claim students are enrolled in their class "who don't belong." The permutations of the truth of matters in these situations are endless. And administrators who naturally wish to satisfy all complaints about placement while ensuring a process that is manageable, efficient, and effective hold the counselors accountable.

The Division of Students Services reminded us that they did not have the resources to administer the pilot program on their own and that they did not want the responsibility for complaints or the consequences those complaints entail. These difficulties caused the faculty, administrators, and staff to more clearly articulate current procedures for addressing students' concerns and to develop new policies for addressing problems arising from DSP. An associate dean bravely agreed to field complaints from students and their representatives, and an English Department coordinator agreed to address complaints from writing faculty. Although the issue may seem mundane and small, I assure you it is a very real one in the context of many schools' regular performance of duty, and, moreover, in this instance DSP caused various placement constituencies to review both broad and specific aspects of the program and to consider new ways of addressing placement needs, as well as immediately implementing lines of communication for discussing current problems and practices.

In the context of the work of the English faculty, the DSP pilot project was in some ways central to the revision of our policies and instructional methods. For example, in the placement folder we included course descriptions, syllabi, and sample writing assignments from three instructors. I suspect I was not the only one who suddenly looked at his policy statement and syllabus in a new light. Just including them in the folder alongside other instructors' syllabi changed my thinking about what I most wanted to communicate to students and how I could best achieve that result. Another instructor was forced for the first time to put an essay assignment into writing for inclusion in the placement folder. This person hitherto had not been compelled by the need nor had the time to rethink this particular aspect of her practice, but because of her experience with DSP, she has begun communicating her assignments both orally and in writing. These achievements may seem insignificant, but they directly affect our attitudes and practices and interactions with students and other members of the college on a daily basis. In a larger sphere, DSP was also part of a movement within the English Department to clearly articulate our course objectives and to regularize our assessment of instructional effectiveness.

As English faculty examined placement procedures in light of the VCCS' shift to a system-wide instrument, DSP provided us with a method we could use to supplement standardized testing. We decided that students who scored within the decision zone (a several point range within which placement decisions are most doubtful) should be offered DSP to assist them with writing placement. We expect only small numbers of students to take advantage of DSP, but we feel confident that it is no worse a method for the "decision zone" than any other, and it has the advantage of generating positive attitudes and performance from all involved.

As a college, we did not move forward with a DSP program for all students, even though the chancellor's directive allows schools to experiment with and assess placement methods like DSP. For one thing, we wanted to wait and see the effects of the system-wide placement test and scores on our program and on the system as a whole. Practicality also affected our decision. The placement folders we put together cost almost $2 each, and even were we to shorten it (we plan to), there's a point beyond which you either swallow the cost or lose the value of the content. Passing the cost onto students is not an option available to us. For the pilot project, the presenter (me) was paid by a grant. If an English faculty member is to make a presentation at each placement test session, who will bear the cost? Should faculty commit themselves to this voluntarily? Just scheduling faculty for the myriad number and times of placement sessions would require significant attention from some as yet unnamed staff member.

We could implement DSP in the counseling session, asking each counselor to provide students with the folder, highlight especially important information, respond to questions, and assist them in the selection of their courses. But for our present mode of operation and our current perceptions about that system, such change would be quite radical and disruptive. Counselors are understandably reluctant to bear the burden of someone else's idea of effective placement management, one that is much more cumbersome than matching test scores with writing courses. And it surely would result in longer counseling sessions, which given current strains on our budgets, staff, and calendar and space resources would create numerous daily problems. Community colleges are more acutely troubled by these issues of monetary and resource costs, as these schools generally are funded at a much lower level than other higher education institutions, and the teaching load for faculty (typically 15 credit hours per semester) limits the amount of time and energy they can devote to other initiatives like DSP. These realities, which form a substantial base of the context of placement in community colleges, are not likely to change.

Aristotle said "politics is the art of the possible," and although we may not like to think kindly of the word "politics" or to consider politics within educational contexts as we pursue our professional ideals, what is politics but the sum total of interests, powers, communications, and environmental circumstances? In this sense, we can trust that it is not only more material to us than our ideals, but also in some measure necessary and therefore good. Because of the considerations just cited, I did not recommend the wholesale adoption of DSP for writing placement. But we recognize that DSP has a role to play in our program, and as we coordinate with faculty across the VCCS, we might find it is especially well suited to the context of particular schools.

DSP encourages us to reassess our assessment methods, and it reminds us that students' self-efficacy may be our best resource as we attempt to both serve and manage them in our schools. Such benefits may be very timely. DSP fosters self-efficacy in ways that accord well with evolving information and communication paradigms that require that people have easy access to clear and multiple kinds of information on which they can base life-affecting decisions. The JTCC English faculty has already adopted DSP for students scoring in the decision zone on the placement test and for students who object either to the test or to our placement policies. If DSP successfully rewrites current placement practices across the country, we will be well positioned to revise our own.

More importantly, DSP realigns our traditional ways of thinking about, measuring, and placing our students, which causes us to examine not only our policies, but also our underlying philosophies and pedagogies. DSP provides students with a rare freedom in our current institutions, but it provides us with freedom, too. I think this is why the idea has spread so rapidly to so many different institutions. The promise of DSP lies not so much in its efficacy at achieving an as yet unmeasurable and an always mythical "correct" or "proper" placement, but in its ability to focus discussion, to raise new questions, and to invigorate professionals seeking to improve their practice.

APPENDIX: VCCS GUIDELINES FOR COURSE PLACEMENT

COMPASS Scores*

Scores	Recommended Course
0-68	English 01 or 03 (Developmental)
60-75	Decision Zone
76-99	English 111 (College-level)

*Each college may adjust placement ranges by adding or subtracting three points in the COMPASS scores.

ASSETT Scores

Scores	Recommended Course
23-40	English 01 or 03 (Developmental)
41-42	Decision Zone
43-55	English 111 (College-level)

REFERENCES

Ansley, Abraham, A. Jr. "College Remedial Studies: Institutional Practices in the SREB States." Atlanta: SREB, 1992. ED345617.

——. "Readiness for College: Should There be Statewide Placement Standards." Atlanta:SREB, 1987. ED333783.

——. "They Came to College? A Remedial/Developmental Profile of First-time Freshman in SREB States." *Issues in Higher Education,* 1991, no 25.

Hamp-Lyons, Liz and William Condon. "Questioning Assumptions about Portfolio-Based Assessment." *College Composition and Communication* 44.2 (1993): 176-190.

Huot, Brian. "Toward a New Theory of Writing Assessment." *College Composition and Communication* 47.4 (1996): 549-65.

Royer, Daniel J. and Roger Gilles. "Directed Self-Placement: An Attitude of Orientation." *College Composition and Communication* 50.1 (1998): 54-70.

Saunders, Pearl. "Current Curricular Principles and Instructional Practices in Community Colleges' Writing Programs." Paper Presented at CCCC, Chicago, 1998.

White, Edward M. *Teaching and Assessing Writing.* San Francisco: Jossey-Bass Publishers, 1994.

—— "An apologia for the Timed Impromptu Essay Test." *College Composition and Communication* 46.1 (1995): 30-45.

White, Edward M. et al. eds. *Assessment of Writing: Politics, Policies, and Practices.* New York: MLA, 1996.

Ziegler, William. "Visible Skills: Using COMPASS Reading and Writing Tests for Placement." Paper Presented at CCCC, Atlanta, 1999.

10

SOUTHERN ILLINOIS UNIVERSITY CARBONDALE AS AN INSTITUTIONAL MODEL

The English 100/101 Stretch and Directed Self-Placement Program

David Blakesley
Purdue University

Erin J. Harvey
New Mexico State University

Erica J. Reynolds
University of Arizona

AN OVERVIEW OF THE WRITING PROGRAM

To understand the material conditions that attended the introduction of directed self-placement (DSP) at Southern Illinois University Carbondale (SIUC) and thus that shaped the rhetoric used to support the change from ACT-Placement to DSP, we need to explain a little bit about the writing program itself.

In Fall 1998, we implemented the English 100/101 *Stretch* program, one modeled on the *Stretch* program at Arizona State University and described by Gregory Glau in "'The Stretch Program': Arizona State University's New Model of University-Level Basic Writing Instruction." English 100 (Basic Writing) would be the new, three credit-hour course specially designed to prepare students to succeed in English 101 (Composition I), 102 (Composition II), and other college-level writing courses. Students who placed themselves into English 100 became participants in the *Stretch* program, which allowed them to take English 100 and 101 with the same experienced instructor in consecutive semesters.

DSP became the new writing placement process. As we conceived it, DSP asked students to select whether they wanted to begin the first-year composition sequence in English 100/101 *Stretch* or in English 101. Students were asked to review their preparation for college-level writing and the course descriptions before making their decision. A first-week diagnostic essay in all sections of English 100 and 101 acted as a check on this process and allowed the WPA to make further recommendations regarding placement. We discuss our reasons for using this diagnostic essay as a supplement to DSP—as well as its benefits and drawbacks—later in this chapter.

SIUC's writing program was well-designed and overseen for many years by outstanding writing program administrators (WPAs), so in many respects, implementing these changes in the program was simply a matter of course. We still felt an enormous amount of pressure, warranted or not, to address what others perceived as substantial problems in the writing ability of the university's junior- and senior-level students. It didn't matter to those placing the blame on the writing program that no one had bothered to ask what we did or why we did it, or that half of our students took their writing courses elsewhere, or that no one had bothered to formally assess the writing of students who passed through our courses, not to mention the writing ability of those students who were reportedly not writing as well as they should be. It was the old and familiar pass-the-buck phenomenon reasserting itself. At the time, everyone was in on the act, from the provost on down. Hence, the pressure.

Two versions of English 101 were offered prior to Fall 1998: 101 Regular (English 101), which included regularly admitted students and special admission (SA) students who had received high scores on a writing placement test; and English 101 Restricted (English 101R), which included only SA students who had received low scores on a writing placement test. English 102 (English 102) was the second course in the sequence. Both courses were required as part of the core curriculum's Foundation Skills sequence.

Prior to Fall 1998, placement in English 101 and English 101R was determined initially by ACT score. Students scoring 19 or below and who were admitted to the university through the Center for Basic Skills (SA students) were given a timed writing test, which was subsequently scored by the English Department. All students scoring higher than 19 on the ACT placed automatically into English 101. SA students who performed well on their test were placed into English 101. Those who did not were placed into English 101R.

There were several differences between English 101 and English 101R. The enrollment caps were 20 and 15, respectively. The courses used different primary rhetorics, with the English 101R course also specially designed to meet the needs of basic writers. More experienced teachers were assigned to teach English 101R. However, both English 101 and English 101R shared identical learning objectives. Students in both courses were encouraged to seek help from SIUC's writing centers. All were expected to move on to the next course in the sequence, English 102, the next semester.

In the 1980s, and when the courses were originally conceived, English 101R included a tutorial component, which required English 101R students to meet with a tutorial group for at least 1 hour per week to get extra help with their writing. That component of English 101R was discontinued in Fall 1987 due to budget constraints and the development of the writing center. Essentially, then, all students placed into English 101R were mainstreamed, once the tutorial component was made voluntary rather than a principal component of the course. Whether a student took English 101 or English 101R, it was expected that he or she would be prepared for English 102 in one semester, regardless of the student's writing ability at the time of matriculation. The Progress grade (PR) could be used in English 101 or English 101R for students who attempted to do the coursework and who attended class regularly but who did not earn a grade of C or better. It was rarely used.

These changes to the program came as a result of campus-wide discussion led by the university's core curriculum director, who had held town meetings in all the academic units on the question of what constituted writing literacy. Those meetings generated all sorts of recommendations (and gripes) from faculty, many of whom were unfamiliar with our curriculum or our attempts to prepare our instructors. Nevertheless, these discussions prompted a host of recommendations, two of which were that the English Department needed to create a basic writing course and a better system of placement. (Many believed that too many students were passed through the courses without learning much.) These recommendations became mandates when they were supported by the university's faculty senate. And thus the WPA's charge was to see that they were addressed.

We began the process of addressing these two recommendations with these observations:

- A significant number of underprepared students were expected to catch up to better prepared peers after one semester of writing instruction in English 101; these students included both those who had placed into English 101R *and*—it is important to note—students who, because they scored higher than 19 on the ACT, never were tested for writing ability prior to enrolling.
- The university had no placement mechanism for determining the preparation and potential for success of regularly admitted stu-

dents, who may have scored above 19 on the ACT but who nevertheless may have had poor writing skills. We believed that as many as 10% to 15% of our students fell into this category, based on our review of grade distribution and the hypothesis that the ACT alone did not directly measure writing ability, only predicting success in writing courses at the high end (i.e., for students scoring above the 80th percentile). A significant number of students who needed extra help with their writing were being placed in a course that was too advanced to meet their needs.

To some extent, these hypotheses were supported by the data that we had begun to collect:

- A significant number of students were failing English 101 one or more times, ultimately resulting in low semester-to-semester retention of students in required writing courses. Students who did poorly in English 101 would either drop out of the university or would postpone re-enrolling in a writing course, both of which were undesirable outcomes for the students and for the university.
- Although the mean GPA of students in English 101R and English 101 sections was very similar, SA students who had passed the English 101R course had a mean GPA in English 102 significantly lower than students who had passed the English 101 course.

Given what we knew and what we believed could happen, we designed the basic writing course and the new placement method, drawing heavily on the Arizona State *Stretch* model and on the placement method outlined by Dan Royer and Roger Gilles in their *CCC* article, "Directed Self-Placement: An Attitude of Orientation." We also relied on the qualitative observations of instructors of English 101 and English 101R, data on the mean GPA of students as they moved through the first-year composition sequence, performance and retention data observed in other writing programs, and what we knew theoretically about the teaching and learning of writing.

Throughout this stage of the process and having received a general mandate, the planning was merely a matter of reviewing the possibilities, weighing their merits, and formulating a strategy. There was no need at this point, or so we felt, to take the range of possibilities to stakeholders other than those who would implement the change in the program itself or those who would need to approve it (the department chair, the college dean, and the university's chief academic officer). It turned out to be fairly easy to persuade these people that DSP was a good alternative form of placement to the one we had been using previously. It was also not difficult to ensure that the new basic writing course be offered for three credit hours, even though we had expected some opposition.

Internally, we decided to adopt DSP as the writing placement mechanism for two reasons.

1. DSP had been successfully implemented at at least one comparable university. Royer and Gilles had persuaded us. It didn't hurt our efforts later that DSP seemed like a relatively inexpensive solution to the problem of writing placement. (Over the course of implementation, we found that rather than pay people to read placement essays, we paid them to talk to students, with the overall expense of doing either roughly equivalent.) More importantly, however, it also communicated the positive message to students that we respected their judgment. We felt that if students chose to take the basic writing course, rather than be forced to take it, that the classroom dynamic would improve dramatically, an important factor in a course in which students' attitudes toward writing is so crucial to writing growth. Setting questions of accuracy and reliability aside for the time being, we felt that DSP could not only positively transform the learning space of the basic writing class, but also that it would make placement a far less dismal affair than it normally is, for students, advisors, teachers, and administrators. At the point of contact between students and teachers, and students and advisors, as Royer and Gilles say, DSP indeed felt right (61).
2. We suspected but were not certain that students could accurately gauge their writing ability. As Erica Reynolds demonstrates in her chapter in this volume, our suspicion turned out to hold some merit. Research has shown that student self-efficacy—task-specific confidence—positively correlates with writing ability.

The tricky part in our implementation came next when it was time to communicate the new policy to the secondary stakeholders. Although we had agreed internally that DSP and *Stretch* could work well together, we still had to rely on others outside the program to make it happen. That meant that the rhetorical dynamic would have to change. We would no longer be talking among ourselves and thus could no longer rely on shared assumptions about how students learn to write. When you remove the bases for easy agreement, cooperation can quickly turn to competition and suspicion. So we knew from the outset that we needed to collect data to support and then to justify the changes we were proposing.

As much as baseline data (such as the mean GPA of students moving through the first-year composition sequence) and qualitative observations of English 101 instructors supported an initiative for change, and as promising as *Stretch* and DSP were for improving students' performance and retention at SIUC, concern among many over the extrapolation of results was understandable. We knew we had to prove that DSP could and did work at SIUC. In what follows, we describe the sometimes difficult institution of combined initiatives, *Stretch* and DSP, and how together they ultimately helped improve the performance, retention, and satisfaction of students who entered the first-year composition sequence in Fall 1998 and continued in their writing courses in subsequent semesters.

THE RATIONALE FOR DSP AT SIUC

Our proposed changes were aimed at mitigating perceived and related problems, such as students' inability to catch up to their better prepared peers in one semester, dramatically high semester-to-semester attrition rates, lack of a placement mechanism for regularly admitted students, and lower GPAs for those SA students who reached English 102. The research by Glau and Royer and Gilles, as well as social psychological studies showing the connections between self-efficacy and writing ability, profoundly shaped the character of our initiatives very early in the process.

To begin with, we found Royer and Gilles' arguments on behalf of DSP convincing, and we had like many others learned to see ACT placement as a stop-gap measure that had probably outlived its usefulness (if it ever had any) at least as a tool for gauging current writing ability or predicting success in writing courses. We saw a high upside to DSP: Royer and Gilles report that when given a choice, 22% of students actually volunteered to take an extra semester of writing instruction, a noncredit course at Grand Valley State University (GVSU). After instituting their new placement method, they also found high student satisfaction and an improved classroom dynamic in both courses. They, like other WPAs and assessment experts, found that consideration of ACT scores, SAT scores, and high school GPAs is not a very valid or reliable way to find out which first-year writing course is best for students (55). Furthermore, as Kathleen Blake Yancey contends in "Writing Assessment: A Position Statement," "Any individual's writing 'ability' is a sum of a variety of skills employed in a diversity of contexts, and individual ability fluctuates unevenly among these varieties" (2). To us, DSP addressed this diversity of contexts, the range of individual abilities among our students, and the university's failure to measure the writing ability of students who might have performed well on the ACT but who could barely write a sentence.

As we mentioned earlier, under the old sequence of courses, regularly admitted students tended to do better as they progressed, whereas SA students tended to do worse. In 1996 and 1997, regularly admitted students earned a mean GPA of 2.69 and 2.73 (on a 4-point scale) in English 101, respectively (see Table 10.1).

In English 102, these same students earned GPAs of 2.92 and 2.86. However, whereas SA students earned a modestly lower mean GPA in English 101 and 101R both years, their mean GPA in English 102 was substantially lower than that of regularly admitted students. For example, in 1996 and 1997, respectively, SA students only earned GPAs of 2.27 and 2.12 once they reached English 102. Clearly, some students needed more preparation and more time to meet the escalating challenges of college-level writing.

Previously, SIUC only tested the writing ability of those students who scored lower than 20 on the ACT. Students who scored 20 or higher were automatically placed in English 101 Regular regardless of their writing competence. However, in Fall 1996, for example, only 75.2% of SA students who were placed in English 101 Regular passed the course (see Fig. 10.1).

Neither ACT scores nor the writing test were proving useful in predicting the success of average students in their first-year writing courses. Students who were not successful were either dropping out of the university or postponing reenrollment. Of course, both were unacceptable outcomes for them and for the university, making it important to find a reliable and cost-efficient placement mechanism for both SA and regularly admitted students to improve their chances at success.

Table 10.1. Tracking Student Performance in English 101 and 102 (Fall 1996–Fall 1997)

	#	Mean GPA in English	Mean GPA in English
English 101/Fall/1996/regularly admitted students	1828	2.69	2.92
English 101/Fall/1996/SA students	258	2.33	2.27
English 101/Fall/1996/SA students	213	2.58	2.32
English 101/Fall/1996/regularly admitted students	1734	2.73	2.86
English 101/Fall/1996/SA students	104	2.50	2.66
English 101/Fall/1996/SA students	341	2.48	2.12

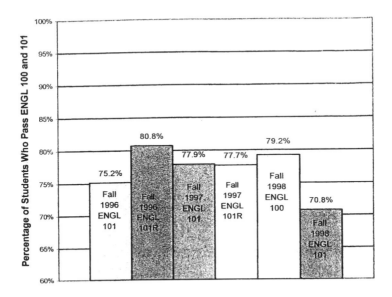

Fig. 10.1 Special admission students in English 100 and 101, 1996-1998.

As we came to DSP, we also had to consider our ability to afford it. Using the ACT as a placement method appeared to be inexpensive, at least in terms of direct costs. Only one academic program (our Center for Basic Skills) tested students with additional measures, depending on ACT score. The English Department did not have to spend any funds at all. Indirectly, however, the costs of using ACT placement may have been far more substantial than we then realized (as discussed later in this chapter). With Royer and Gilles, we fantasized about having the time and resources to conduct interviews with each incoming student to discuss his or her writing ability, to read high school writing samples, to survey reading interests, and even to gauge maturational growth over the summer following high school. However, conducting interviews and assessing writing samples would likely be far too costly for our writing program, in terms of both time and money. We reviewed the feasibility and validity of conducting placement tests and readings in the context of enrollment patterns and an incoming class of more than 2,300 students. We concluded that testing all students for writing ability was neither feasible (costing at least $20,000 per year) nor prudent, especially given our uncertainty about whether any timed writing or high stakes writing situation could predict readiness for chances of success in English 101, 102 or higher level writing courses.

Early in our development of rationale, we visited one of the most frequently asked questions in relation to DSP: Can students really make the right choice, in terms of writing composition placement, on their own? Research on self-efficacy and its influence on writing indicate that they can (Reynolds 3). Studies conducted by McCarthy, Meier, and Rinderer, Bruning, Murphy, and Shell, and Johnson and Pajares, have shown that self-efficacy, as outlined by social psychologist Albert Bandura, is a situation- and subject-specific personal confidence in one's ability to successfully perform tasks at a given level *and* a strong predictor of actual ability. Students who feel strongly efficacious that they will be able to perform specified writing skills are indeed able to do so. Furthermore, strongly efficacious writers produce writing that is superior in macro-level qualities to writing produced by their low self-efficacious peers. These research findings support Royer and Gilles' claim that students who appraise their ability too highly have a challenge before them. On the other hand, students who believe English 098 (basic writing) is the best course for them are happy to have the opportunity to improve themselves (65). In a mock advisory session in Spring 1998, we had already recorded similar motivation. One student put it this way: "I would work that much harder if I placed myself in English 101—to prove that I could do it." When students begin their first semester feeling like they don't measure up and that they are being forced into remedial work, they can feel very resentful (among other things). Consequently, teachers end up spending more time boosting morale than getting down to the real work of teaching and learning to write. By combining *Stretch* with DSP, we hoped that a multi-dimensional solution to the ongoing problems we faced would benefit our students without being overly complicated pedagogically or administratively. The *Stretch* program also offered an extra incentive for those English 100 students to enroll in English 101 in the contiguous semester.

As we chose DSP, we also had the opportunity to design our new basic writing course (English 100) and to reconceptualize the other courses in the first-year composition sequence. We were greatly impressed by Glau's description of a *Stretch* program at Arizona State University, in part because he had carefully measured the consequences of the curricular change, which we hoped to do as well. He reports improved performance and retention for students who have the same instructor and group of students from their first to second semester of writing:

> When we compare the students who registered in the *Stretch* Program sequence of WAC 101-ENG 101 over the last two academic years (1994-95 and 1995-96) to those who took our old ENG 071-ENG 101 sequence over the last five years it was offered, we find that about 23 percent more WAC 101 students go on to take ENG 101 here, and nearly 30 percent more WAC 101 students pass ENG 101. (83)

At Arizona State, a significant proportion of students indicated that instructor continuity was the best thing about the program. Glau adds that the benefits of building a sense of such a writing community is important in that students remain together for an entire year (82). Additional research provides a possible explanation for this improved performance and retention. Daly suggests that apprehension and low self-efficacy in conjunction with poor evaluations and avoidance techniques become a vicious cycle for writers. Writing self-efficacy is developed over a period of time and evaluative feedback from peers and instructors helps to shape a student's sense of writing self-efficacy. Past successes and failures with writing foster or diminish an individual's strength of self-efficacy; however, assuming that feedback is legitimate (be it positive or negative), the degree of self-efficacy a student feels about his or her writing is likely to be justified. Students who feel highly apprehensive report having experienced previous failures in terms of writing, whereas students with low apprehension report having experienced success.

While working in a *Stretch* program, students and teachers are provided with a continuity that fosters trust, confidence, a much more thorough understanding of the needs each student writer experiences, and an additional 15 weeks to address those needs and nurture confidence. Additional studies have shown that a student's degree of apprehension, which is a tendency to either approach or avoid particular situations, is—like self-efficacy—a very strong predictor of success. Daly and Miller ("Studies"); Daly; Daly, Faigley, and Witte; and Daly and Wilson have shown that students with low apprehension with regard to writing are more competent writers in terms of both skills and performance than are their highly apprehensive peers. We predicted that better outcomes in their courses would translate into a higher motivation to stay enrolled in the university by ensuring a sense of continuity in writing development, increasing confidence, and improving the chances for success in English 102.

It should be evident by now that our choice of DSP was not whimsical nor merely one of convenience. Instead, we weighed research on placement methodology (relying heavily, for instance on Edward White's research in books like *Teaching and Assessing Writing*), relied on quantifiable performance data, measured a variety of economic factors, and considered the psychology and apprehension of writing in college, and then, of course, the degree to which our university wanted and needed change in the writing program. In the next section, we report our results.

RESULTS OF THE IMPLEMENTATION OF STRETCH *AND* DSP

We collected baseline data to track student performance in the first-year composition sequence, beginning with the Fall 1996 semester. The data has been useful in testing the efficacy of the new program in improving the performance and retention of students entering in Fall 1998. In Spring 1999, we reported intermediate and positive results to the administration. In Spring 2000, we completed our study of the first group of students to use DSP and to pass through the new sequence of courses.

As well as collecting and analyzing data on performance and retention, we designed two surveys for students: one for the beginning of the Fall 1998 semester and another for the end of that first semester. We designed the precourse survey to learn how and where our dissemination methods could be improved and to see how confident students felt about their placement decision. The postcourse survey was designed to elicit reflection on the placement process, such as how the diagnostic essay affected a student's motivation to do well, the grade he or she expected to receive, confidence about writing ability, and whether or not the right choice had been made with regard to placement.

Before we discuss our survey results and the dynamic of introducing DSP to the university community and into our writing program, we offer this summary of how well the change seems to have worked with regard to student performance and retention. Very often, this sort of data has the most currency when arguing the value of change across contexts, whereas the dynamics of introducing such initiatives as *Stretch* and DSP very often depend more greatly on the resources and ingenuity of WPAs in matching goals to institutional contexts (see Blakesley's chapter in this volume). We discuss the particulars of the strategies we used at SIUC after we provide this summary of student performance and retention (see also Table 10.2):

1. On the premise that success fosters a sense of self-efficacy, it was encouraging to find that students who take English 100 had a substantially higher pass rate (9% higher) in their first course than did their peers in English 101.
2. We noticed a pattern in the success rate of SA students. The Fall 1998 SA students (both English 100 and 101 groups) had a mean GPA of 2.44 as a group, which is .12 higher than it was for the 1996 English 101R group of students and .32 higher than it was for the 1997 group of English 101R students. We were particularly excited to see this improvement because courses themselves now have more challenging student learning objectives.

3. Of those students who say they heard about DSP prior to enrolling for the course, 21% chose English 100. In the first 2 years (1998 and 1999), 582 students chose to take English 100.
4. The promise that students who begin with English 100 will do as well if not better than their peers by the end of the composition sequence was fulfilled.
    a. The pass rate in English 102 (91.4%) for regularly admitted students who begin with English 100 was 3.5% higher than it was for students who began the sequence with English 101 (87.9%).
    b. SA students who began with English 100 had a 6% higher pass rate in English 101 than did those who began with English 101. They had a 1% higher pass rate in English 102.
    c. The Fall 1998 group of SA students, whether they began with English 100 or 101, had a higher pass rate than the same population in previous years. The Fall 1998 group had an overall pass rate of 83.6% in English 102, a 3.2% increase over the Fall 1996 group (80.4%) and 4.6% increase over the Fall 1997 group (79.0%).
5. By early Spring 1999, we saw an immediate impact on retention when the number of students in writing courses from semester to semester increased 11%, representing a net gain of 59 students.
6. We were also able to see encouraging evidence of improved satisfaction and performance when one of the students who began with English 100 in Fall 1998 later won the Andrew P. Smith Memorial Writing Across the Curriculum Award for an essay that she wrote in her Spring 1999 English 101 course. The student attributed her success to her instructor and to the DSP/*Stretch* program.

DIRECTED SELF PLACEMENT'S EFFECT ON ACADEMIC ADVISING

The pre-major advisors all state that regardless of some difficulties, this program has been the most successful institution of a complicated enrollment program they have ever seen at SIUC. (Virginia Rinella, chief pre-major advisor, Fall 1998)

In addition to positively effecting student performance, DSP fostered some better relationships across traditionally isolated academic units. We met

Table 10.2. Tracking Student Performance in ENGL 100, 101, and 102 (Fall 1996–Fall 1998+)

Course/Semester/Year/Group	# of Students	Mean GPA in ENGL 100	Pass Rate in ENGL 100	Mean GPA in ENGL 101	Pass Rate in ENGL 101	Mean GPA in ENGL 102	Pass Rate in ENGL 102
English 101/Fall/1996/ regularly admitted students	1828			2.69	78.0%	2.92	85.9%
English 101/Fall/1996/ SA students	258			2.33	75.2%	2.27	77.5%
English 101R/Fall/1996/ SA students	213			2.58	80.8%	2.32	83.9%
All SA students in English 101/Fall/1996/ regular or restricted	471				77.7%		80.4%
English 101/Fall/1997/ regularly admitted students	1734			2.73	79.8%	2.86	87.5%
English 101R/Fall/1997/ SA students	63			2.47	77.8%	2.53	88.1%
English 101/Fall/1997/ SA students	104			2.5	77.9%	2.66	86.4%
English 101R/Fall/1997 SA students	341			2.48	77.7%	2.12	76.7%
All SA students in English 101/Fall/1997 regular or restricted	445				77.8%		79.0 %

Table 10.2. Tracking Student Performance in ENGL 100, 101, and 102 (Fall 1996–Fall 1998+) (cont.)

Course/Semester/ Year/Group	#of Students 100	Mean GPA in ENGL 100	Pass Rate in ENGL 100	Mean GPA in ENGL 100	Pass Rate in ENGL 100	Mean GPA in ENGL 100	Pass Rate in ENGL
English 100/Fall/1998/ regularly admitted students	71	3.1	88.7%	2.64	76.9%	2.94	91.4%
English 100/Fall/1998/ pre-major students	124	2.9	88.7%	2.38	71.6%	2.44	84.4%
English 100/Fall/1998 SA students	77	2.85	79.2%	2.46	76.7%	2.44	84.4%
English 101/Fall/1998/ regularly admitted students	1360			2.72	76.7%	2.44	84.4%
English 101/Fall/1998 pre-major students	367			2.70	76.3%	2.91	87.7%
English 101/Fall/1998/ SA students	390			2.29	70.8%	2.44	83.6%
All SA students in 1998 group	450			2.35	71.6%	2.44	83.6%

with chief academic advisors beginning in Fall 1997, almost a year before students would begin taking courses in the new sequence, but not that long before the time when students would be asked to choose English 100 or English 101, something they would need to do in Spring 1998 when they made registration appointments. Our frequent visits to individual academic advising units was ongoing throughout every subsequent semester and proved to be an invaluable catalyst for positive change. Most academic advisors had never met with the faculty who administered curricular programs, despite the obvious reasons for doing so. The relationship was often seen on both sides as antagonistic. Advisors believed that faculty would make changes capriciously, without fully considering the consequences for students and their advisors. Advisors were often criticized for not ensuring that students took foundation courses when they were supposed to, and by students, for simply not having courses available for them to take (even though that responsibility fell to the departments and the central administration). Consulting advisors often and personally turned out to be perhaps the most important step we took in ensuring the success of DSP at SIUC.

Whenever change is implemented, people will offer various opinions about its rationale. They might agree generally that it's time for the change, but there will be divergent opinions about the rationale and, of course, the means of achieving goals. Because academic advisors would be (or would continue to be) the university's first contact point with students when they communicated their placement decisions, we knew it would be critical that all advisors not only understood the new placement mechanism, but also the new curriculum so that they could answer questions asked by the new students they would advise. Our first, and perhaps most important challenge, was to help advisors understand the new student learning objectives for the courses. It was not enough for them to be familiar with the battery of statements on the DSP brochure, where students could go for additional advice (i.e., high school English teachers and counselors, the English Department), or the objectives and procedural aspects of administering the diagnostic essay. (The actual brochure we used with students is included in Appendix A)

Understandably, curricular change of this magnitude will be met with at least initial hesitancy on the part of some faculty and administrators, particularly as the English 100/101 *Stretch* and DSP change affected mandatory core curriculum classes and involved an entire incoming class of students. Although most departmental advisors were receptive to and even enthusiastic about *Stretch* and DSP, we must admit that the level and quality of student advising was inconsistent across academic units. For DSP to work in the way that we intended and to serve all incoming students fairly, undergraduate advisors needed to help us make students aware of their choices. Too many (52%) of the students in the first year of implementation claimed that they had never heard of the process prior to the first day of class. One student, for instance, maintained, "I was not informed about the two different classes, which I think is justly unfair." In some cases, advising units were not sending the brochure to students prior to advising, nor were they providing an opportunity to discuss the options during their appointment. In other cases, students were registering over the phone, never meeting with an advisor to discuss their options. We should note, however, that in our precourse survey, we found that 93% of the students who knew about DSP highly or moderately valued their right to choose which course to take. Particularly indicative of satisfaction was one student's comment, "I think it's a great program for students because some students move faster than others and it [*Stretch*/DSP] puts them at their own pace." We still believe that students who are satisfied with their choices (and the right to make them) have an improved chance of success.

Because it can help foster good relationships between academic advisors and WPAs (or more generally, writing programs), DSP encouraged positive attitudes toward the writing program among students and across the institution, which in turn can make accomplishing other programmatic goals easier. As many WPAs know, perception matters when it comes time to argue for change, resources, or better working conditions. In working closely with advisors across campus, we had ambassadors with a stake in the success and quality of the writing program.

STUDENT ATTITUDES TOWARD DSP

In Fall 1998, the first group of students to enter the new sequence of composition courses was surveyed at the start and end of the semester to determine student satisfaction with the DSP process, the Stretch program, and the advising they received prior to enrolling at the university. The two surveys were designed to elicit information on what factors students considered when they made their choice between the two courses. We also analyzed the data to see whether gender had any influence on choice of course (some have questioned whether females might choose English 100 at a higher rate due to a lack of confidence in their writing, or whether males would choose English 101 at a higher rate because of a false sense of confidence). A sample of the end-of-semester survey is included in Appendix B.

In the precourse survey, there were 2,025 respondents. As depicted in Fig. 10.2, 48% of the respondents recalled hearing about DSP. That percentage should have been 100%, of course, so in the next year, the WPA

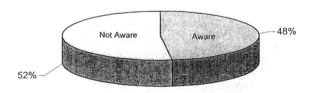

Fig. 10.2. Awareness of DSP.

took steps to better promote awareness of the program, to better inform students and advisors, and to make sure that instructors were well trained so that they could advise students on the first day of classes. Still, however, we knew that because SIUC students did not attend a common orientation prior to enrolling (as students do at GVSU), it would be extremely difficult to make sure all students were well informed. As Royer and Gilles noted, the WPA's direct contact with students is clearly the best way to ensure that self-placement is directed, and to the degree that contact is limited, the directive nature of DSP loses its efficacy.

As Fig. 10.3 shows, when students knew about DSP, 21% chose English 100, 79% English 101. These results are consistent with those found at GVSU, where students chose their equivalent course at a 22% rate (Royer and Gilles 58).

When students were advised about DSP, they appreciated the opportunity they had been given. Figure 10.4 shows that 93% of the students found the information from the brochure and/or advisors helpful (of those who reported receiving such information).

In Fig. 10.5, we see that 93% of the students who knew about DSP highly or moderately valued their right to choose which course to take. This result is important because a key benefit of this placement method is that for students who are satisfied with their placement in a writing course, especially a basic writing course like English 100, the chances for success are improved dramatically. With traditional placement methods (such as ACT), many students find that despite some success in high school with writing, they end up being told that based on their test scores, they must take an extra class (at some universities that extra course carries no credit). Not only do students distrust test results, but as Royer and Gilles suggest, they start such a class with a chip on their shoulder (59). Teaching basic writing is

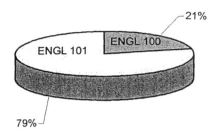

Fig. 10.3. Placement choice of students aware of DSP.

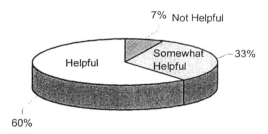

Fig. 10.4. Helpfulness of DSP information.

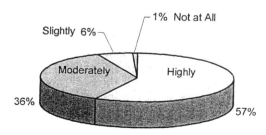

Fig. 10.5. Do students value their right to choose?

especially difficult, so when students feel disenfranchised at the start, the teacher's task becomes even more difficult. As we have mentioned, research suggests that writing apprehension can severely impact a student's writing ability. DSP encourages a positive and honest assessment of the students' writing from the outset, making the classroom one in which teachers and students can begin the real work of teaching and learning to write rather than spending time boosting the morale of students told by a test that they aren't college-level writers right after they have been admitted to college.

In Fall 1998, students reported at both the start and end of the semester that they were very confident with their choice of course. Figure 10.6 shows that 97% of all students in English 100 and 101 began the semester somewhat or very confident that they had chosen their course correctly.

Figure 10.7 shows how the students felt by the end of English 100. At that time, 84% of the students in English 100 reported that they had chosen their course correctly. That is a high percentage given the likelihood that students who do exceptionally well in the course might feel that they would have done equally well in English 101. Even so, an overwhelming majority believes the right choice was made.

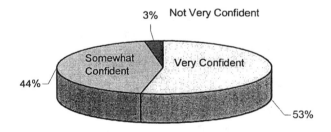

Fig. 10.6. Level of confidence in placement at beginning of course.

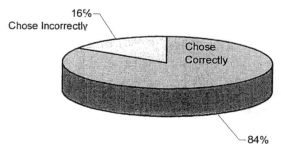

Fig. 10.7. Did students make the right choice in English 100?

Figure 10.8 shows that by the end of the course, 97% of the English 101 students felt they made the right choice. Whether that high a percentage actually did choose correctly is a matter for debate. About 20% of the students do not pass the course, so one wonders whether those students did indeed make the correct choice. It would be useful to study this response more thoroughly with some follow-up questions because one consequence of DSP should be a feeling of greater responsibility on the student's part for the outcomes of his or her education. It would be ideal if students came to believe that grades in courses were earned and not simply received.

Figures 10.7 and 10.8 also provide important information regarding the validity of DSP. According to Brian Huot, "[W]e should ask students whether or not they were still pleased with their decisions about the course because it seems to me that this would be the only way to check on the consistency of placement decisions, since students decide which course to take" (e-mail to WPA-L, April 8, 2000). Student satisfaction is just one of many measures to consider when determining validity, of course, but in this case, it is an important one.

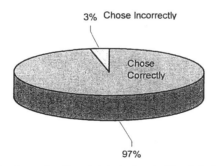

Fig. 10.8. Did students make the right choice in English 101.

GENDER AND DSP

Because DSP is an indirect measure of writing apprehension and because people tend to associate apprehension with lack of confidence, some believe that females will be more likely than males to place themselves in basic writing, on the premise that cultural biases predispose females to be less confident than males about their abilities. In their study of writing apprehension, Daly and Miller found, however, that males were significantly higher in writing apprehension than females ("Studies" 255). Our enrollment results from Fall 1998 support Daly and Miller's finding, and add validity to the premise that DSP is at least an indirect measurement of writing apprehension, which correlates with actual writing ability.

SIUC AS AN INSTITUTIONAL MODEL   227

Figure 10.9 shows the breakdown by gender: 131 males said they chose English 100, whereas 78 females say they did. Figures 10.10 and 10.11 show the results of correcting those figures as percentages of the total population who chose.

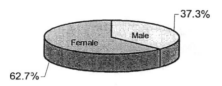

Fig. 10.9 Percentage of students by gender who chose English 100.

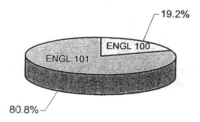

Fig.10.10. Percentage of females who chose English 100 or 101.

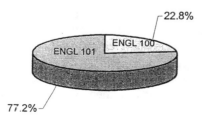

Fig. 10.11. Percentage of males who chose English 100 and 101.

Males chose English 100 at a 3.6% higher rate than did females, a result we would expect to see given that males tend to have greater writing apprehension than females and if, as Daly and Miller contend, females tend to be rated significantly higher in composition writing than males (252). That the results of DSP are consistent with what the research says about writing ability across genders testifies in yet another way that it has validity as a writing placement method.

WHAT OUR DIAGNOSTIC ESSAY SHOWED

For both political and research purposes, the WPA included a diagnostic essay in the placement process. To those who distrusted the idea of DSP, the diagnostic essay was a safety net because it would give students another chance to consider their decision. The results of the diagnostic essay were important to us also because they could help show that DSP might work at least as well as a timed writing in determining placement in a composition course.

On the second day of every English 100 and 101 class, instructors supplied students with a single prompt and gave them 50 minutes to write an essay responding to it. Instructors were then asked to score the essays holistically with a supplied rubric and return them to the WPA for review within 24 hours. (After Fall 1998, these essays were read blind by the instructor of another section of the same course.) After receiving packets of essays for every English 100 and 101 section, the WPA and placement coordinators spent approximately 2 days reviewing and evaluating essays, particularly those identified by instructors as warranting a recommendation to switch to or from English 100/101 *Stretch*. Recommendations were made in a referral form letter (signed by the WPA) and enclosed in a student's exam booklet. Essays were returned to each instructor to be distributed on the Day 3 of class. On Day 4, students who switched met with their new class.

While acknowledging the limited validity of such an in-class writing exam for determining placement, we were able to extrapolate results from the diagnostic to outline some tendencies related to the DSP process. Of the students who participated in DSP, 10% seemed to be placing themselves too highly. Students who accepted a gentle recommendation to reconsider their choice of courses and who then switched courses performed well in their new course. For example, students who moved from 101 to 100 did well in their new course (with a mean GPA of 2.81). Students who moved from 100 to 101 were also successful (with a mean GPA of 3.46). Conversely, students who did not accept the recommendation of the WPA to reconsider their choice of courses had a failure rate in English 101 higher than 50%. Students who chose not to accept the recommendation to move to English 100/101 *Stretch* were asked to make regular appointments with a Writing Center tutor. Students who were referred to the Writing Center during the diagnostic process were entered into a log to monitor whether they sought this extra help. In Week 6 of classes, the director tracked these students and sent them a package including a letter, a brochure explaining the benefits of working with a tutor, and a map to the main writing center and conveniently located satellites. This package, handed out by instructors in class, was meant to ensure that all students were made aware of their options in terms of university support outside the writing classroom and to secure information for the WPA regarding at risk students. As might be expected, we discovered that students who chose not to move from English 101 but who sought extra tutoring did better in their course than those who did not.

DPS'S EFFECT ON TEACHERS AND TEACHER TRAINING

Because instructors also became advisors in this system, it was important to train graduate assistants from administrative and pedagogical perspectives, beginning with their pre-semester workshops when they first began teaching in the program, and continuing through the time when they too would teach English 100/*Stretch* or become placement coordinators. All of our graduate assistants (GAs) had to understand the placement process for it to work effectively. No longer would students show up on our doorstep by some process mysterious to both instructors and students alike.

In addition to discussing DSP/*Stretch* at length and throughout the initial 8-day pre-semester workshop, the WPA set up particular support mechanisms for new English 100 teachers: periodic meetings, a listserv, and an experienced GA-consultant for them to meet with as needed. The meetings occurred before, during, and after each semester and were attended by English 100 instructors, the WPA, and GAs interested in teaching English 100 in the future. At these meetings, we addressed common concerns, such as the challenge of interpreting and achieving course goals, monitoring Writing Center visits, and—as the semester drew to a close—strategies for making a smooth transition to English 101. The listserv was a way to address more immediate, individual concerns. An English 100 guide provided general course information, a course description, and student learning objectives. It also included suggestions for paper topics, rhetorical principles to emphasize for each paper, and suggested readings. (Compared to

English 101, English 100/101 *Stretch* sections required four rather than six major papers in the first semester to allow students more time to draft, edit, and revise. Students were also asked to write in response to shorter assignments more frequently, about familiar subjects, and to known audiences.)

In addition to this support, we provided a detailed script for the first 2 weeks of class that outlined tasks leading up to and including the diagnostic essay. That script emphasized the importance of the instructors' in-class briefing regarding *Stretch,* DSP, and the diagnostic essay exam, as well as the need to conduct precourse surveys. Placement coordinators noticed that many students had found it helpful to discuss their options with instructors, whereas other students still wanted to speak to an advisor before they made their final decision. In some cases, instructors accompanied students to the program's main office. It was clear that instructors were playing a key role in the placement process, which we think has positive results for them as well as for their students.

Graduate students have served as placement coordinators for each semester since implementation. These students had special interests in assessment and/or writing program administration and after becoming placement coordinators, were involved in all aspects of the initiative: disseminating information across campus, soliciting feedback, managing the diagnostic essay exam, advising students, and assisting with enrollment after the first 2 days of the semester. They spent time studying core readings on assessment, such as White's "Defining Purposes and Issues in the Assessment of Writing Ability" and "Using Tests for Admissions, Placement, and Instructional Evaluation" (*Developing Successful College Writing Programs*); Yancey's "Writing Assessment: A Position Statement"; Royer and Gilles *CCC* article; and, Glau's article from *WPA: Writing Program Administration.*

The basis for appointing GAs to teach English 100 or the former English 101R was at least 1 year of teaching experience at SIUC and a special interest in teaching basic writers. In previous years, it had been difficult to find enough GAs to teach the English 101R sections, partly because of the experience it demanded, but also because of its reputation as a no-win situation for students who needed more help with their writing than they could get in one semester. We found, however, that GAs were eager to teach in the English 100/101 *Stretch* sequence, perhaps because they valued the opportunity to teach the same students for a full year.

Erica and Erin's roles as placement coordinators over the first year of implementation, peer mentors, and graduate teaching assistants put them in a unique position to see how *Stretch* and DSP played out from an instructor's perspective. Compared to what it was for those teaching English 101R before Fall 1998, the morale of GAs teaching English 100 was much better.

By and large, despite some difficulties, instructors were enthusiastic. The anxiety brought on by entering a classroom full of students who felt they were forced into some sort of remedial, noncredit-bearing course, was gone. For the first time, teachers who were interested in teaching basic writing students were being greeted by students who had chosen to enroll in a basic writing course. The litany of complaints and resentful comments overheard at the beginning of every basic writing course's semester ("I don't understand why I'm here because I was in AP English in high school," "I didn't have enough time to finish that essay in 45 minutes," or "My mom's an English teacher!") were replaced by more enthusiastic first-day murmurings. The instructors felt, understandably we think, that they met their students for the first time on common ground with common goals.

Although most instructors reported a good deal of satisfaction with the new system, some concerns arose among others. The weight of institutional pressures on the WPA to ensure the success of the new DSP/*Stretch* initiative did not go unnoticed by the instructors. There were those who worried that in order to make the new system a success, they might be expected to see to it that their students received grades of C or higher, thereby allowing the students to continue in the contiguous English 101R course. A few instructors felt that the importance of implementing the DSP/*Stretch* system might in fact supercede their own integrity in assessing students' work. Whether or not these sentiments were actually merited is difficult to ascertain, but the fact that they were espoused at all points out the importance of ensuring that instructors grade fairly, that they do not evaluate student writing to meet quotas, and that they respond effectively to student needs. Because it was a new system, it was especially important to attend to how the changes would affect what in any normal semester will be of concern to the WPA: fair and effective evaluation of student writing.

There were also some instructors disappointed to learn that some of their *Stretch* students who had taken the first course in the sequence with them chose to enroll in courses taught by different instructors the next semester. (Fewer than 10% of all students chose to change instructors midstream, and some of them did so because of scheduling problems.) What purpose, they asked, does the *Stretch* sequence hold if students are allowed to opt for another instructor the next semester? We did allow students to choose a different instructor in the contiguous semester, but it rarely happened, and we did so because we hoped to preserve the right of the student to choose courses (and teachers). In most cases, students lobbied hard to take their same instructor for English 101. When students did have to switch, their new instructors (who had also taught English 100 in the previous semester) paid special attention to helping them make the adjustment and to rebuild the camaraderie they had felt with their previous group.

CONCLUSION

It is not hard to imagine that students came to the basic writing course more motivated to learn than they might otherwise have been under a more traditional placement method (i.e., and with chips on their shoulders). As placement coordinators of the new system, Erica and Erin witnessed first hand the decisions with which students struggled, some more painfully than others. Students would arrive at the makeshift desk in the writing program office with many questions. Some had already conferred with their parents, advisors, and high school English teachers. Most importantly, all of them had discussed the decision with current teachers. Both students and teachers realized that the choice students were making was an important one. We like to think that the time they spent thinking about their writing histories and abilities, about course goals, and about their desire to succeed was much better spent than it might otherwise have been had they simply strolled into a large room, taken an essay exam, and then waited for the results to determine their fate.

We have seen throughout this process of implementing DSP that an (apparently) minor change in one aspect of a writing program's administration can have far-reaching effects on students, teachers, and the university community. Traditionally, we have relegated the question of placement to forces beyond our control, or to processes that can disenfranchise if not alienate students. Why? In part, we believe, because managing a placement process that does otherwise is indeed a complex and challenging job, one few WPAs have the time or the motive to attempt. We have found, however, that in addition to improving the experience and learning of the students in our courses, we improved the writing program in numerous other ways, the morale of the instructors in our most important course, and the program's visibility and integrity across the university.

APPENDIX A—CONTENTS OF THE DIRECTED SELF-PLACEMENT BROCHURE

DSP and English Composition at SIUC

To succeed at SIUC, you will have to make many informed and mature decisions about which major to pursue, which courses to take, and how to manage and prioritize responsibilities. At SIUC, we believe that you can and should begin exercising your judgment early. **Directed Self-Placement**

(DSP, for short) allows you to decide whether to begin the English Composition sequence in the English 100/101 Stretch Program or in English 101. We want you to reflect on your preparation for college-level writing, to consult with teachers, advisors, and family members, and then to choose the right course. (You will also write a diagnostic essay the first week of class and be asked to reconsider your original placement if the results warrant that recommendation.) Finally, all students are required to participate in DSP and should take responsibility for making this important decision. Before you meet with your advisor to register for courses, carefully review this guide. Past results show that students who are well informed also earn higher grades in whichever option they choose. So please consider this information carefully!

Option 1: English 100/101 Stretch

The *Stretch* program is carefully designed to ensure that students develop the writing skills they will need to successfully complete the English Composition requirement and excel at the university. In the *Stretch* program, students take English 100 and 101 in consecutive semesters with the same instructor. Both instructors and students thus have time to address specific writing needs at a pace and in a sequence that helps students excel. Students who choose English 100/101 *Stretch* improve their chances for success in English 101 and 102. English 100, 101, and 102 are each offered for three credit-hours. Depending on your major, English 100 may count for elective credit for degree requirements. English 101 and 102 satisfy the core curriculum requirement in the Foundation Skills area.

In English 100, you will practice the forms of writing that will be expected of you in English 101, such as argumentation and analysis. You also will learn the writing and reading skills that help you gain confidence in your ability to communicate your ideas clearly. You will usually write about subjects familiar to you. If one or more of these characteristics describe you, consider enrolling in English 100:

- ☐ Generally, I don't read when I don't have to.

- ☐ In high school, I did not do much writing.

- ☐ My high school GPA was about average.

- ☐ I'm unsure about the rules of writing.

- ❏ I've used computers, but not often for writing and revising.
- ❏ My ACT score was below 20.
- ❏ I don't think of myself as a strong writer.
- ❏ I have been advised to take English 100 following a diagnostic writing.

Option 2: English 101

Generally speaking, you are well prepared for English 101 if you have done quite a bit of reading and writing in high school. English 101 instructors will assume that you can summarize and analyze published material from magazines, newspapers, books, and scholarly journals. They will also assume that you have written a variety of essays in a variety of forms, including persuasive and analytical writing. If most of the following statements describe you, you should take English 101 first:

- ❏ I enjoy reading newspapers, magazines, and books.
- ❏ In high school, I wrote several essays per year.
- ❏ My high school GPA placed me in the top third of my class.
- ❏ I have used computers for drafting and revising essays.
- ❏ My ACT score was above 20.
- ❏ I consider myself a good reader and writer.

Further Course Information

You can find out more about these courses on the World Wide Web at out our Directed Self-Placement Home Page:

> http://www.siu.edu.departments/english/writing/wstudies.html

See the reverse side for some Frequently Asked Questions . . .

[Page 2 Starts Here]

Frequently Asked Questions: Directed Self Placement and English 100/101 Stretch

Q. Why would a student choose to begin with English 100?

A. When a student chooses English 100, he or she automatically becomes a part of the *Stretch* program, which allows students to work with the same experienced instructor in both English 100 and 101. Having the same instructor and peers for two semesters ensures a sense of continuity in writing development, increases confidence, and improves chances for success in English 101 and 102. Students in *Stretch* programs generally earn higher grades in more advanced writing courses.

Q. Does English 100 count as a credit toward graduation?

A. In nearly all cases, yes. Students receive 3 hours of course credit for English 100. English 100 does not substitute for core requirements, but these 3 hours may be applied toward the degree if the student's major allows for elective credit. Students should check with their advisors to determine whether English 100 will fulfill degree requirements in their major.

Q. How do students in English 100 ensure that they have the same instructor for English 101?

A. Students will be told which section of English 101 to register for and a spot will be reserved for them in that section until the 13th week of the semester. (The English 101 course will be offered at the same time on the same days as their English 100 course.) Students who would like a different instructor for English 101 will just register for a different section.

Q. What if the diagnostic essay shows that the student should move from English 100 to 101 or from 101 to 100?

A. The Director will advise these students that they should consider moving but will not require them to move. Students will be told which sections will be open to them if they would like to move, and they will be asked to see Donna Vance in Faner 2390 to get a closed-class card for the appropriate section if they do. Students who do not move from English 101 to 100 after advised that doing so would be in their best interest will be given instructions for setting up appointments with Writing Center tutors.

Q. If a student fails English 101, can he or she restart with English 100?

A. Yes. The student will just select English 100 when registering for the next semester's courses.

Q. If a student receives a PR in English 101, can he or she restart with English 100?

A. Yes. The student would enroll in English 100 the next semester and then take English 101 the semester after that. The student has one academic year to make up a PR grade before it turns to an F, so if the student completes the English 100-101 sequence satisfactorily within the year immediately following, the PR grade would not turn into an F automatically.

Q. How can students and advisors learn more about the *Stretch* program, the English Composition courses, and DSP?

A. The English Department site on the World Wide Web includes useful information on these topics:

> http://www.siu.edu.departments/english/writing/wstudies.html

If would like to meet with a Placement Coordinator to discuss your placement in English 100 or 101, please contact Dr. David Blakesley or Ms. Donna Vance by phone at (618) 453-6811 or by email at dblake@siu.edu. The Writing Studies office is open Monday - Friday from 8 a.m. to 4 p.m.

APPENDIX B: FINAL SURVEY

For All English 100 and 101 Instructors
Student Survey: English 100/101 *Stretch* Program

Note to Instructors: Please read the following script to your students, then ask them to complete the survey, which we will be using to gauge the effectiveness of DSP, the *Stretch* program, and the Writing Center services. Collect the completed surveys from your students, then return them to Donna Vance in Faner 2390 in the same envelope. If you have any questions, see Dr. Blakesley, Erin Harvey, or Ms. Vance.

Survey Script

At the beginning of the semester you were asked to consider whether you should begin to satisfy the core curriculum writing requirements by enrolling in the English 100/101 *Stretch* program or in English 101. You also wrote a diagnostic essay and some people were asked to reconsider their choice of courses.

The following survey is designed to aid in the improvement of the DSP initiative, the core curriculum writing courses, and the SIUC Writing Center services. We would appreciate receiving further feedback from students. Please answer the questions as honestly and thoroughly as you can. If you do not complete the survey as directed, your survey can't be used and you input will be lost.

We are not asking for your name and all responses will be kept confidential. **The survey takes only about 10 minutes to complete.**

Does anyone have any questions?

Student Survey: Directed Self-Placement
ENGL 100 / 101 Stretch Program

For Question 1, please check one only

1. Please check where you go to for advising.

    ___ College of Agriculture (AG)
    ___ College of Applied Sciences and Arts (AP)
    ___ College of Business and Administration (BA)
    ___ College of Education (ED)
    ___ College of Engineering (EN)
    ___ College of Liberal Arts (LA)
    ___ College of Mass Communication and Media Arts (MC)
    ___ College of Science (SC)
    ___ Pre-Major Undeclared (PMJU)
    ___ Pre-Major Special Admission (PMJS)

For Questions 2-4, please check the appropriate answer

2. Sex   ___ female   ___ male

3. Which course are you completing this term?   ___ 100   ___ 101

4. What grade do you expect to receive in the writing course your are completing?

   __ A __ B __ C __ D __ F __ INC __ PR

For Question 5, please check all statements that apply to you

5. Which, of the following factors have influenced the grade you expect to receive?

POSITIVELY INFLUENCED

- __ Good attendance and participation
- __ Effectively drafting and completing assignments
- __ Help from instructor
- __ Help from a Writing Center tutor
- __ Other _____

NEGATIVELY INFLUENCED

- __ Poor attendance
- __ Late/missing assignments
- __ Difficulty understanding instructions
- __ Difficult material
- __ Other _____

For Question 6 and 7, please check the appropriate answer

6. Do you think you made the right choice of courses? __ Yes __ No

7. Did your performance on the Diagnostic Exam positively or negatively affect your motivation to do well?

   __ Positively   __ Negatively   __ Don't Know

For Question #8 and #9, please check one statement only

8. How confident are you about your writing ability?

   __ Very confident   __ Somewhat confident   __ Not very confident

9. How confident are you that you will do well in your next composition course?

___Very confident ___ Somewhat confident ___ Not very confident

Were you advised to visit one of the Writing Centers this semester?

___ Yes ___ No

10. Did you visit one or more of the three Writing Centers?

___ Yes ___ No

If you responded yes to Question 11 to indicate that you **have visited** the Writing Center, answer Questions 12-15, and question 18.

If you responded no to Question 8 to indicate that you **have not visited** the Writing Center, skip ahead to Questions 16-18.

For Questions 12 or 16, check all statements that apply to you

12. Which of the following reasons contributed to your decision to use the Writing Center's services:

a. ___ I was advised to.
b. ___ I believed that if I used the Center my essays and grades would improve.
c. ___ I believed that if I did not use the Center, my teacher would take points off my grades.
d. ___ I believed that by attending the Center I would improve as a writer.
e. ___ I believed that attending the Center would increase my confidence as a writer.
f. ___ I felt that my teacher would appreciate my extra effort.
g. ___ Other: _____

13. Of the reasons you selected in Question 12, which one do you see as most important (Item a-g)? ___

14. Do you plan to visit the Writing Center again? ___ Yes ___ No

Please explain why or why not: _____

_____

15. Approximately how many conferences have you had at the Writing Center thus far this semester?

   ___ 1
   ___ 2-3
   ___ 4-5
   ___ 6 or more

16. Which of the following reasons best describe why you have not visited the Writing Center?

   a. ___ I did not know about the Centers until I read this survey.
   b. ___ I don't feel I need the services offered.
   c. ___ I don't fully understand the services the Writing Centers offer.
   d. ___ I feel I am receiving enough individual help with my writing from my instructor.
   e. ___ I am receiving sufficient help from a friend, classmate, or other person.
   f. ___ I have not used the Center because I'm afraid my teacher would count off for such extra help.
   g. ___ I have not used the Center because I'm afraid my peers would look down on me for doing so.
   h. ___ I haven't yet had time to visit one of the Centers but plan to in the near future.
   i. ___ I'm too busy this semester to use the Writing Center.
   j. ___ Other: _____

17. Of the reasons you selected in Question 16, which one do you see as most important (Item a-j)? ___

18. Please add any suggestions or comments you would like to make about DSP, the use of the diagnostic exam to advise students, or the Writing Centers.

REFERENCES

Bandura, Albert. *Social Foundations of Thought and Action: A Social Cognitive Theory*. Englewood Cliffs, NJ: Prentice Hall, 1986.

Bruning, Roger H., Carolyn Colvin Murphy, and Duane F. Shell. "Self-Efficacy and Outcome Expectancy Mechanism in Reading and Writing Achievement." *Journal of Educational Psychology* 81 (1989): 91-100.

Daly, John A. "Writing Apprehension and Writing Competency." *Educational Research* 72 (1978): 10-14.

Daly, John A., Lester Faigley, and Stephen P. Witte. "The Role of Writing Apprehension in Writing Performance and Competence." *Journal of Educational Research* 75 (1981): 16-21.

Daly, John A., and Michael D. Miller. "The Empirical Development of an Instrument to Measure Writing Apprehension." *Research in the Teaching of English* 9 (1975a): 242-49.

——. "Further Studies on Writing Apprehension: SAT Scores, Success Expectations, Willingness to Take Advanced Courses and Sex Differences." *Research in the Teaching of English* 9 (1975b): 250-56.

Daly, John A., and Deborah A. Wilson. "Writing Apprehension, Self-Esteem, and Personality." *Research in the Teaching of English* 17 (1983): 327-41.

Glau, Gregory. "The 'Stretch Program': Arizona State University's New Model of University-level Basic Writing Instruction." *WPA: Writing Program Administration* 20 (1996): 79-91.

Huot, Brian. Directed Self Placement and Reliability. Online posting. 8 April 2000. WPA-L <http://list.asu.educgi-bin/wa?A2=ind0004&L=wpa-I&P=R16665>.

Johnson, Margaret J., and Frank Pajares. "Confidence and Competence in Writing: The Role of Self-Efficacy, Outcome Expectancy, and Apprehension." *Research in the Teaching of English* 28 (1994): 313-31.

McCarthy, Patricia., Scott Meier, and Regina Rinderer. "Self-Efficacy and Writing: A Different View of Self-Evaluation." *College Composition and Communication* 36 (1985): 465-71.

Reynolds, Erica. *The Role of Self-Efficacy in Directed Self-Placement: An Analysis of Confidence, Apprehension, and Gender Components.* Thesis. Southern Illinois U of Carbondale, 1999.

Royer, Daniel J., and Roger Gilles. "Directed Self-Placement: An Attitude of Orientation." *College Composition and Communication* 50.1 (1998): 54-70.

White, Edward M. *Developing Successful College Writing Programs.* Foreword by Richard Lloyd-Jones. San Francisco, CA: Jossey Bass, 1989.

——. *Teaching and Assessing Writing.* 2nd edition, Revised and Expanded. Portland, ME: Calendar Islands Publishers, 1998.

Yancey, Kathleen Blake. *Writing Assessment: A Position Statement.* 1997. http://www.ncte.org/positions/assessment.html. National Council of Teachers of English. 10 October 2001.

11

RESPONDING TO DIRECTED SELF-PLACEMENT

Michael Neal
Clemson University
Brian Huot
University of Louisville

With the publication of "Directed Self-Placement: An Attitude of Orientation" in 1998, Royer and Gilles fueled a nationwide discussion about large-scale student placement into first-year writing. The 1990s saw a steady stream of scholarship on placement (Harrington; Haswell and Wyche-Smith; Howard; Robertson) that set the stage for the article and the dialogue about directed self-placement (DSP) that emerged from it. As an assessment methodology, DSP differs from most current procedures for placing students into first-year writing courses in that the assessment does not produce data or information on which educators make more or less informed decisions regarding the appropriate first-year writing course for individual students. Rather, students are provided with information about the courses offered by the institution for first-year students and offered assistance, often with a survey but supplemented with the option of speaking to an academic advisor to understand their own literacy histories and experiences. Students ultimately gauge their own history and experience with writing in order to make the most appropriate and accurate choice of courses themselves.

As long as colleges and universities have offered multiple levels of first-year writing, they have also been forced to use some form of placement to decide on which students should enter what classes. As Royer and Gilles point out in their two chapters, for the most part, writing placement has involved students taking some sort of test, with faculty and program administrators deciding into which courses students should be placed. Although Royer and Gilles see DSP as replacing traditional direct writing assessment—typically single sample, impromptu essays scored holistically—many placement decisions are still made based on scores from the verbal section of the SAT or ACT, purposes for which these exams were never intended. The survey Huot published nearly 8 years ago indicated that half of the 1,100 responding institutions (40% of the 2,700+ colleges and universities on the MLA mailing list) still used some indirect (a euphemism for a writing test in which students' writing ability is judged on their performance in answering multiple-choice questions on grammar, usage and mechanics) writing assessment. Newer indirect placement exams like COMPASS or ACUPLACER (its pen-and-paper equivalent) score a student's ability to edit a provided text. In its 2000 marketing literature, COMPASS claimed to have placed more than 750,000 students, a number that continues to grow. The use of indirect assessment for placement, including COMPASS, is documented by several chapters in this volume. On the other hand, DSP has become so pervasive in the thinking of people who design and construct placement procedures that Cynthia Leweicki-Wilson, Jeff Sommers, and John Tassoni describe their placement procedures for a branch campus of Miami university as a rationale for not using DSP.

Theoretically, the case for DSP is strong. Drawing on the progressive educational theories of John Dewey and the tradition of American Pragmatism, Royer and Gilles contend that students are the ones best able to make decisions about their educational future, their experiences with reading and writing and the future performance. Additionally, they argue and are supported by others in this volume (Blakesley; Chernekoff; Reynolds) that when students choose to take a prerequisite for the most commonly required first-year writing course, that this course is transformed, because students are committed to writing and learning in ways they cannot when they are placed into such courses by others. Although the mainstreaming of students into first-year writing is supported theoretically and empirically (Elbow; Gleason; Grego and Thompson; Soliday), DSP provides a viable alternative in which students are offered various levels of instruction and choose the course that best suits their needs as they understand them.

As the chapters in this volume demonstrate, locally constructed and controlled versions of DSP have been implemented in English departments and writing programs across the country. A relative newcomer to the world of writing assessment, DSP captures the minds and imaginations of writing administrators—and for good reason. In this response chapter, we begin first by exploring claims made by proponents of DSP as to its potential practical and theoretical value. We examine the theories and assumptions that underlie scholarship and research in DSP, and we investigate the ways that it has been and is being implemented in writing programs. In addition to the claims made about DSP, we also pose questions and concerns that need to be addressed by administrators who are interested in deciding whether DSP is the best possible placement system for their programs or departments. Most importantly, we outline the need for continued validity inquiry into DSP. We point to a number of issues that a validation of DSP needs to address, citing critiques that are recently emerging in assessment literature. We also note how some of the programs described in this volume have already made a strong case for the use of DSP at their institutions and have begun the larger process of validation just described. Our intent is to supplement the work in this volume by addressing the kinds of concerns that can only make DSP a more attractive and authoritative choice for placement.

CLAIMS ABOUT DSP

Perhaps the most compelling and dominant claim regarding DSP is that it shifts the focus of the placement out of the hands of administrators, granting students a remarkable amount of agency. In this volume, Janice Chernekoff advocates student decision making at multiple levels of the student's educational careers: "Educators cannot expect that students will instantly turn into mature decision-makers and active citizens upon graduation from college if we also insist on them being passively evaluated and tested throughout college" (133). In this way, Chernekoff sees testing systems as impairing student agency and responsibility. Others echo this concern, noting that within DSP, students are required to research and make important decisions that will influence their own opportunities for success. Because students are more invested in their own education than anyone else in the university system, it seems fair to allow them to participate in a meaningful way in choosing the first-year writing course that best suits their immediate needs. In this collection, this warrant is echoed throughout: "[C]ontrol, agency, and decision making are returned entirely to the student" (23); "For now, it is important to note that a unique feature of directed self-placement is that it permits the construction of a self within a community because it fosters agency, choice, and self-determination" (57); "DSP conveys to students the message that writing is something that they can take some control over. Because of it, students are a little less at the mercy of what they perceive to be the subjective and whimsical opinions of composition instructors. In other words, DSP provides students with a means to intercede in the external evaluation of their writing" (146).

Advocates of DSP also note the advantages of students in developmental writing classes choosing the course rather than being required to take it. Basic writing courses often carry not only the stigma of remediation, but also the financial burden of having students pay for classes that often do not result in college credit. Students who place themselves into noncredit writing classes might have a better attitude about the class as well as the institution than those placed into the same classes by a more traditional method of placement: "DSP communicated a positive message to students that we respect their judgment. We felt that if students chose to take the basic writing course, rather than be forced to take it, that the classroom dynamic would improve dramatically, an important factor in a course in which students' attitudes toward writing is so crucial to writing growth" (211). Blakesley and Reynolds note an important factor in student learning and development, that of attitude. Students with open, receptive attitudes toward the material in a class are more prone to excel than those who are resistant to the content of the course or resentful of being placed into it. Closely connected to student attitude in developmental writing are the attitudes and experiences of teachers in developmental writing courses. Blakesley, Reynolds, and Chernekoff address the working conditions of instructors of developmental writing: "Instructor morale in the basic writing course, ENGL 100, is substantially higher than it was among teachers of the ENGL 101R prior to Fall 1998" (208); "Faculty teaching DVE reported that attitude and performance of students taking this course were markedly improved over previous semesters" (135). It seems clear that students placing themselves into developmental courses increases the morale of both students and teachers in those courses.

There are some claims for DSP, however, with which we cannot agree. For example, we cannot agree with Royer and Gilles' claim that traditional placement is a waste of resources that could be used for curriculum development, faculty workshops, or other writing program features more directly related to teaching and learning of writing. Assessment is never an isolated activity; it always has unintended effects that have a range of implications, depending on the assessment and the institution. As students of writing assessment, we note that proponents of holistic scoring in the early 1980s (White) touted it as the perfect way to engage faculty in conversations about student writing and their own teaching. As portfolios became a writing assessment option, their scoring was noted as an important venue for teachers to talk about their students and teaching (Elbow and Belanoff). And in the 1990s, team-scored exit portfolios were noted as an important aspect for faculty development and writing program unity (Durst, Roemer, and Shultz). Depending on the local context and the specific assessment scheme, local assessment programs can have important benefits for teachers and their students. Additionally, DSP does not necessarily mean a complete reduction in costs attributed to placement. Blakesley noted that the DSP placement system he helped to develop at Southern Illinois University costs no less than the system it replaced because advisors spend so much time helping students make decisions, and Chernekoff observed that DSP has hidden costs not visible at first.

However strongly the contributors to this volume feel about the advisability of DSP, there is simply no overriding evidence to assume that other forms of placement are suspect. We respect the fact that Royer and Gilles and other volume contributors were unhappy with their placement procedures and that this unhappiness started them on the road to develop DSP. In fact, since we like DSP so much, we are almost glad they were unhappy with their earlier uses of a writing placement exam. However, it may be that most institutions that use student writing are satisfied with their placement procedures. At least that's what a national survey showed in 1994 (Huot). In fact, institutions that used a writing sample were satisfied at a higher rate than those who did not (58). As well, the scholarly literature documents how several placement programs that use the reading of student writing have demonstrated theoretically and empirically that they place students in courses accurately (Harrington; Haswell and Wyche-Smith; Hester, Neal, O'Neill and Huot; Robertson; Smith) to the satisfaction of teachers (Hester, Neal, O'Neill, and Huot; Robertson; Smith) and students (Robertson; Hester, Neal, O'Neill, and Huot). So, although we heartily support DSP, we cannot support even the most faint implications that other forms of writing placement are inherently flawed. In fact, in the next section on validity and DSP, we outline some procedures for ensuring that DSP solidify its role as perhaps the placement procedure of choice. We would support such a position for DSP not because of flaws in other forms of placement, but because DSP gives students a central role in the decision-making process, creates basic writing classes in which all students have chosen to be in the class and uses less institutional resources. Our position is that the institutions might consider using DSP for placement not because other forms of writing assessment are bad, but because DSP might be better for them. Because as we document here, validity inquiry looks at the accuracy and appropriateness of decisions based on some assessment procedure, the advisability of an assessment depends on a specific locale and institution.

VALIDITY AND DSP

For us, the most important questions we or anyone else can raise about the use of a specific assessment is to look at the validity of the decisions made on its behalf. In order to achieve a high degree of validity, we must be able to document that decisions based on the results of the writing assessment are reasonably accurate and appropriate (Messick). In many ways, we are concerned with the dismissive attitude given to validity by strong proponents of DSP. Royer and Gilles seem to be annoyed by questions or concerns about validity: "It's interesting even here how—in the face of what seems so obvious—the concern for validity and reliability still pesters Hesse's recollection of the event" (this volume 4). Rather than an annoyance, we see a validity argument as absolutely necessarily in establishing a new form of placement or in maintaining a traditional form. No amount of "common sense" or administrative concern can counterbalance the need for a placement system that has a high degree of validity and thus is defensible. On the other hand, as we point out later, validity is about making an argument, so the argument for DSP will focus on the strengths of the decisions we can make based on its use.

Before looking at validity arguments for DSP, it is probably best for us to talk a little bit about what validity is and why we believe it to be the major consideration for understanding the worth of any assessment procedure. In Composition Studies, validity is often referred to as whether or not a test measures what it purports to measure. This definition can be found in the educational measurement literature back in the 1950s, but it has not been an operative or acceptable definition for several decades (Shephard). Such a definition withstands very little scrutiny. For example, we could intend a test to measure which students fit a traditional measure for a college student and design an assessment that would identify students who are non traditional in some ways and use the test to prevent these students from entering college.[1] In this way, we could prevent nontraditional students from entering college and as long as that's what we intended to do, then the text would be valid. Unfortunately, this measure would be deemed a valid test and would accrue to it an acceptability that, in fact, does not exist. In the rather vast literature on test validity, the most commonly cited definition comes from Samuel Messick who holds that validity is "an integrative evaluative judgment of the degree to which empirical evidence and theoretical rationales support the *accuracy* and *appropriateness* of *inferences* and actions based on test scores or other modes of assessment" (13). In Messick's definition, validity becomes a much more complex activity that requires theoretical and empirical input. Messick goes on to say, "To validate an action inference requires validation not only of score meaning but also of value implications . . . and of the social consequences of using scores for applied decision making" (13). Under such a definition, our earlier scenario looks quite different in terms of validity because we would need to consider the consequences involved in making decisions to deny entry to certain kinds of students.

Validity is never completed or finished; it is an ongoing process because as long as we use an assessment method to make decisions, then we need to continue to build an argument about the accuracy and appropriateness of these decisions. In fact, the evolution of placement procedures have depended upon validity inquiry. William L. Smith's groundbreaking research that influenced the field to move away from holistic scoring for placement was based on his attempt to validate the decisions his program was making about students. In much the same way, DSP was created because Gilles and Royer were unhappy with the way their placement system was working, and they began to look for alternatives. Validity inquiry is another way of talking about reflective practice in assessment (Moss). In Pamela Moss' terms, *validity* is the test of the test. In terms of DSP, it is the test of the decisions students make about their placement into first-year writing courses. In practical and ethical terms, validity is about making sure that the tools we use work in a matter that aids and encourages the educational process for the students it affects. In more sobering terms, validity is a safeguard against those who label English Department assessment initiatives in negative terms: "Authorizing English departments to isolate themselves intellectually in order to engage in technically amateurish evaluation of their programs" (Scharton 61). In our minds, engaging in validity inquiry is a win–win situation because it strengthens the position of DSP, while providing a recognizable framework to establish the viability of DSP in ethical, practical, theoretical, and empirical terms.

There are two important points to make about more sophisticated and current notions of validity. First, validity is not about whether or not a test is valid, but rather about the decisions based on behalf of a test. Second, validity is always in terms of degree; it is always partial. Lee J. Cronbach, who wrote some of the earliest validity theory in the 1950s and who with Messick has been one of validity's most important theorists, talks about validity in terms of argument, noting that a validity argument "must link concepts, evidence, social and personal consequences and values" (4). Seeing validity as argument is helpful in many ways because it makes visible the rhetorical nature of assessment claimed in the abstract by Kathleen Blake Yancey and others. Understanding validation as an argument is also consistent with its current conceptions of always being partial or to a degree because no argument will convince everyone. Validation also speaks not to a test or static construct but to the decisions or actions of those using the tests, since arguments attempt to change the thoughts and actions of its audience. In thinking about constructing a validity argument for DSP, we must acknowledge that we cannot claim that it is a valid form of placement, but rather we must look at specific uses of DSP and attempt to validate the actions being taken on its behalf.

In building a validity argument for DSP or any other form of writing assessment, we must look at the decisions being made and the sample of behavior upon which the decisions are made. For example, when Yancey talks about three waves of writing assessment—indirect measures like multiple-choice and editing tests, holistically scored essays, and portfolios—she is essentially talking about the sample of student behavior on which decisions are made because in each case the decision focuses on a different sample of student behavior. On the other hand, another part of the assessment process is the way in which the decisions are being made. In traditional holistic scoring, the decisions are made by independent readers trained on a specific rubric in order to that they might agree on a numerical score. Studies of placement readers using protocol analysis in which readers talk as they read and score show that readers often make decisions based on what classes students are being placed into and then look for the number on a rubric (Pula and Huot). In DSP, students make decisions about the courses they have an option to place into based on their understanding of their abilities and the curriculum. A major portion of the validity argument for DSP depends on the accuracy and appropriateness of the decisions students make. This volume presents several studies (Blakesley; Chernokoff; Cornell and Newton; Reynolds and Harvey) that document the quality of students' decisions based on the grades they receive in the courses. This kind of evidence goes a long way in answering questions about the quality of student decision-making and the ability of students to make that kind of decision. In questioning student decision making ability, we are not necessarily criticizing students or the ability to make important educational decisions. Rather, we are, in Cronbach's term, *testing rival hypotheses* much in the same way that any successful argument considers oppositional points of view. That is, it seems that with help students are the best people to make these decisions; a process of validation provides evidence to support this.

Although it appears that this volume does a good job in considering student decision making in terms of grades, we are concerned that teachers are involved more in the process. In some ways it seems to us that this is by design, since DSP is meant to be student-centered. Royer and Gilles argue that in traditional placement "teachers know and students do not" (62); whereas in DSP that is reversed and students are the ones that know. Although we agree with the critique of traditional placement, we are uncomfortable with the dichotomy that either teachers or students know while the other does not. It seems to us that in terms of placement students know some things while teachers know others. Clearly, students know more about their histories and abilities as writers, and the surveys and other instruments used honor that knowledge. On the other hand, teachers know about the curriculum and instruction at their own institutions. Teacher knowledge is certainly a part of the practice of having instructors counsel with students, a practice that seemed to be emphasized at Southern Illinois University (Blakesley). What's missing from all of the studies of DSP in this volume is a consideration of teacher input about placement. We suggest that any validation of DSP or any other placement procedure needs to consider teacher satisfaction.

In addition to teacher satisfaction, we think it is important for validation research on DSP to look more closely at the kinds of decisions students are making. Although DSP does allow students the autonomy favored by a pragmatic philosophy and the progressive educational theories of John Dewey, it seems to us that DSP has failed to consider more complicated theories of agency and power. Reynolds, in her chapter on self-efficacy, concludes that students can accurately assess their literacy abilities: "There is a very definite correlation between an individual's strength of perceived efficacy regarding writing skills and actual ability to perform those skills" (80). However, other scholarship, such as a recent publication by Ellen Schendel and Peggy O'Neill points toward different conclusions. Schendel and O'Neill cite a 1999 article by Kruger and Dunning which suggests that undergraduate students do not accurately assess their own abilities:

> Students who score lowest when it comes to estimating their ability on a series of tests (humor, logic, and grammar) overestimate their competency, and students who score highest on the test underestimate their abilities. Kruger and Dunning also found that with instruction, students can improve their self-evaluation skills. An implication of their finding for writing teachers is that students can learn and develop the metacognitive skills they need to accurately evaluate their own performance, but students do not necessarily arrive in our classrooms or at college orientation with this ability. (218)

Schendel and O'Neill suggest that students may not have developed necessary self-assessment skills that would allow them to choose the most appropriate writing course for their needs. Of particular concern are those students who are not traditionally privileged within the university, thus discouraging them from appropriately estimating their abilities. For these students, self-assessment can become in Foucauldian terms a method by which students are forced to unwittingly participate in their disciplining, providing institutions with information and power over their lives (Schendel and O'Neill 203-4). We are not suggesting that students are unknowing dupes of their own predetermined subjectivity and are unable to choose outside of the roles that society and culture create for them. On the other hand, it seems naïve not to recognize that individuals can be heavily influenced by their gender, social class or ethnicity. In fact, Lewiecki-Wilson, Sommers, and Tassoni outline a hybrid placement system for nontraditional community college students in which students write about themselves as writers and teachers make recommendations based on this writing because they have found that this particular group of students are heavily influenced in their decision making. We urge DSP to consider the ways in which individuals can be influenced in their decision-making as part of the argument for its validity.

One last issue that we urge for the validation of DSP is some consideration of the courses about which students decide. Although it is true that it is the student's decision about which course to enter, the courses themselves are created outside of the control of students. Validity inquiry needs to consider the rationale for even using an assessment (Messick). For example, Shephard critiques the use of school readiness testing because she argues that that there is no conclusive evidence that students who sit out a year before starting school benefit from the experience. In the same light, before we argue for the accuracy or appropriateness of a specific form of placement, we need to provide evidence that the students who are placed or place themselves into a prerequisite course benefit from the experience. In some ways, this has probably been one of the biggest shortcomings of placement in general. In this volume, two institutions provide evidence about the value of basic writing courses, and while Southern Illinois University offers evidence that its *Stretch* course does help students perform better in subsequent courses, DePauw cannot.

Overall, we think this volume provides a strong beginning in terms of its effort to argue for the validity of the decisions made by students in a range of DSP programs in various institutions. Our call for institutions to provide more information about teacher satisfaction, the possible influences of culture, gender, class and ethnicity on student decision making, and the benefits of basic writing courses should only strengthen the theoretical and empirical base from which individual institutions can argue for the validity of decisions made on behalf of its placement program.

CONCLUSION

One thing we hope we have made clear in this chapter is that we find the collection of chapters and research on DSP in this volume to be a marvelous beginning toward the establishment of DSP as an important form of writing assessment. Although this volume is focused on DSP, it is also a strong response to those who would lament the lack of models for writing placement or who might claim that there is little or no research about placement procedures. As well, we hope that this volume encourages others interested and involved in placement and placement research to consider sharing their experiences publicly. Certainly this volume, in its depth and variety can function as a model for those who would publish about placement and other forms of institutional research on assessment and other subjects important to effective writing program administration. What should also function as a model in this volume are the ways the contributors have invested their time in researching the various ways in which placement impacts students and institutions. Although we feel our discussion about validity can help direct the energies of those who would design and implement their own form of DSP, it is very clear that all of these chapters emphasize the importance of research into placement and assessment.

Although we can celebrate the strong start that DSP has made, reflected in this volume, we also urge those working with DSP to continue their research. Unfortunately, none of the chapters in this volume frame their research as validity inquiry nor do they take advantage of the principals for inquiry that validity theory can provide. This disconnection of DSP research to validity is not surprising, considering that assessment in Composition has not utilized a robust and current understanding of validity. On the other hand, as DSP leads the way on placement and research into placement we hope that it will also become a model for the kinds of validation research that will not only solidify the status of DSP as a placement procedure but that it will also furnish composition scholars with a model for validity inquiry into assessment procedures of all kinds. Just as DSP has rejuvenated the discussion and interest in placement, we hope it can also provide leadership on doing assessment and validating the decisions we make on its behalf.

It seems to us that DSP has the potential to not only enrich our understanding of placement but to provide writing program administrators with an increased impetus to become involved with assessment on their own campuses. The kind of theoretical and practical reasoning that supports DSP can also be invaluable as compositionists and writing program administrators tackle other assessment problems important to their institutions and programs. Although we predict that DSP will be with us for some time and should give many institutions the opportunity to revise their placement procedures and improve their writing programs, we are also hopeful that others will follow Roger Gilles and Dan Royer's example in taking charge of local assessment initiatives in ways that can continue to help all of us who struggle with writing assessment.

REFERENCES

Cronbach, Lee J. "Five Perspectives on Validity Argument." *Test Validity*. Ed. Harold Wainer. Hillsdale, NJ: Lawrence Erlbaum, 1988. 3-17.

Durst, Russel K., Marjorie Roemer, and Lucille Schultz. "Portfolio Negotiations: Acts in Speech." *New Directions in Portfolio Assessment*. Eds. Laurel Black, Donald A. Daiker, Jeffrey Sommers and Gail Stygall. Portsmouth, NH: Boynton/Cook, 1994. 286-300.

Elbow, Peter and Pat Belanoff. "Portfolios as a Substitute for Proficiency Examinations." *College Composition and Communication* 37 (1986): 336-39.

Gleason, Barbara. "Evaluating Writing Programs in Real Time: The Politics of Remediation." *College Composition and Communication* 51 (2000): 560-88.

Grego, Rhonda and Nancy Thompson. "Repositioning Remediation." *College Composition and Communication* 47 (1996): 62-84.

Harrington, Susanmarie. "New Visions of Authority in Placement Test Rating." *WPA: Writing Program Administration* 22 (1998): 53-84.

Haswell, Richard and Susan Wyche-Smith. "Adventuring Into Writing Assessment." *College Composition and Communication* 45 (1994): 220-36.

Hester, Vicki, Michael Neal, Peggy O'Neill and Brian Huot. "The Results and Implications of a Six-Year Pilot Program Using Portfolios to Place Students in First-Year College Composition." American Educational Research Association Annual Meeting, April, 2000.

Howard, Rebecca. "Applications and Assumptions of Student Self Assessment." *Self Assessment and the Development of Writing Ability*. Eds. Jane Smith and Kathleen Yancey. Cresskill, NJ: Hampton P, 2000. 35-59.

Huot, Brian. "A Survey of College and University Writing Placement Practices." *WPA: Writing Program Administration* 17 (1994): 49-67.

Lewiecki-Wilson, Cynthia, Jeff Sommers and John Paul Tassoni. "Rhetoric and the Writer's Profile: Problematizing Directed Self-Placement" *Assessing Writing* 7 (2000): 1-18.

Messick, Samuel. "Validity." *Educational Measurement*. Ed. Robert Linn. American Educational Research Association and Macmillan, 1989. 13-104.

Moss, Pamela. "Testing the Test of a Test: A Response to the Multiple Inquiry in the Validation of Writing Tests." *Assessing Writing* 5 (1998): 111-22.

Pula, Judith J., and Brian Huot "A Model of Background Influences Holistic Raters." *Validating Holistic Scoring for Writing Assessment: Theoretical and*

Empirical Foundations. Eds. Michael M. Williamson and Brian Huot. Cresskill, NJ: Hampton, 1993. 237-65.

Robertson, Alice. "Teach Not Test: A Look at a New Writing Placement Procedure." *WPA: Writing Program Administration* 18 (1994): 56-63.

Royer, Daniel J. and Roger Gilles. "Directed Self-Placement: An Attitude of Orientation." *College Composition and Communication* 50.1 (1998): 54-70.

Scharton, Maurice. "The Politics of Validity." *Assessment of Writing: Politics, Policies, Practices.* Eds. Edward M. White, William D. Lutz and Sandra Kamusikiri. New York: Modern Language Association, 1996. 52-75.

Schendel, Ellen and Peggy O'Neill. "Exploring the Theories and Consequences of Self-Assessment through Ethical Inquiry." *Assessing Writing* 6 (1999): 199-227.

Shephard, Lorrie. "Evaluating Test Validity." *Review of Research in Education* 19 (1993): 405-50.

Smith, William L. "Assessing the Reliability and Adequacy of Using Holistic Scoring of Essays as a College Composition Placement Program Technique." *Validating Holistic Scoring for Writing Assessment: Theoretical and Empirical Foundations.* 142-205.

Soliday, Mary. "From the Margins to the Mainstream: Receiving Remediation." *College Composition and Communication* 47 (1996): 85-100.

White, Edward M. *Teaching and Assessing Writing.* San Francisco: Jossey Bass, 1985.

Yancey, Kathleen Blake. "Looking Back as We Look Forward: Historicizing Writing Assessment." *College Composition and Communication* 50 (1999): 483-503.

AUTHOR INDEX

A
Adams, P.D., 21, 29, 155, *178*
Ansley, A.A., Jr., 195, 196, *206*

B
Bandura, A., 74, 75, 79, 82, 83, 87, 91, 92, 93, *102,* 165, *178,* 215, *240*
Bartholomae, D., 21, *29*
Belanoff, P., 23, *29,* 244, 246, *254*
Benesch, S., 21, *29*
Bers, T.H., 96, 97, *102*
Blakesley, D., 33, 40, *47*
Blythe, S., 33, *47*
Brodkey, L., 133, *146*
Bruning, R.H., 76, 77, 78, *102,* 215, *240*
Burke, K., 28, *29,* 32, 34, 36, *46*

C
Camp, R., 49, 50, 51, *70*
CCCC Committee on Assessment, 19, *29*
Cherry, R. D., 51, 52, *70*
Condon, W., 51, *70,* 194, *206*
Conway, J.K., 18, *29*
Cooper, G., 180(*n*2), *187*

Crobach, L.J., 249, 250, *254,*
Crowley, S., 32, 39, *46*

D
Daly, J.A., 79, 81, 83, 84, 85, 86, 87, 88, 89, 90, 91, 92, 93, 94, 95, 99, *102,* 216, 226, 228, *241*
Davies, B., 133, *146*
Dewey, J., 51, *70,* 58, 60-61, 64, 67, *68*
Donovan, R., 19, *30*
Douglas, M., 31, 32, *46*
Durst, R.K., 247, *254*

E
Elbow, P., 20, 21, 23, 26, 28, *29,* 55, 70, 184(*n*5), *187,* 244, 246, *254*

F
Faigley, L., 88, 89, *103,* 216, *241*
Fox, P.W., 98-99, *103*
Freire, P., 37, *46,* 114, *125,* 133, *146*

G
Gilles, R., 37, *47,* 108, *125,* 130, 132, 133, 137, *147,* 188, 199, 200, 201, 202, *206,* 210, 211, 212, 214, 215, 223, 230, *241,* 243, 244, 246, 250, *255*

Glau, G., 39, *46,* 212, 215, 216, 230, *241*
Gleason, B., 33, 38, *47,* 244, *254*
Grabill, J.T., 33, *47*
Grant, G., 28, *30*
Greenberg, K., 19, 21, *30*
Grego, R., 21, *30,* 244, *254*

H

Hamp-Lyons, L., 51, *70,* 179(*n*1), 180(*n*2), 181(*n*3), 194, *206*
Harrington, S., 243, 247, *254*
Haswell, R., 20, 22, *30,* 243, 247, *254*
Hester, V., 247, *254*
hooks, b., 133, *146*
Horton, M., 114, *125*
Howard, R., 243, *254*
Huot, B., 49, 50, *70,* 199, *206,* 226, 241, 244, *247,* 250, *254*

J

James, W., 57-58, 59, 60, *71*
Jessel, D., 95, 96, 97, 98, *103*
Johnson, M.J., 74, 79, 82, 83, 84, 85, 86, 87, 88, 93, *103,* 215, *241*
Jones, W., 21, *30*

K

Kidda, M., 21, *30*
Knudson, R.E., 95, *103*

L

Lederman, M.J., 19, *30*
Lewiecki-Wilson, C., 244, 252, *254*
Locke, E., 82, *103*
Lundeberg, M.A., 98-99, *103*

M

McCarthy, P., 73, 74, 75, 76, 77, 78, 79, 82, 83, 84, 85, 86, 87, 88, 89, 92, *103,* 215, *241*
McClelland, D.C., 27, *30*
McKenna, E., 179(*n*1), 180(*n*2), 181(*n*3)

McLeod, S., 83, *103*
Meier, S., 73, 74, 75, 76, 77, 78, 79, 82, 83, 84, 85, 86, 87, 88, 89, 92, *103,* 215, *241*
Messick, S., 248-249, 252, *254*
Meyer, P.R., 51, 52, *70*
Miles, L., 33, *47*
Miller, M.D., 79, 81, 83, 84, 85, 86, 88, 90, 93, 94, 95, 99, *102,* 216, 226, 228, *241*
Moir, A., 95, 96, 97, 98, *103*
Moss, P., 249, *254*
Murphy, C.C., 76, 77, 78, *102,* 215, *240*

N

Neal, M., 247, *254*

O

O'Neill, P., 247, 251-252, *254, 255*

P

Pajares, F., 74, 79, 82, 83, 84, 85, 86, 87, 88, 93, *103,* 215, *241*
Parker, F.E., 21, *30*
Peirce, C.S., 57, 58, *71*
Porter, J.E., 33, *46*
Pula, J.J., 250, *254*
Puncochar, J., 98-99, *103*

R

Reynolds, E.J., 215, *241*
Ribaudo, M., 19, *30*
Rinderer, R., 73, 74, 75, 76, 77, 78, 79, 82, 83, 84, 85, 86, 87, 88, 89, 92, *103,* 215, *241*
Roberts, T-A., 98, 99, *103*
Robertson, A., 243, 247, *255*
Rodby, J., 22, *30*
Roemer, M., 247, *254*
Rose, M., 111, *125*
Royer, D.J., 39, *47,* 130, 132, 133, 137, *147,* 182, 188, 199, 200, 201,

202, *206,* 210, 211, 212, *214,* 223, 230, *241,* 244, 246, 250, *255*
Ryzewic, S., 19, *30*

S

Saunders, P., 195, *206*
Scharton, M., 249, *255*
Schendel, E., 251-253, *255*
Schultz, L., 247, *254*
Schunk, D.H., 91, 94, *103*
Shell, D.F., 76, 77, 78, 215, *240*
Shephard, L., 248, *255*
Shor, I., 114, *125*
Smith, K.E., 96, *102*
Smith, W.L., 20, *30,* 54, *71,* 97, 247, 249, *255*
Soliday, M., 153, *178*
Sommers, J., 244, 252, *254*
Stitt, B.A., 96, *103*
Stock, P.L., 179(n1), 186, *188*
Sullivan, P., 33, *47*

T

Tassoni, J.P., 244, 252, *254*
Thayer, H.S., 70, 71

Thompson, N., 21, *30,* 244, *254*
Turner, J., 21, *30*

W

Wellesley College Center for Research on Women, 96, *103*
White, E., 20, *30,* 51, *71,* 73, 82, *103,* 194, *206,* 216, 230, *241,* 246, *255*
Wiener, H., 19, *30*
Williamson, M., 66, *71*
Wilson, D.A., 90, 91, *103,* 216, *241*
Witte, S.P., 88, 89, *103,* 216, *241*
Wood, R., 82, *103*
Wyche-Smith, S., 22, *30,* 243, 247, *254*

Y

Yancey, K.B., 49, 50, *71,* 212, 230, *241,* 249, 250, *255*

Z

Ziegler, W., 198, *206*

SUBJECT INDEX

A

academic advisors, 35, 40-42, 44, 46, 101, 112, 114, 141, 164, 176, 185, 211, 218, 221-223, 229, 232, 233, 235-236, 247
ACUPLACER, 244
agency, 20-22, 24, 46, 57, 60-62, 66, 68, 74, 101, 178, 245, 251
anxiety, 75, 76, 83, 84, 86, 93, 152, 230
apprehension, 9, 10, 64, 76, 79, 83-102, 165, 216, 225, 226, 228
assessment methods, 50, 51, 196, 205
at-risk students, 4, 42, 143, 149, 150, 153, 160, 161, 164, 165, 168, 172, 174, 178, 187
attitude, 5, 8, 58, 60, 95, 130, 135, 140, 141, 143, 246, 248

B

Bandura, Albert, 74, 79, 82, 93, 102, 165, 178, 199, 215, 240
basic writer, 21, 64, 65, 68, 134, 171, 209, 230
basic writing, 9, 10-12, 21, 24, 27, 28, 64, 67, 90, 101, 108, 109, 113, 132, 143, 150, 169, 172, 209, 210, 211, 215, 223, 226, 231, 232, 246, 247, 252
bureaucracy, 5, 35, 36, 43
Burke, Kenneth, 28, 29, 32, 34, 36, 46

C

choice, 2, 8, 24, 32, 40, 43, 44, 49, 55, 56, 57, 59, 60, 61, 62, 67, 69, 74, 87, 97, 98, 100, 112, 118, 133, 135, 138, 142, 160-162, 165, 166, 168, 172-174, 176-178, 182, 184, 185, 195, 212, 215-217, 222, 224-226, 228, 229, 232, 237, 238, 243-245, 247, 250
community, 1, 3, 5, 18, 20, 21, 38, 44, 57, 60-64, 67, 117, 129, 134, 144, 145, 193, 195-197, 199, 200-205, 216, 217, 232, 245, 252
COMPASS, 194, 196, 197, 198, 199, 200, 205, 206, 244
complaints, 45, 65, 130, 133, 142, 143, 198, 200, 202, 203, 231
Computerized Placement Test, 194

confidence, 6, 9, 10, 11, 64, 73, 74, 76, 79, 80, 82, 83, 86, 90, 91, 93, 96, 98-100, 109, 131, 133, 153, 160, 163, 168, 178, 211, 215-217, 222, 225, 226, 233, 235, 239

consequence(s), 5, 7, 22, 34, 49, 50, 56, 57, 58, 59, 60, 62, 69, 80, 132, 133, 183, 184, 196, 203, 215, 221, 226, 249

correct placement, 193

cost(s), 6, 40, 73, 82, 100, 154, 155, 157, 168, 195, 201, 204, 213, 214, 247

course portfolio, 66

curriculum, 2, 4, 5, 7-9, 10, 11, 26, 32, 33, 45, 49, 50, 51, 53, 54, 55, 69, 70, 90, 94, 102, 108, 116, 143, 152, 153, 155-157, 162, 169, 174, 181, 186, 187, 194, 209, 221, 233, 237, 246, 250, 251

D

decision making, 2, 5, 22, 38, 62, 127, 134, 136, 245, 249, 250, 252

democracy, 60, 61

developmental courses, 68, 196, 201, 246

developmental writing, 8, 108, 181-183, 186, 199, 200, 246

Dewey, John, 57, 58, 61, 67, 69

diagnostic essay 39, 45, 164, 208, 217, 221, 228, 230, 233, 235, 237

E

economic factors, 216

educational choices, 146

Educational Testing Service, 96, 132, 194

Elbow, Peter, 5, 15, 21, 29, 55, 70, 168, 184, 187, 244, 246, 254

ESL, 29, 96

Ethnicity, 95, 103

F

females 10, 82, 85, 94, 95, 96, 98, 99, 102, 166, 169, 170, 172, 174, 176, 177, 222, 226, 227, 228

first-year writing, 8, 9, 10, 11, 15, 19, 22, 28, 50, 52, 54, 56, 62, 108, 110, 111, 113, 115, 132, 171, 177, 178, 180, 182-185, 187, 212, 213, 243, 244, 245, 249

Freire, Paolo, 37, 46, 114, 125, 146

G

gateway, 16, 17, 19, 45

gender, 4, 10, 57, 76, 83, 94, 95, 96, 97, 99, 102, 164-166, 167, 169, 170, 222, 227, 252

grade inflation, 10

grading, 4, 6, 11, 19, 23, 28, 51, 55, 68, 112

grammar, 42, 56, 88, 97, 117, 138, 143, 163, 244, 251

guiding (students), 53, 64, 89, 101, 111

H

Hawthorne effect, 7, 202

holistically scored, 76, 89, 107, 195, 198, 250

holistic scoring, 194, 246, 249, 250

Honors, 137, 138, 144, 181

I

inquiry, 6, 57-60, 62, 66, 68, 153, 245, 247, 249, 252, 253

institutional context, 34, 217

instructor's perspective, 230

J

James, William, 5, 33, 47, 57, 58, 59, 60, 70, 147

M

mainstreaming, 4-6, 12, 33–34, 150–151, 156–158, 177–178, 244–245

males, 10, 85, 94-100, 102, 166, 169, 170, 172, 173, 176, 177, 222, 226-228
mandatory placement, 11, 149, 157
motivation, 8, 12, 18, 19, 69, 144, 160, 172, 173, 178, 215, 216, 217, 238
multicultural, 151
multilingual, 117

O

orientation, 2, 5, 40, 53, 54, 58, 60-63, 65, 67, 82, 94, 108, 110, 113, 115, 116, 127, 129, 130, 131, 138, 139, 141-144, 146, 154, 161, 176, 184, 185, 223, 251
outcomes, 74, 77-79, 143, 210, 213, 216, 226
outcome expectancy, 74-80, 86
overconfidence, 160

P

pedagogy, 4, 7, 32, 94, 107, 108, 133, 187
Peirce, C.S. 5, 57, 58, 59, 71
persistence 12, 74, 149, 150, 164, 172, 173
placement booklet, 111, 112, 118
placement complaint, 65
placement decisions, 8, 9, 54, 57, 68, 99, 101, 102, 107, 108, 182, 194, 200, 203, 221, 226, 244
placement essays, 8, 20, 56, 153, 154, 211
placement instrument, 107, 111, 113, 116, 117, 196, 199
placement method, 2, 8, 9, 12, 34, 37, 50, 51, 54-56, 62, 65, 68, 69, 82, 101, 108, 112, 132, 137, 145, 193, 195, 199, 204, 210, 212, 213, 216, 223, 228, 232
placement problem, 11, 60, 128
placement process, 2, 6, 7, 19, 21, 22, 27, 45, 53, 54, 55, 57, 68, 108-113, 115-117, 118, 143, 208, 217, 228-230, 232
placement system, 6, 7, 27, 55, 113, 131, 137, 158, 177, 186, 245, 247, 248, 249, 252
placement testing, 3, 19, 20, 21, 22
placement tests, 7, 19, 20, 37, 108, 114, 131, 185, 198, 202, 214
portfolio placement, 7, 8, 55, 56, 158, 178, 181, 182, 183, 184, 185, 186
Pragmatism, 57-59, 69, 70, 71, 244
pragmatist, 5, 49, 51, 53, 55, 57-63, 65, 67, 69, 71
predictor, 64, 74, 84, 86, 87, 93, 101, 194, 215, 216

Q

questionnaire, 76, 80, 109, 111, 114, 115, 139, 161, 162, 174, 184

R

race, 164, 165, 167, 169
readiness scores, 164, 165, 166, 169, 170
reliability, 4, 7, 9, 20, 51, 53, 56, 78, 131, 194, 211, 248
remediation, 33, 150, 158, 246
retention, 4, 40, 50, 102, 130, 156, 210, 212, 215, 216-218

S

SAT, 53, 83-85, 88, 94, 97, 100, 103, 108, 130, 131, 134, 137, 138, 140, 143, 151, 153-167, 170, 171, 177, 183, 190, 193, 194, 195, 212, 241, 244
satisfaction, 50, 115, 141, 142, 146, 174, 212, 218, 222, 226, 231, 247, 251, 252
self-efficacy, 9, 10, 57, 64, 73-89, 91-99, 101-103, 136, 165, 197, 199, 200, 201, 205, 211, 212, 215-217, 223, 251

self-esteem, 9, 64, 90, 91, 98, 172, 201
stakeholders 34, 38, 41, 210, 211
standardized tests 88, 100, 155, 169, 170, 178, 193, 195, 199
standardized test scores 50, 113, 151, 177, 178, 190
status quo, 10, 32, 35-38, 44, 45
Stretch, 39, 43, 45, 46, 207, 208, 210-212, 215-218, 221, 222, 228-230, 231, 233, 235-237, 241, 252
student attrition, 154
student performance, 34, 35, 40, 44, 52, 217, 218
subjectivity, 39, 252

T

test placement, 3, 197
timed writing, 53, 54, 63, 100, 101, 162, 208, 214, 228
traditional placement, 1, 55, 68, 69, 82, 101, 113, 200, 223, 232, 246, 250
transform, 62, 211
true placement, 12
tutorial programs, 186

V

validity, 3, 4, 7, 20, 33, 34, 49, 51, 55, 66, 69, 108, 131, 194, 195, 214, 226, 228, 245, 247, 248, 249, 250, 252, 253

W

writing apprehension, 9
Writing Center, 10, 109, 110, 117, 118, 145, 177, 179, 180, 181, 183, 185, 187, 229, 235-240
writing confidence, 83, 178
writing skills, 74, 76, 79, 80, 81, 82, 85-88, 92, 93, 96, 101, 111, 117, 131, 135, 140, 141, 162, 163, 195, 210, 215, 233, 251